Television and Political Advertising
Volume 2:
Signs, Codes, and Images

COMMUNICATION

A series of volumes edited by:
Dolf Zillmann and **Jennings Bryant**

Zillmann/Bryant • Selective Exposure to Communication

Beville • Audience Ratings: Radio, Television, Cable, Revised Edition

Bryant/Zillmann • Perspectives on Media Effects

Ellis/Donohue • Contemporary Issues in Language and Discourse Processes

Winett • Information and Behavior: Systems of Influence

Huesmann/Eron • Television and the Aggressive Child: A Cross-National Comparison

Gunter • Poor Reception: Misunderstanding and Forgetting Broadcast News

Olasky • Corporate Public Relations: A New Historical Perspective

Donohew/Sypher/Higgins • Communication, Social Cognition, and Affect

Van Dijk • News as Discourse

Wober • The Use and Abuse of Television: A Social Psychological Analysis of the Changing Screen

Kraus • Televised Presidential Debates and Public Policy

Masel Walters/Wilkins/Walters • Bad Tidings: Communication and Catastrophe

Salvaggio/Bryant • Media Use in the Information Age: Emerging Patterns of Adoption and Consumer Use

Salvaggio • The Information Society: Economic, Social, and Structural Issues

Botan/Hazleton • Public Relations Theory

Zillmann/Bryant • Pornography: Research Advances and Policy Considerations

Becker/Schoenbach • Audience Responses to Media Diversification: Coping With Plenty

Television and Political Advertising

Volume 2:
Signs, Codes, and Images

edited by

Frank Biocca

Center for Research in Journalism and Mass Communication
University of North Carolina at Chapel Hill

LEA LAWRENCE ERLBAUM ASSOCIATES, PUBLISHERS
1991 Hillsdale, New Jersey   Hove and London

Lawrence Erlbaum Associates, Inc., Publishers
365 Broadway
Hillsdale, New Jersey 07642

Library of Congress Cataloging-in-Publication Data

Television and political advertising.

   Contents: v. 1. Psychological processes —
v. 2. Signs, codes, and images.
   1. Advertising, Political. 2. Advertising,
Political — Psychological aspects. 3. Television
in politics. I. Biocca, Frank.
JF2112.A4T46 1990   659.1'932   89-71468
ISBN 0-8058-0662-8 (v. 2)
Printed in the United States of America
10 9 8 7 6 5 4 3 2 1

Contents

Part IV:
Regulating Signs and Images

Preface

The sizzle, sputter, and hiss of political discourse is increasingly confined to 30-second barrages. The television "spot" is the haiku of political thought. Much must be crammed into 30 seconds, but even more must be inferred when the message is received and unpacked in the mind of the voter.

The chapters in these volumes examine the artifice of the televised political ad and attempt to peer into the minds of the voters who view them. This work is the labor of the National Political Advertising Research Project (NPARP). NPARP's mission was to study the psychological and symbolic processing of political advertising.

Back in the spring of 1987, I felt that we needed a better understanding of how these ads structure political information and how that information is represented in the minds of voters. Through the generous assistance of the Gannett Foundation, funding was obtained to support research projects at universities and research centers around the country. The project was administered by the Center for Research in Journalism and Mass Communication at the University of North Carolina at Chapel Hill.

The NPARP focused solely on television advertising. Television is the most influential political advertising medium. We reasoned that to better understand the psychological processing of political advertising, it was first necessary to better understand the processing of television as a medium.

From a pool of over 80 research proposals, a group of 17 was chosen for funding. They constituted a team whose research goals were most focused on the mission of the project. The project sought research that was theory driven and would advance our fundamental understanding of how political ads interact with cognitive structures and what role the medium of television plays in those cognitions. It was also important to understand the social circulation of the codes of representation found in ads and political discourse. It was clear that progress toward a better understanding of the political ad could only come about through the simultaneous application of various theoretical and methodological paradigms. The contents of volumes 1 and 2 reflect this philosophy.

A project like this always involves the assistance and good graces of a number of bright and supportive people. I know all the participants are very grateful that support of their research was made possible through the help of Gerald Sass of the Gannett Foundation and Richard Cole, Dean of the School of Journalism at the University of North Carolina. I personally would like to acknowledge the assistance of a number of colleagues and research assistants, who at one time or another helped keep me from sinking in a sea of paper: Rich Beckman, Tom Bowers, Sara Carpenter, Prabu David, Juming Hu, Joe Keefer, Phil Myers, Jane Rhodes, and Mary Alice Sentman. I also want to acknowledge the help and patience of my most treasured colleague, Zena Biocca.

Frank Biocca
Project Director
National Political Advertising Research Project
Center for Research in Journalism and Mass Communication

1

Generating Meaning in the Pursuit of Power

1

What Is the Language of Political Advertising?

Frank Biocca
University of North Carolina at Chapel Hill

> The study of the diffusion and restriction [of political doctrines] calls for a general theory of language as a factor in power. . . . Part of the changes wrought by power are brought about by the use of language, and one of our tasks is to assimilate the special theory of language in politics to a general theory of power . . . *symbols (words and images) affect power as they affect the expectations of power.*
>
> —Lasswell et al. (1949)

What is the "language of politics"? Is it just traditional rhetoric? Not really. An understanding of verbal language provides us with few tools to discuss the full content of the televised political message: the determined gestures of a politician in front of a waving American flag, the image of a crying midwestern farmer standing in the middle of a wheat field, the white middle-class nightmare evoked by the face of Willy Horton,[1] or the reassuring, avuncular smile of a Ronald Reagan, a smile connected to a thousand late night movies. As Lasswell, Leites, and associates (1949) put it, "Symbols (words and images) affect power" (p. 19).

---

[1]The face of Willy Horton refers to an image that appeared in a Bush campaign commercial in the 1988 election. The face of this murderer-rapist and his parole within a program approved by the democratic candidate, Michael Dukakis, led to controversy regarding not only the issue but the very ad itself, and the *meaning* of the face of Willy Horton. Democratic candidate Jesse Jackson suggested that the ad was racist, because for White middle-class voters the face did not refer to an individual but to a general "Black menace." He suggested that the Bush campaign knew that was how the ad was going to be "read" and that the strategy was, therefore, racist.

3

In the modern campaign Lasswell's "language of politics" has become the language of television—words and images spewing out of the slick machinery of American politics. In this part of Volume 2, I consider the language of television. In this chapter and the ones that follow, I explore how the structures of the political commercial, the ad's form and content,[2] attempt to guide the viewer/voter's cognitive processing.

In advanced electronic democracies like the United States, electoral politics are increasingly a matter of competing for claims to key political symbols (Edelman, 1964, 1977; Elder & Cobb, 1983; Nimmo & Combs, 1983). The candidate's symbolic properties are carefully molded (Sabato, 1981), and symbolic attacks by opponents are quickly repulsed (Hahn & Gustanis, 1987). All this is seen as necessary to create, restructure, and manage the *perception* (meaning) of the candidate, as well as the *issues* of the election. All parties seem moved by the rule: He who defines the symbolic terrain, wins.

THE POLITICAL CONSULTANT AS SEMIOTIC ENGINEER

The political consultant is an engineer in a thriving political industry—the manufacture of meaning (Kern, 1989; Sabato, 1981; Spero, 1980). For most Americans, the candidate exists only inside the television set, pasted together from small clips of videotape. The discourse of American politics bounces around the confines of the four corners of the television screen. The telegenic Kennedy believed that the television set had made his election possible (Sabato, 1981).[3] The wooden Michael Dukakis lamented that the television set had defeated him ("Dukakis speech," 1990).

Where once the political ad was a backyard product fashioned by rough and earnest rules, the modern televised ad is all steel, chrome, and silicon aimed at the heart and mind of the undecided voter. The

---

[2]In the discussion of television we often see the opposition between form and content. In some cases form means the hardware of the medium or the executional variables of production. Content is often defined as the images, words, narratives, and so forth. I do not use this opposition here.

What is often called *content* (i.e., narrative, dialogue, etc.) has formal properties. Content is made up of just another set of forms. Any representation is a form or the product of forms and structures. Therefore, my use of form and structure should not be interpreted as limited to a discussion of the permanent properties of the medium (i.e., the screen, the pixilized image, etc.) or to technique (i.e., camera motion, cuts, etc.).

[3]Some might say he remains immortalized, a video icon, in those grainy clips that are played over and over on the screen that gave him political life. For many born too late, he is but a sad figure, waving at the crowd, riding in a limousine to his death.

consultant engineers the machinery of appearances. This is a political skill as old as the father of political consulting, Machiavelli (1952):

> Men in general are as much affected by what things seem to be as by what they are; often, indeed, they are moved more by appearances than by the reality of things. (p. 22)

Political advertising is a treacherous arena where appearances and meanings are constructed and destroyed.[4]

Many students of political advertising turn to political consultants to get a deep insight into how political advertising really works (e.g., Diamond & Bates, 1984; Kern, 1989; Sabato, 1981). But the consultants themselves are at a loss. In their more honest moments, they admit that they are baffled. One consultant confessed, "We're all kind of probing in the dark. We're out there experimenting with what works" (Sabato, 1981, p. 122). According to Tony Schwartz, dean of political consultants and creator of the well-remembered Johnson "Daisy" commercial, he and his fellow political consultants "don't know why they are doing what they are doing. They just mechanically learn some new technique, but they don't really understand it" (Sabato, 1981, p. 17). The political consultant may speak the language of political advertising, but cannot articulate its rules.

This should not be surprising. After all, speakers of English can use the language proficiently without being able to explain its syntax. Political consultants may be proficient political communicators without being able to reliably and precisely pinpoint the rules of the language of political advertising. They can communicate meaning without necessarily knowing how exactly the meaning of the ad is structured, how it works, or how it is received in the many and varied viewing environments.

POLITICAL ADS HAVE SEMANTIC STRUCTURES

If communication research is the study of the transfer of meaning, then we need to specify the ways in which the political ad generates meaning.

---

[4]The Reagan presidency is a watershed in our sensitivity to the theatrical and symbolic character of politics, especially elections. The actor-president was hailed not for his intelligence, great wisdom, or foresight, his skills as chief administrator of the nation, or his great integrity or moral virtuousness, but for his ability as a "great communicator." If there were any doubt about the relationship of the "dream industry" to the political process, they were quickly erased. It is perhaps not surprising that the post-Reagan era is marked by increased unease about the value of political discourse and the resultant validity of the electoral process itself (see Shyles, chapter 9, this volume).

In Volume 1 of this series, I outlined a model for analyzing the mechanisms by which a voter extracts meaning from political ads (Biocca, in press). This was a psychological approach.

But the application of cognitive theories to the study of political advertising is not enough to understand how the ad imparts meaning to a viewer. An analysis of the *semantic processing* of political ads presumes an analysis of the *semantic structures* of the message. The assumption underlying these two volumes, and this chapter, is that *structural models* of the message must emerge simultaneously with theories of viewers' *mental models* (Johnson-Laird, 1983) of those same messages. To unpack the meaning of a political ad, we must understand not only the cognitive processes of reception but the social construction, circulation, and transformation of the codes the ad contains. Understanding the cognitive processes of the viewer is only half the answer. It would seem that a *theory of the message* must emerge simultaneously with a *theory of the cognitive processing of the message*. One cannot be successful without the other.

A message is a blueprint of a psychological process. Upon exposure the viewer builds a message—not always the one intended by the blueprint, but always one *influenced* by it. With certain semantically open political ads, the blueprint leaves out many details and allows the viewers to inhabit their own constructed meanings.

This group of chapters is a programmatic discussion of the analysis of political ads and shares the assumption that "media discourses should be analyzed in terms of their structures at various levels of description" (Van Dijk, 1988, p. 2). It outlines a broad framework for organizing the systematic study of the message structures within political ads.

In its analysis of the ways in which political ads structure meaning, this part of the volume will proceed in discussing four levels of analysis, moving from more atomic structures to more global structures. This is represented in Fig. 1.1. The general areas discussed are:

1. analysis of specific *signs* used in political commercials;
2. analysis of the *codes* of televised political ads;
3. analysis of the *discourse* (discursive structures) of political ads and their references to other social discourses; and
4. analysis of the mechanisms of *semantic framing* of political ads.

More global structures, such as semantic frames, do not necessarily subsume the others, but rather represent different levels or strategies of analysis.

The analysis that follows flows from a number of research streams. The analysis of the relationship between message structures and psycho-

Levels of Structural Analysis of Political Ads

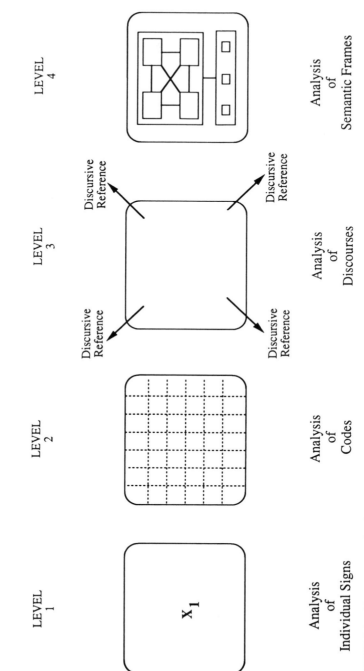

FIGURE 1.1. The structure of political ads can be analyzed at various levels, including the analysis of individual signs, codes, discourses, or semantic frames.

logical processes has also been the goal of the traditional fields of rhetoric (e.g., Baird, 1964; Gregg, 1984); persuasion (Petty & Cacioppo, 1986; Reardon, 1981); and content-analytic strategies, including Lasswell's venture into quantitative semantics (Lasswell et al., 1949). A number of theories of representation are referred to and built on, most notably cognitive theories of semantic processes (e.g., Johnson-Laird, 1983), discourse analysis (e.g., Van Dijk, 1988; Van Dijk & Kintsch, 1983), film theory (e.g., Bordwell & Thompson, 1986; Metz, 1974), and some of the more reader-oriented or systematically Peircean[5] representatives of semiotic theory (Eco, 1976; Sebeok, 1986).

FIVE GOALS OF A THEORY OF POLITICAL ADVERTISING

The structural analysis of political ads is a first step toward advancing five principal goals of a theory of political advertising:

1. to precisely analyze the semantic and syntactic structures of specific political ads (a linguistics [semiotics] of the political ad);
2. to relate structural properties of ads to viewers' mental models of the meaning generated by the ads (a psycholinguistics [psychosemiotics] of political advertising);
3. to determine generalizable patterns for groups of ads, for example, those of a candidate, an election, negative ads in general, or ads for various types of offices, such as congressman, senator, or president (a sociolinguistics [sociosemiotics] of political advertising);
4. to specify generalizable properties of political advertising as a genre (a stylistics and formal criticism of the political ad)[6]; and
5. to analyze the role of political advertising in the use, distribution, and construction of political ideology (the cultural study of political advertising).

---

[5]*Peircean* refers to the work of the American philosopher and semiotician, Charles Peirce. Peirce's work can be interpreted as presenting a neo-Kantian or psychological approach to signification. Peirce was a colleague of the famous American psychologist, William James, and he once conducted some perception experiments. Semioticians who tend to adopt a Peircean perspective are more inclined to discuss signification as a psychological process, or at the very least a process occurring in what Peirce referred to as a "quasi-mind." A quasi-mind could also be a form of artificial intelligence.

[6]At this point, the study of codes begins to overlap with the analysis of discourses. It can be argued that codes are in some ways ossified discourses.

Although the structural and interpretive analyses of ads can be an intellectual end in itself, the analysis of message structures is seen as a method for generating hypotheses and models of textual communication strategies. For example, consider Goal 2, a psychosemiotics of the political ad. An analysis of the structural properties of ads might at later stages generate highly specific *hypotheses* about how structure contributes to forging new semantic connections in the minds of voters. Exploration, if not confirmation, of these hypotheses is left to different, empirically based psychological (Biocca, in press) and naturalistic (Lindlof, 1988; Morley, 1980) research strategies.

It is in the very nature of meaning to change and evolve with usage. Therefore, a sophisticated structural analysis of the codes of an ad can give us some means of zeroing in on changes in the construction and reception of political advertising over time. Anyone who looks at the political advertising of the 1950s is struck by how phenomenally naive, plastic, and static the ads seem. Yet, in the 1950s they appeared natural and conventional. The techniques of the ads and the poses of the politicians suited the schemata of the voter and embraced the forms of the video culture that surrounded the politician and the viewer. A successful analysis of these forms and structures would contribute to the other four goals in our understanding of political advertising.

REFERENCES

Baird, C. (1964). *Rhetoric: A philosophical inquiry.* New York: Ronald Press.
Biocca, F. (in press). Viewer's mental models of political commercials: Towards a theory of the semantic processing of television. In F. Biocca (Ed.), *Television and political advertising, Vol. 1: Psychological processes.* Hillsdale, NJ: Lawrence Erlbaum Associates.
Bordwell, D., & Thompson, K. (1986). *Film art.* New York: Alfred A. Knopf.
Diamond, E., & Bates, S. (1984). *The spot: The rise of political advertising on television.* Cambridge, MA: MIT Press.
Dukakis speech barks at '88 sound bites. (1990, April 22) *Raleigh News and Observer,* p. 6A.
Eco, U. (1976). *A theory of semiotics.* Bloomington, IN: Indiana University Press.
Edelman, M. (1964). *The symbolic uses of politics.* Urbana, IL: University of Illinois.
Edelman, M. (1977). *Political language: Words that succeed and policies that fail.* New York: Academic Press.
Elder, C., & Cobb, R. (1983). *The political uses of symbols.* New York: Longman.
Gregg, R. B. (1984). *Symbolic inducement and knowing: A study in the foundations of rhetoric.* Columbia, SC: University of South Carolina Press.
Hahn, D. F., & Gustanis, J. J. (1987). Defensive tactics in presidential rhetoric: Contemporary topoi. In T. Windt & B. Ingold (Eds.), *Essays in presidential rhetoric* (pp. 23–54). Dubuque, IA: Kendall Hunt.
Johnson-Laird, P. (1983). *Mental models: Towards a cognitive science of language, inference, and consciousness.* Cambridge, MA: Harvard University Press.

Kern, M. (1989). *30-second politics: Political advertising in the eighties.* New York: Praeger.

Lasswell, H., Leites, N., & Associates (1949). *Language of politics: Studies in quantitative semantics.* Cambridge, MA: MIT Press.

Lindlof, T. (1988). Media audiences as interpretive communities. In J. A. Anderson (Ed.), *Communication yearbook 11* (pp. 81–107). Beverly Hills, CA: Sage.

Machiavelli, N. (1952). *Great books of the Western world: Vol. 23. The prince.* Chicago: Encyclopaedia Britannica.

Metz, C. (1974). *Film language: A semiotics of cinema.* New York: Oxford University Press.

Morley, D. (1980). *The nationwide audience: structure and decoding.* London: British Film Institute.

Nimmo, D., & Combs, J. E. (1983). *Mediated political realities.* New York: Longman.

Petty, R., & Cacioppo, J. (1986). *Communication and persuasion: Central and peripheral routes to attitude change.* New York: Springer-Verlag.

Reardon, K. (1981). *Persuasion: Theory and context.* Beverly Hills, CA: Sage.

Sabato, L. J. (1981). *The rise of political consultants.* New York: Basic Books.

Sebeok, T. (Ed). (1986). *Encyclopedic dictionary of semiotics* (Vols. 1–3). Berlin: Mouton de Gruyter.

Spero, R. (1980). *The duping of the American voter, dishonesty and deception in presidential television advertising.* New York: Lippincott & Crowell.

Van Dijk, T. (1988). *News as discourse.* Hillsdale, NJ: Lawrency Erlbaum Associates.

Van Dijk, T., & Kintsch, W. (1983). *Strategies of discourse comprehension.* New York: Academic Press.

2

Some Limitations of Earlier "Symbolic" Approaches to Political Communication

Frank Biocca
University of North Carolina at Chapel Hill

> There are more things in a text than are dreamt of in our text theories. But there are also *fewer* things than are dreamt of.
>
> —Eco (1979)

Are there blueprints to the structure of an ad? How does the ad's structure influence the construction of meaning? Because meaning is not constructed purely by chance within each individual voter, we can safely postulate that a relationship exists between the structure of the political ad and the psychological processes of the viewer. The political consultants assume this to be true every time they design an ad.

In political communication, as elsewhere, the search for blueprints of the political message have been sought by both practitioners and critics of political discourse at least as far back as the day Aristotle first espoused his theories of rhetoric (Aristotle, 1926). In the American political communication literature, there is a stream of analyses of the use of significant symbols in politics (Arnold, 1962; Edelman, 1964; Elder & Cobb, 1983; Lasswell, 1960; Lasswell, Lerner, & Spier, 1979, 1980a, 1980b; Nimmo, 1974; Nimmo & Combs, 1980). Much of this work shows the influence of presemiotic[1] and early semiotic theories, such as those from the Chicago school of sociology, and especially the

---

[1]Presemiotic analysis is defined here as a relatively unsystematic analysis of the symbolism of various texts, especially one that does not subscribe to a neolinguistic or psycholinguistic model of communication codes.

work of the anthropologist Sapir (1949), and the symbolic interaction-
ists (Blumer, 1969; Duncan, 1968; Mead, 1962), as well as the thought of
the philosopher Cassirer (1923) made popular by outstanding students
such as Susanne Langer (1957).[2]

What distinguishes this literature is a sincere effort to explain the
symbolic aspects of political communication and how the symbols
reflect and shape the emotions and world views of political actors and
voters. The functions of illusion and myth in political communication,
the historical connectedness of political discourse, and the deep pas-
sions evoked by references to symbolic political entities suggested by the
words "flag," "country," "homeland" and "enemy," are discussed.
The blood and passion of two world wars haunts this work with horrific
images of the power and costs of ideology.

Unfortunately, this literature often infuses the concepts of symbol,
image, and myth with a misty mysticism. Political symbols seem to guide
political communication like distant polar stars. At other times, political
symbols appear to have the haunting, quasi-religious properties of Jung's
archetypes (Lasswell, 1965). Their semantic richness and power are
explained by reference to neo-Freudian externalization (see Edelman,
1964; Lasswell, 1965) and the unconscious (e.g., Rolle, 1980).

This approach often leads the theorist to expand the reach of the
concepts and to reify the notion of symbol. As the limited set of
concepts is used to explain a wider scope of communication, they
become overgeneralized and unmanageably fuzzy. The analyses over-
reach themselves; too few analytical tools are used to explain too many
social and psychological phenomena.

THE MANY MEANINGS OF "SYMBOL" AND "IMAGE": EXAMPLES OF CONCEPTUAL PROBLEMS

If we are to adopt a theoretical vocabulary that can help us in our
analysis of political ads, the concepts must be reasonably clear and
potentially open to validation. Let's consider two popular concepts in
political communication: political "symbol" and candidate "image."
These can be valuable concepts. Unfortunately, they are often crippled
by the conceptual confusion noted earlier.

---

[2]To a lesser degree we can also see the indirect influence of the semiotic work of Charles
Morris (1932). The notion of myth that is circulated in these texts borrows heavily from
early anthropological theorists of myth (Malinowski, 1948) and the continuance of that
tradition in anthropology (Campbell, 1983). More rarely do you find more rigorous, if
somewhat rigid structuralist approaches to myth (e.g., Levi-Strauss, 1973; Leymore, 1975).
See the fine bibliographic essay in Nimmo (1974).

For example, consider a definition by Edelman (1964), who is often cited as a seminal theorist of political symbolism and political imagery (e.g., Elder & Cobb, 1983; Graber, 1986; Kern, 1989; Nimmo, 1974). Edelman wrote:

> Every symbol stands for something other than itself, and it also evokes an attitude, a set of impressions, or a pattern of events associated through time, through space, through logic, or through imagination with the symbol. (p. 6)

It is clear from this definition that the concept of *symbol* is intended to cover a lot of psychological terrain. In this definition, the symbol can be a unit of cognition or can comprise whole sequences of symbolic processing. It can be a narrative, a logical term, a form of spatial memory, an attitude, and so on. Psychologically, these are substantially different, but the distinctions are lost. Analyses get blurred when the terms *symbol* and *image* are used to label a variety of social, semiotic, and psychological processes.

The related concept of *sign* is one of the most basic concepts in semiotic theory (Sebeok, 1986). In the political symbolism literature, *sign* is used either as a synonym for the *symbol,* a synonym for *signifier,* or the term *signal* (for "standardized" semiotic definitions; see Sebeok, 1986). In the writing of Elder and Cobb (1983), the concept of *symbol* is synonymous with the semiotic concept of *sign* (signifier): "A symbol is any object used by human beings to index meanings that are not inherent in, nor discernible from, the object itself." Semioticians might recognize the Scholastic formula, *Aliquid stat pro aliquo.* But the "objects" appear to have their own inherent meaning and are not symbols in and of themselves.

On the other hand, in Nimmo's (1974) writing the concept of *sign* is synonymous with semiotic concept of *signal* (Sebeok, 1986). For example, "a sign is a sensation . . . images give meaning to a sign" (Combs, 1974, p. 6). Here, *sign* refers to a presemantic, sensory signal.

The concept of *image* also appears to have a variety of meanings. In some cases, *image* is used to refer to the complete semantic representation of person or organization. In other passages, it is used in a much narrower sense and refers to the types of mental images discussed in cognitive psychology (Kosslyn, 1980). These latter images are presented as spatial representations available from memory. For example, one theorist wrote that "an image is a subjective representation of something previously experienced" (Nimmo, 1974, p. 5). In this case, political images are closer to Lippman's sense of "pictures in our head" (Lippman, 1922).

Images, to some, serve the same function as schema in schema theory (Rumelhart, 1980). Nimmo (1974) devoted a number of pages to the discussion of the perceptual, cognitive, affective, and connative components of images. In this case, an image is defined by whole sets of cognitive procedures.

For others, *symbols* and *images* are synonymous with *attitudes* and *issues*. Elder and Cobb (1983) state that the "substantive meaning (of symbols) is based on a person's internalized beliefs and values regarding the external world and the way it operates." They also include questionable examples of symbols, such as "right to life" and "gun control," in their typologies of political symbols (Elder & Cobb, 1983).

Finally, when fully expanded, the concepts of *symbols* and *images* become synonymous with the concepts of ideology, that is, the logic of ideas animating the thought and behavior of voters and political actors. Elder and Cobb (1983) include self-schematic (Markus, 1977; Markus & Sentis, 1982) and group identification as the "meaning" of symbols:

> The second type of meaning that a person may assign to a symbol arises from his self-conception and the people and groups with whom he identifies. (p. 41)

In other cases, symbols and images refer to whole world views. Elder and Cobb wrote, "They provide him with a picture of the world covering the full range of environmental influences he experiences" (p. 45). Here the concept suggests a global semantic universe similar to Eco's (1979) encyclopedia. These properties are sometimes reserved for what Elder and Cobb following Mead (1962), called *significant symbols* and, sometimes, *key symbols*.

At different points, the concepts of *image* and *symbol* are synonymous. Sensing this confounding, one writer suggested early on to his reader, "The relationship between symbols and images obviously is close" (Nimmo, 1974, p. 6). Can it be too close? Can the distinction disappear, such that the analytical value of each concept also starts to disappear? The end result of this varied usage of important concepts like "symbol" and "image" is a conceptual blur bordering on confusion.

When the concepts of *symbol* and *image* become synonymous with the concepts of *sign, issue, mental image, ideology,* and so forth, the analysis becomes indistinct. The foreword of one of the more recent books in this tradition acknowledges the problem and states that they have attempted to be "more constructively taxonomic and more rigorously empirical in (their) argument" (Elder & Cobb, 1983, p. 000). But the problem appears to persist.

Some reflection on the problem seems to suggest two root causes.

First, the concepts are used to simultaneously describe various stages in the communication process: (a) social processes, (b) structural properties of the message, and (c) psychological processes of voters. In some cases, the effects of the properties of a symbol or message are included in the analytical language used to describe the message. Therefore, the descriptions are forced to expand in order to take in these various stages of communication. The distinction between message forms and message effects is lost. Second, there is little or no distinction made between various units of signification and meaning. Momentary processes, long-term memory structures, and various types of mental representations are collapsed when a single term is used to describe all of them.

In the analysis that follows, there is no attempt to simultaneously describe the structures *in* a message and the psychological and social processes that result *from* the message. Psychological processes are discussed elsewhere (Biocca, in press).

In the next chapter, I make the distinction between various levels or types of symbolic structures and elemental signs. In subsequent chapters, types of codes and semantic frames are discussed.

REFERENCES

Aristotle (1926). *The art of rhetoric* (J. Freese, Ed.). London: William Heineman.

Arnold, T. (1962). *The symbols of government.* New York: Harcourt, Brace, Jovanovich.

Biocca, F. (in press). Viewer's mental models of political commercials: Towards a theory of the semantic processing of television. In F. Biocca (Ed.), *Television and political advertising, Vol. 1: Psychological processes.* Hillsdale, NJ: Lawrence Erlbaum Associates.

Blumer, H. (1969). *Symbolic interactionism.* Englewook Cliffs, NJ: Prentice-Hall.

Campbell, J. (1983). *Historical atlas of world mythology.* San Francisco: Harper & Row.

Cassirer, E. (1923). *Philosophy of symbolic forms.* New York: Harcourt, Brace, Jovanovich.

Nimmo, D. (1974). *Popular images of politics.* Englewood Cliffs, NJ: Prentice-Hall.

Duncan, H. D. (1968). *Symbols in society.* New York: Oxford University Press.

Eco, U. (1979). *The role of the reader.* Bloomington, IN: Indiana University Press.

Edelman, M. (1964). *The symbolic uses of politics.* Urbana, IL: University of Illinois.

Elder, C., & Cobb, R. (1983). *The political uses of symbols.* New York: Longman.

Gnaber, D. (1986). Political Languages. In D. Nemmo & K. Sanders (Eds.), *Handbook of political communication.* Beverly Hills: Sage.

Kern, M. (1989). *30-second politics: Political advertising in the eighties.* New York: Praeger.

Kosslyn, S. (1980). *Images and mind.* Cambridge, MA: Harvard University Press.

Langer, S. (1957). *Philosophy in a new key.* Cambridge, MA: Harvard University Press.

Lasswell, H. (1960). *Psychopathology and politics.* New York: The Free Press.

Lasswell, H. (1965). *World politics and personal insecurity.* New York: The Free Press.

Lasswell, H., Lerner, D., & Speier, H. (Eds). (1979). *Propaganda and communication in* world history: The symbolic instrument in early times (Vol. 1). Honolulu: University Press of Hawaii.

Lasswell, H., Lerner, D., & Speier, H. (Eds). (1980a). *Propaganda and communication in world history: Emergence of public opinion in the west* (Vol. 2). Honolulu: University Press of Hawaii.

Lasswell, H., Lerner, D., & Speier, H. (Eds.) (1980b). *Propaganda and communication in world history: A pluralizing world in formation* (Vol. 3). Honolulu: University of Hawaii.

Levi-Strauss, C. (1973). Structualism: The structural study of myth. In V. W. Gras (Ed.), *European literary theory and practice* (pp. 289–316). New York: Delta.

Leymore, V. L. (1975). *Hidden myth: Structure and symbolism in advertising*. London: Heineman.

Lippman, W. (1922). *Public opinion*. New York: Harcourt, Brace, Jovanovich.

Malinowski, B. (1948). *Magic, science and religion, and other essays*. Boston: Beacon Press.

Markus, H., & Sentis, K. (1982). *The self in information processing. Social psychological perspectives on the self*. Hillsdale, NJ: Lawrence Erlbaum Associates.

Markus, H. (1977). Self-schemata and processing information about the self. *Journal of Personality and Social Pscyhology, 35,* 63–78.

Mead, G. H. (1962). *Mind, self, and society*. Chicago, IL: University of Chicago Press.

Morris, C. (1932). *Six theories of mind*. Chicago, IL: University of Chicago.

Nimmo, D. (1974). *Popular images of politics: A taxonomy*. Englewood Cliffs, NJ: Prentice Hall.

Nimmo, D., & Combs, J. E. (1980). *Subliminal politics: Myths & mythmakers in America*. Englewood Cliffs, NJ: Prentice-Hall.

Reardon, K. (1981). *Persuasion: Theory and context*. Beverly Hills, CA: Sage.

Rolle, A. (1980). The historic past of the unconscious. In H. Lasswell, D. Lerner, & H. Speier (Eds.), *Propaganda and communication in world history: Vol. 3. A pluralizing world in formation* (pp. 403–260). Honolulu: University Press of Hawaii.

Rumelhart, D. (1980). Schemata: The building blocks of cognition. In R. J. Spiro, B. J. Bruce, & W. F. Brewer (Eds.), *Theoretical issues in reading comprehension: Perspectives from cognitive psychology, linguistics, artificial intelligence, and education* (pp. 33–58). Hillsdale, NJ: Lawrence Erlbaum Associates.

Sapir, E. (1949). *Culture, language, and personality; selected essays*. Berkeley, CA: University of California Press.

Sebeok, T. (Ed.). (1986). *Encyclopedic dictionary of semiotics* (Vols. 1–3). Berlin: Mouton de Gruyter.

3

Looking for Units of Meaning in Political Ads

Frank Biocca
University of North Carolina at Chapel Hill

> There is an increasing *rapprochement* between philology and psychology—between the science of language and the science of what we do with language.
>
> —Langer (1957)

Do we really understand the effect of an ad by looking at the whole as a unit? Many analysts of political advertising seem to think we do. Much of the theoretical analysis of political commercials is carried out at the level of the whole commercial.

Descriptions of types of political ads may be well suited to broad taxonomic or content-analytic studies. Attempts are made to classify ads as to their genre, that is, issue/image, and so forth (Jamieson, 1984; Joslyn, 1980) and to identify stylistic or strategic trends (e.g., Shyles, 1984a, 1984b). But these broad classifications become stretched when they are used as a springboard to a discussion of effects, presumably psychological or social ones, that assume intervening psychological processes (e.g., declining voter turnout in response to negative advertising). We might learn a lot more by analyzing the ads at a more microscopic level.

An eon of psychological processing goes on within the mind of the viewer during the span of 30 seconds. Waves of words, images, and sounds crash into the consciousness of the viewer. Complex psychological processes capture the rush of signification (e.g., vision: Marr, 1982; identification: Marcel, 1983; Seymour, 1979). It is true that certain patterns of semantic activation might be consistently responsive to broad taxonomic properties (genres) of ads. But broad classifications of ads (e.g., issue/image, attack, comparative) make for blunt tools; the analyst can only hammer away at the structure. But a more probing dissection of the political ad calls for a more precise instrument—a scalpel instead of a hammer.

For example, consider the distinction between issue and image ads— a preoccupation, some might say an obsession, among writers of political advertising (e.g., see the issue/image references in Kaid & Wadsworth, 1985). Few political ads can be reliably classified as either "issue ads" or "image ads." A breakdown of a political ad into smaller components, such as scenes or verbal statements, shows that most are composed of statements that either suggest some future policy action or stance (issues) and references that suggest general personal characteristics or vague, policy-related constructions (images). Effects researchers who make the distinction often assume that some parallel exists between the structural distinction—image versus issue—and some difference in psychological processing, for example, affective (emotional) versus semantic (rational) processes. Although there are some exceptions (e.g., Garramone, 1983), attempts to relate such broad structural categories to psychological processes may be problematic, because neither "issue ads" nor "image ads" are truly consistent in their persuasive approach.

This problem raises the following question: If we are *not* going to take the complete ad as the starting point in our analysis, how then should we begin? Maybe we should attempt to construct the ad the way the mind builds it, from elementary perceptions interpreted within an overarching context or frame. As a step toward building theoretical models, the political ad might be broken up into a set of elements or signs. Perhaps we might look at how these elements are used to generate meaning within the context of communication (semiotic) codes, discourses (discursive structures), and semantic frames (overarching topical, schematic, or rhetorical structures).

USING THEORETICAL UNITS OF COMMUNICATION AND MEANING: SIGNS, SEMEMES, SEMANTIC LINKS, AND NODES

As is true with any segment of video, the political ad can be broken into smaller units, such as specific words, nonverbal gestures, static images, and sounds. The very act of decomposing the ad into words, images, and sounds allows the analyst of political advertising to look for units of meaning within the ad. In a word, these are *signs* (Eco, 1976). We set aside, for the moment, questions as to whether we should look for smaller units than the sign, and whether the sign is the ideal level at which to work our analysis (Eco, 1979).[1]

Figure 3.1 presents a graphic representation of a theoretical unit of meaning in the political ad, the sign. A sign is some elemental unit that has meaning for someone. In our analysis of the political ad, we assume that there are some elemental units that carry meaning, the video equivalent of morphemes in linguistics.

In many ways a sign is not an object, a part of the ad, but a cognitive process, a *sign-function* (Eco, 1976). A sign can be defined as a link (correlation) between something social (psycho-physical), an expression unit (signifier) and something psychological, a macrosemantic unit (signified). The latter is sometimes called a *sememe*[2] (Calabrese, 1986; Eco, 1976). These are useful theoretical units. Elements in a political ad, such as a candidate's gesture, an object in a scene, can be discussed as potentially activating certain meanings in the minds of viewers.

But what is a sememe? From one viewpoint (Katz & Fodor, 1964), the meaning content of the sememe for the stimulus object "flag" might be just some dictionary entry, a set of semantic features (markers) that

---

[1]The use of the concept of sign in semiotic theory owes a great deal to a sometimes unacknowledged analogical connection to the morpheme, often interpreted incorrectly as a word unit (lexeme). As in the work of Saussure, there is an assumption of a correspondence between an identifiable expression unit and some limited semantic unit. But if we look at the structure of a television shot with a goal to understanding its psychological processing, what is the unit? There is not an identifiable unit for the perceptual system, for example. Semiotics acknowledges the existence of smaller units. Eco (1979) wrote, "The linguistic sign is not a unit of the system of signification; it is, rather, a detectable unit in the system of signification" (p. 21). For example, continuing in a tradition, Eco (1976) referred to *figurae*. Figurae are units like the letter "a." These are units in a *code* and not necessarily psychological units. But they are psychological units to the degree that the psychological processing of the code requires the specific processing of the individual units first, which is not necessarily the case (e.g., word superiority effects and other evidence of nonatomistic processing).

In specific discussion of media like television, Metz (1974) seriously considered the concept of film as a language and gave up on the notion of identifying a sign for film language: "Cinema has no phonemes; nor does it, whatever one may say, have words" (Metz, 1974, p. 65), although this leaves aside the more global semantic question of identifying units in the filmic images that are parsed by the viewer.

[2]Meaning exists *only* for someone. It is, therefore, misleading to talk of the meaning of a sign in the abstract, although the theoretical need to generalize and the regularities of social communication push us to discuss an interpersonal and stable conception of meaning. When we do talk of meaning in general, we are really talking about the fact that the associations stimulated by a sign (considered as its expression or form only) is highly correlated *across individuals*. This correlation, evidenced by coordination of behavior, is the very stuff of culture.

A Theoretical Unit of Signification in the Political Ad

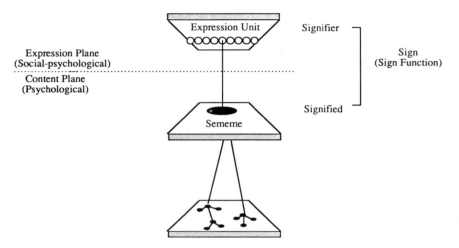

Semantic Features, Procedures, Propositional Links

FIGURE 3.1. This figure represents a theoretical unit of signification in the political ad. The ad is composed of units of meaning (*signs*). Each sign is a psychological link (sign function) between an expression unit (*signifier*) present in the message and some psychological content (meaning) associated with the expression unit. This pattern of associations triggered by a sign has been called a *sememe*.

indicate whether the concept "flag" does or does not possess that feature. For example, the concept for "flag" might contain values from a set of semantic primitives like "animate-inanimate." This seems intuitive, if somewhat Platonic. But the dictionary model, although powerful in some respects, has a number of drawbacks (Eco, 1976; Johnson-Laird, 1983).

Semantic theory offers the aforementioned approach and a range of other possible approaches (Lyons, 1977). But which is best for the study of political advertising? A little introspection is helpful here. We know that the meaning of certain elements, such as "the flag," is not just some unit; rather, the meaning is composed of other elements, associations perhaps. For some people, "the flag" denotes the U.S.A. and connotes patriotism. It may activate stories about Betsy Ross, the meaning of the stars, or images of a childhood Fourth of July. But the total meaning of the stimulus "flag" is reasonably stable within individuals, although not all of the meanings of flag are necessarily activated upon viewing a token of the type, that is, an individual flag. Even though a sememe—a macrounit of semantic processing—may not be strictly measurable, it is parallel to some minimal, consistent, and repeatable pattern of activation among elements of memory. The representation of these elements of memory are potentially accessible when the sign, a flag, is shown to the individual. These elements could be said to be connected to the sign, "flag," by a set of *links,* semantic links, to *nodes*[3] that contain the associations. Therefore, the sememe becomes a set of connections in a semantic network.

In Fig. 3.1, the sememe is shown to be made up of a set of connections to nodes, the tokens of other concepts in semantic memory. The meaning of the sign, the mental operation carried in response to some expression unit, is theorized to be the activation of a set of semantic links to associated concepts triggered by the use of the sign.[4] As is common in semantic network models, the concepts are considered to be composed of a finite pattern of links that connect primitive concepts. The links vary in type and strength. For example, a simple set relation might be linked by the simple "is a" link, as in the proposition, "Bush *is a* Republican." *Is a* is not just a term, but a representation of an operation in which the mind defines set membership: Bush $= f$ (Republican). Other types of semantic links might include logical procedural links, such as "agent," "cause," "instrument" (Anderson, 1983; Rumelhart, 1977). It must be emphasized that a specific sign does not trigger an exact set of semantic features when it is used, in the same way that "flag" in a political commercial does not mean the exact same thing in all contexts.

This approach to the signs in the political ad can suit both semiotic and cognitive theories. For the philosopher Charles Sanders Peirce (1966), the meaning of a sign is a potentially infinite regression of other signs. For the semiotician Umberto Eco (1976), the sign is a trip into the encyclopedic maze of semantic memory. For neural network models of semantic memory, a sign is a set of multiple connections to nodes, where

---

[3]It would be a mistake to identify a sign with a node in semantic memory. Some discussions of network models frequently use lexemes to illustrate nodes when discussing semantic networks (in such cases, equivalence of sign = node might be considered). More often the operative analogy is the computer bit. More fully articulated network models—for example, the connectionist neural network—do not use the sign or symbol as fundamental unit, but rather the "pseudoneuron." In such cases, information is not stored as a node or within nodes, but in the patterns, connections, or excitation across nodes.

[4]Charles Sanders Peirce, an early and very astute theorist of semiotics, pointed out that the meaning of a sign must be a set of other signs. As in a dictionary, the explanation of a word is often other words. Whether we assume the brain to be a symbol manipulator or, for semantic memory, a cluster of associational links between units vaguely resembling neurons, the meaning of a sign must be other signs, other systems and media of representation.

the pattern of connections themselves rather than nodes contain meaning (Rumelhart, McClelland, & PDP-Research-Group, 1986a, 1986b).

The important point to distill from this discussion is that the meaning of a sign lies not in expression itself, or in some definition, but in a set of connections to other concepts *at the moment* the sign is processed. Not all of these connections are activated every time the sign is used. The meaning is not really fixed, as it is in a dictionary. In some ways, the meaning of the sign does not precede the text (Kristeva, 1969). Meaning is a momentary set of operations influenced by the psychological context in which those operations are carried out using more stable semantic links of the concept stored in the memory of the viewer. There is not quite a dictionary of meanings, at least not in any rigid sense of the word, "dictionary." The sign is always a possibility of meaning. That meaning is not contained in the physical form of the sign itself, but in the mind of the viewer in the process of *making meaning* from a political message.

Discussions of political ads too easily succumb to statements about how the ad "carries" meaning. Analysts assign and search for the meaning of the ad in its *expression,* rather than in its *interaction* with the viewer (i.e., Leymore, 1975; Williamson, 1978). It is misleading to think that the political ad "contains" and "transports"[5] the meaning. It is better to perceive the ad as *evoking* meaning that is already resident in the viewer. The ad *activates* a pattern of semantic processing in the viewer that will change upon repeated viewing of the ad (see discussion in Biocca, in press). It follows that an ad only "creates" meaning by forging new associations (new configurations) of sememes in the mind of the viewer. This is not unique to political advertising; it is true of all communication.

Figure 3.2 suggests that we keep in mind the dividing line between the social and the psychological when discussing signs used in political ads. It is here that we must begin to consider the social aspect of the sign so

---

[5]Surely, given the "transportation" notion of communication, a message must transport *new* information to a receiver. Otherwise, how would an individual ever learn new information? Here we must distinguish between knowledge (semantic and procedural memory) and experience (contact with the field of changing stimuli). A message is a new experience. But whatever information is generated in the viewer depends on whether the structures of semantic and procedural memory used to interpret the message are significantly modified. To the degree that the experience of the ad is considered part of a category (e.g., images of "liberal" candidates), then it may modify the category "liberal." A new distinction may be made in a semantic field (e.g., the category "democratic socialist" is placed in a voter's semantic field that contains poles of "communist" and "capitalist"). In any case, the concept of getting information or meaning from an ad is best conceptualized with an associationist model that sees the information as a minor modification of links in semantic memory, rather than the traditional "transportation" or "filter" model of communication that tends to see information as "delivered," "partially received," "not received," or "rejected."

as to better understand the psychological aspect. The expression unit—a word on this page, for example—can be publicly circulated and experienced by others. That is the whole point of advertising. It is this public circulation of signs and codes and the social construction of meaning that make communication codes so profoundly political. In elections the sign is used in the narrowly political sense to suggest legitimacy, mobilize voters around the sign ("symbol"), and alter the meaning of opponents (Edelman, 1964; Elder & Cobb, 1983).

The second part of the sign, the sememe or signified, is found within the individual voter. Sememes are not experienceable across individuals; only signifiers are. Sememes are not transferable. To communicate, a communicator translates the sememe into an expression unit (encodes),[6] which can then be preserved, transported, and displayed to other people (Innis, 1950, 1951). The sememe is subject to significant variation across voters, depending on the subculturally influenced communication experiences of the voter. These are partially related to demographic, psychographic, and life-style measures. The sememe will be slightly different for each individual.[7] It may even be different within the same individual at two points in time.

But whereas sememes vary within individual voters, individuals do

---

[6]The term *encoding* has different meanings in the mass communication literature and in the psychological literature. In the mass communication and semiotics literature, it refers to the act of objectifying thought into a coded signal, just as I am translating my thoughts into words as I write. This meaning is inherited from information theory.

In psychology, encoding is used most often in perception to designate the process by which information present in a retinal image is translated into some code used by the cognitive system. In communication this would be closer to the concept of decoding. Unfortunately, both fields inherit their usage of the term *encoding* from information theory.

In this article, I am using the mass communication or semiotic usage.

[7]Communication between two human beings is made possible by an operating assumption that is always wrong. As communicators, we tend to assume that the sememe activated by a sign in us will be same in others. Of course, correlation of sign to sememe is not perfect across individuals. But communication is possible, because these associations are not random. They are constrained by the relatively stable properties of the physical world around us and the fact that we perceive this world through a perceptual system that segments the physical universe in a somewhat similar fashion across individuals (e.g., Gibson, 1979; Marr, 1982).

Actually, we do more than just assume semantic isomorphism between ourselves and others. We make assumptions about the model reader for our communication. The model reader is a mental construct of the other, the person we are talking to face-to-face, or the "average" viewer/voter (see the discussion in Biocca, in press). This is a generalized "other" in Mead's sense (Mead, 1964). The message is encoded in anticipation of its reception by this model reader. But it might be argued that the *default* model reader is a projection of our self (self-schema) onto the listener. In any case, even when we are constructing a message for the "perspective of the other," we inevitably construct the model reader from a model of our self.

not really freely *create* meaning at random. As in other forms of social communication, the meaning of the signs used in political discourse is constrained by social convention (e.g., "the flag represents our country") and by the circumstances or context of usage (e.g., "hands or fists raised in a demonstration mean defiance" whereas "a hand or fist raised on the classroom is a request to speak or question"). Even when we are attempting to subvert the shared meaning of a sign, we cannot fully escape the constraints of convention.

These social conventions are systematized into *codes,* systems that evolve out of interpersonal association between expression units and sememes or semantic primitives (Eco, 1976). The codes are internalized as sets of links, nodes, and operations that constitute a large part of the semantic memory of the individual voter.

REFERENCES

Anderson, J. (1983). *The architecture of cognition.* Cambridge, MA: Harvard University Press.

Biocca, F. (in press). Viewer's mental models of political commercials: Towards a theory of the semantic processing of television. In F. Biocca (Ed.), *Television and political advertising, Vol. 1: Psychological processes.* Hillsdale, NJ: Lawrence Erlbaum Associates.

Calabrese, O. (1986). Seme. In Thomas Sebeok (Ed.), *Encyclopedic dictionary of semiotics* (Vol. 2, pp. 879–884). Berlin: Mouton de Gruyter.

Eco, U. (1976). *A theory of semiotics.* Bloomington, IN: Indiana University Press.

Eco, U. (1979). *The role of the reader.* Bloomington, IN: Indiana University Press.

Edelman, M. (1964). *The symbolic uses of politics.* Urbana, IL: University of Illinois.

Elder, C., & Cobb, R. (1983). *The political uses of symbols.* New York: Longman.

Garramone, G. (1983). Image versus issue orientation and effects of political advertising. *Communication Research, 10,* 59–76.

Gibson, J. J. (1979). *The ecological approach to visual perception.* Boston: Houghton Mifflin.

Innis, H. (1950). *Empire and communication.* Oxford: Clarendon Press.

Innis, H. (1951). *The bias of communication.* Toronto: University of Toronto Press.

Jamieson, K. H. (1984). *Packaging the presidency, a history and criticism of presidential campaign advertising.* New York: Oxford University Press.

Johnson-Laird, P. (1983). *Mental models: Towards a cognitive science of language, inference, and consciousness.* Cambridge, MA: Harvard University Press.

Kaid, L. L., & Wadsworth, A. J. (Eds.) (1985). *Political campaign communication: A bibliography and guide to the literature, 1973–1982.* Metuchen, NJ: Scarecrow Press, Inc.

Katz, J., & Fodor, J. (1964). *The structure of language.* Englewood Cliffs, NJ: Prentice-Hall.

Kristeva, J. (1969). *Semiotike: Recherches pour une semanalyse.* Paris: Seuil.

Langer, S. (1957). *Philosophy in a new key: A study in the symbolism of reason, rite, and art.* Cambridge: Harvard University Press.

Leymore, V. L. (1975). *Hidden myth: Structure and symbolism in advertising.* London: Heineman.

Lyons, J. (1977). *Semantics, Vol. 1.* Cambridge, UK: Cambridge University Press.

Marcel, A. J. (1983). Conscious and unconscious perception: Experiments on visual masking and word recognition. *Cognitive Psychology, 15,* 197–237.

Marr, D. (1982). *Vision: A computational investigation into the human representation and processing of visual information.* San Francisco: W. H. Freeman and Company.

Mead, G. H. (1962). *Mind, self, and society.* Chicago: University of Chicago Press.

Metz, C. (1974). *Film language: A semiotics of cinema.* New York: Oxford University Press.

Peirce, Charles S. (1966). *Collected papers.* Cambridge, MA: Harvard University Press.

Rumelhart, D. (1977). Understanding and summarizing brief stories. In D. Laberge & M. Collins (Eds.), *Basic processes in reading: Perception and comprehension* (pp. 265–304). Hillsdale, NJ: Lawrence Erlbaum Associates.

Rumelhart, D., McClelland, J., & PDP-Research-Group (Eds). (1986a). *Parallel distributed processing: Explorations in the microstructure of cognition: Vol. 1, Foundations.* Cambridge, MA: The MIT Press.

Rumelhart, D., McClelland, J., & PDP-Research-Group (Eds). (1986b). *Parallel distributed processing: Explorations in the microstructure of cognition: Vol. 2, Psychological and biological models.* Cambridge, MA: The MIT Press.

Shyles, L. (1984a). The relationships of images, issues and presentational methods in televised spot advertisements for 1980's American presidential primaries. *Journal of Broadcasting, 18*(4), 405–421.

Shyles, L. (1984b). Defining "images" of presidential candidates from televised political spot advertisements. *Political Behavior, 6*(2), 171–181.

Seymour, P. (1979). *Human visual cognition.* London: Collier MacMillan.

Williamson, J. (1978). *Decoding advertisements: Ideology and meaning in advertising.* London: Marion Boyars.

4

The Role of Communication Codes in Political Ads

Frank Biocca
University of North Carolina at Chapel Hill

> I said in my acceptance speech at Atlanta that the 1988 election was not
> about ideology but about competence. I was wrong. It was about phrase-
> ology. It was about 10-second sound bites. And made-for-TV backdrops.
> —Dukakis ("Dukakis . . . , 1990)

When we discuss codes, we are talking about the social construction of
meaning. We venture beyond the mind of an individual voter and are
immediately brought into the sphere of social exchange—into the sphere
of politics.

Social meanings communicated by codes are fluid. The political
communicator dips into the pool of codes to draw up the contents of an
ad and to shape the vaguely articulated meanings floating in the minds of
the electorate.

> Nothing is left to chance: every aspect has been included for some
> purpose—from the color to the background scenery to the inflections in
> the announcer's voice. (Sabato, 1981, p. 111)

For a political consultant to work with the use of "color" and "background scenery," there is an assumption that there are codes that most
of us share about those things. The consultants assume—and often test
to make sure—that the selection of items is reasonably in tune with the
meanings that viewers bring to their decoding of the signs.

Let's start with a simple definition. Fiske (1987) began his book,

Television Culture, with a straightforward definition of codes that stated:

> A code is a rule-governed system of signs, whose rules and conventions are shared amongst members of a culture, and which is used to generate and circulate meanings in and for that culture. (p. 4)

The political consultant's selection of elements for the "background scenery" in a political ad is based on his or her knowledge of those rules. This notion of a rule-governed system implies that the pattern of association and opposition that a code contains is *negotiated* in a culture. A rule can be handed down to members of the culture. It can be created and agreed to by a subculture. But most of all, it is inferred (abducted) as a general principle by an individual eager to be "tuned into" the social environment. A rule can also be violated because of ignorance or for shock effect. It may evolve differently within various social groups. So it is with codes. Whether a code is strong or weak depends on whether the rules consistently evoke certain responses and meanings.

If codes were simply a matter of strong convention, we as analysts of political advertising would be faced with a simple task. It would be theoretically possible to collect the code's correlation between signifiers and signified and construct a kind of dictionary for all the nonlinguistic codes of the political ad. A survey of an electorate could be used to determine the semantic space occupied by each sign (e.g., lexical multidimensional space as in Osgood, Suci, & Tannebaum, 1957). There could be a kind of Rosetta Stone of political codes. Armed with this knowledge, an analyst would simply decode the ad by looking up and summing the semantic units that correspond to the signs in an ad.

But, of course, this is too simplistic. Codes, like the meanings they impart, are variously circulated within the culture. They are *inflected* (subject to variations in use and meaning) by different subcultures. Finally, codes are volatile correlations of expressions to semantic contents, open to change, even inviting violation and invention in the pursuit of informational or aesthetic effects (Eco, 1976).[1] If this were not the case, political consulting would be a deadly science rather than an art.

---

[1]This is especially true in esthetic communication, where esthetic play often involves the violation and twisting of codes, in order to produce new meaning, to get the observer to engage in metasemiotic contemplation, or to invent new codes from the destruction of old ones. In the last case, the communicator is recycling expression units and placing them in new contexts with new syntactic and semantic associations.

A full discussion of a theory of codes would take us far outside the scope of this chapter and toward a discussion of general semiotics, semantics, and the philosophy of language (see, for example, Eco, 1976; Hervey, 1981; Lyons, 1977; Sebeok, 1986). The serious study of the structure and content of television, let alone political advertising, is still too rudimentary for us to even attempt to integrate advanced semantic theories.

But much could be gained. There are few issues in the theory of codes that cannot be tied directly to a discussion of the functions, structures, and the effects of political ads.[2] So with this in mind, we take a step toward the analysis of the structural components of political ads by considering how the ads could be decomposed and analyzed as a set of codes, rather than our remaining at the level of the whole ad. The analyst must first fracture the expression continuum. Only by working with the pieces can we come to see how the whole exerts its power.

It would be foolish to think that there are codes unique to the political ad. The category *political advertising* is a fragile distinction we make within the flow of television content. It is distinguished by the speakers of its discourse, that is, politicians and their organizations and the purpose of the discourse, which is the attainment or maintenance of the support of the viewer in a democratic election. The political ad shares many of its codes with other genres or "texts" on television.[3] Also, the political ad is certainly not the only political content on television; it only has the most *overt* political content. An analysis and study of the

---

[2]See Eco's (1976) chapters on codes and sign production. This literature has not been well integrated into a discussion of American political advertising, which is still dominated by anecdotal studies. European studies of political communication are more likely to adopt a semiotic perspective. Nonetheless, in the absence of a more advanced discourse on political advertising, some of the more rigorous and systematic theories of general semiotics, as exemplified by the work of Eco, can have tremendous value in the analysis of political advertising, by providing some valuable theoretical and analytical tools for decomposing the structural properties of the political ad.

[3]Part of this is due to the fact that the producers of such ads often produce some of the other texts on television, that is, product advertising and news and entertainment programming. A frequent observation in the history of the development of political ad genres has been that the personnel who produce them have frequently relied on the techniques and motifs of the product commercial (Diamond & Bates, 1984; Sabato, 1981). In a political culture that considers political discourse to be above and removed from the "vulgarity" and "triviality" of commercial discourse, this has produced great unease and fear that the politician, the mythical "leader of the free world," has become a product. At the heart of this unease is the conflict between the concept of "leader," who creates and forms public opinion and guides behavior, and the notion of "product," which slavishly pursues public whims and is transformed so as to please (e.g., this dilemma is featured in the film, *The Candidate*).

codes of the political ad must acknowledge that the boundary of video content captured by the phrase *political communication* is essentially fuzzy, tentative, and always subject to revision.

ANALYSIS OF THE SHOT IN THE POLITICAL AD

The political ad is a collection of individual images, shots, and scenes. The shot and even the single image do not correspond to a "word" in some language of television. Nonetheless, it has been argued that television has the properties of language; it has a syntax (Carroll, 1980; Metz, 1974).

A single frame of video or a shot are among the smallest syntactic units of television. But even a single frame is already a complex collection of signs and codes; it is a text. This is a point emphasized by Metz (1974):

> The cinema has no phonemes; nor does it, whatever one may say, have words . . . the image (at least in the cinema) corresponds to one or more sentences, and the sequence is a complex segment in a *discourse*. (p. 65)

Keeping this in mind, let's consider some of the codes that might contribute to the meaning of the politician who is the subject of the commercial.

Codes Associated with Composition, Camera Position, and Camera Movement

Codes associated with the use of the camera are a good place to start in our analysis of the codes of the political commercial. A formal system in television is built around the way the commercial positions the viewer's point-of-sight: camera distance, focal length, horizontal camera angle, vertical camera angle, and height. These variables are definitely structural, subtle, and unique to film media. The placement of the camera in relation to the objects filmed—a politician, for example—can influence the meaning of what is filmed.

The most basic codes are those that cue perception. At its most basic level, the placement of the camera contributes to the composition of the shot. It is clear that point-of-sight and focal length influence the processing of the perceptual codes involved in the calculation of space, time, and motion in the diegetic space of the video image (Hochberg,

1986). In a companion article (Biocca, in press) I suggested that the placement and movement of the camera influence psychological processes, the perceptual *point-of-sight* and the more schematic concept of *point-of-view* (Branigan, 1984).

What is the most common shot in political commercials? Certainly, it's the "talking head" shot. The political commercial is a kind of television portraiture. Normally, the "featured" head is that of the politician. The framing (Arnheim, 1982) and composition of the shot establish a physical distance between the viewer and the politician. The location of the camera vis-à-vis the politician defines a horizontal and vertical angle of sight for the viewer, perspective relationships within the image, and an implied relationship to the gaze of the politician. The camera literally positions the viewer in relation to the candidate and activates social codes associated with that physical location.

For example, the camera can suggest intimacy between the viewer and the politician by activating codes of physical distance. Here the codes of representation and point-of-sight may be intereacting with proxemic codes of physical space (Hall, 1974). The camera's distance from the politician can influence the viewer's perceived closeness and the likeability of the politician (Baggaley, 1980; Kepplinger, 1990). A study comparing responses to live or televised versions of a presidential debate (Biocca, 1990a) found that the closer the television camera is to a politician in a political debate, the more the audience likes what he says, even after controlling for the verbal content of the politician's statements. This finding could be due to the fact that in a closeup, the politician is able to communicate more information through his facial expressions. But this may not be the most influential factor. The hypothesis that proxemic codes are the cause of the increased liking of the candidate is suggested by the finding that the effect continues over a variety of exposure durations (Schulz, van Lessen, Schlede, & Waldman, 1976, discussed in Kepplinger, in press). We would expect that the effect of redundant information from a facial expression (which can be negative) would diminish over time, whereas the effect of proxemic social codes would continue.

Because camera angle suggests our physical position relative to the candidate, it can also carry the proxemic codes suggested by the expressions "He's way above me" or "He's beneath me." It can communicate perceived power relations between viewer and viewed. In an almost animalistic way, it can communicate a primitive political relation between the leader and the led.

Extreme camera angles not only take more time to process but tend to produce negative evaluations (Kepplinger, 1990). This may be due to the difficulties in perceptual processing resulting from the atypicality of extreme camera angles. But it may also result in the activation of the proxemic social codes (codes of physical distance between people) discussed later. Lower camera angles, which place the viewer in an "inferior" position to the viewed, appear acceptable and neutral, but angles in which the viewer looks down from a "superior" position may lead to unfavorable evaluations of the person viewed. When these angles are extreme, they can make the viewer highly conscious of his or her position in space, and possibly uncomfortable with this position. But the research in this area does not show a consistent effect for specific camera angles (see Beverly & Young, 1978; Kepplinger, 1990; Kepplinger & Donsback, 1986; Mandell & Shaw, 1973; McCain, Childberg, & Wakshlag, 1977; Tiemens, 1970). This should not be surprising. The codes activated by camera angle are no doubt interacting with other codes that are simultaneously processed. *Together* they construct the meaning and effect of a particular shot.

The composition of the shot in a political commercial, that is, the relation of objects to each other and to the frame, may activate another set of codes. For example, tightly framed pictures of people and politicians can lead the viewer to perceive the individuals as less dynamic (Kepplinger, in press). The location of objects within a frame also appears to be coded and can be suggestive of power, activity, and potency (Herbner, Van Tubergen, & Whitlow, 1979).

The camera is not fixed; it often moves within the shot. Camera motion conveys a great deal of perceptual information. Therefore, it can affect the meaning of objects represented in a scene. Film and television production researchers have long speculated about the meanings potentially imparted by various camera movements (e.g., Pryluck, 1976; Zettl, 1973, 1976). Although the perceptual psychology of camera motion has received some study (Biocca, 1989a, 1989b; Gibson & Rosenblatt, 1955; Gibson, 1966; Hochberg, 1986; Kipper, 1986), the relationship of camera motion to semantic processing of political figures has received limited empirical exploration (Biocca, 1990a). Even though it remains to be explored, we can assume that the camera motion can contribute to the perceived activity or potency of the represented politician (actant).

The codes of camera angle and shot composition have received some attention in the political communication literature (see also Kaid & Davidson, 1986). These codes can have an effect not only on the momentary perceptions, but on the viewer's understanding and memory for represented events. But there may be much more to codes activated by these subtle structural features than has been examined thus far.

Facial and Kinesic Codes in Political Person Perception

Because many ads involve "talking heads," it is clear that nonfilmic codes, associated with facial expression, and kinesics[4] will play a role in the voters' semantic processing of the political commercial. All of these are clearly coded structural features essential for both production (i.e., acting) and the viewer's reception of the political ad. Analysis of these subtle codes is supported by an extensive literature (e.g., Burgoon, 1989; Key, 1977; Ekman, 1982, 1985).

Television magnifies the importance of the candidate's facial expressions to the point where it can be a major part of the candidate's "message." The face of the candidate is a rich display. Whenever the candidate's face appears on the screen, it imparts meaning. Viewers automatically read the meaning of the candidate's subtlest facial expressions, including those that suggest evidence that the candidate is lying (Ekman, 1982, 1985). The fact that Kennedy looked squarely into the camera during the 1960 debate, whereas Nixon was more shifty eyed, may have made Kennedy look more credible and personable (see Hemsley & Doob, 1978, on eye contact).

Movement communicates meaning. The study of such codes is called *kinesics* (Birdwhistell, 1970). How a candidate physically moves in space is a source of meaning in the political ad. In the average political commercial, candidates are often shown in their "stump speech" poses, pointing, slicing the air, and pounding the podium to punctuate their verbal message and communicate "forcefulness" and "passion." The sometimes frenetic hand gestures suggest that some of the candidates have been coaxed to thrash about.

Our mental image of candidates often includes noted physical movements. To some television viewers, Ford's physical clumsiness communicated incompetence. Captured by the camera and paraded on television news, such displays became a significant part of the meaning of Gerald Ford. Ronald Reagan, the senior citizen, consciously speeded up his stride when the cameras were pointed his way. He had been coaxed to not let the camera "see" his age. Most political ads show candidates on the march, diving into seas of hands, jogging, waving, and smiling—a bundle of vigor and energy.

Television's focus on "talking heads" may magnify the importance of these nonverbal communication skills. Commentators find the increasing emphasis on such "political skills" disturbing:

---

[4]Kinesics is the study of body movement, especially communication through body movement.

The . . . political process is in very bad shape indeed if governments are to be elected on the basis of a man's laugh, or his walk, or a habit of drumming his fingers on the table top. (journalist quoted in Sabato, 1981, p. 120)

Objects, Spaces, Color, and Light as Codes: The Mise-en-Scene

It is common in the political advertising literature to see references to the visual content of the mise-en-scene of shots featuring the candidate. For example, Kern (1989) classifies a group of ads according to their location or setting. He makes reference to objects and elements in these locations, such as a "flag-draped office," to identify signs that are intended to impart semantic properties to the politician. Kaid and Davidson (1986) content-analyze the setting of the commercial in their analysis of incumbent and challenger "videostyles." Similar casual references to the semantic effects of background, objects, color, and lighting can be found in a number of the popular treatments of political advertising (e.g., Diamond & Bates, 1984; Sabato, 1981). Such discussions often reflect the intuitive insights of the advertising industry and rules of thumb developed by practitioners.

But like much of the literature on political advertising, the analysis of such elements is rarely systematic. There is no underlying theory of signification, and the classification of signs is defined by a set of assumed and unmeasured emotional and cognitive effects: identification, empathy, attention, and so on.

More elaborate discussion of the elements of the mise-en-scene can be found in film theory (Bordwell & Thompson, 1986). But some of these treatments are often hinged to discussions of film style, history, or production. They may not deal systematically with the relationship of such elements to the viewer's experience of the film, especially its effects on perceptual and semantic processing. Nonetheless, film theory provides some of the most detailed discussions of the codes of the mise-en-scene.

As I demonstrate in the chapter on semantic framing (see chapter 6, this volume), the objects, spaces, and people in a political ad are a part of the meaning of the candidate modeled in the mind of the viewer. Rather than list various codes operative in the mise-en-scene, I incorporate reference to such codes in the discussion of semantic frames to show how the elements of the mise-en-scene can transfer semantic features to the represented candidate. The semantic properties of the scenes adjust the links of the candidate/concept to associated concept nodes. In this manner the commercial alters the meaning of the candidate. Each element in the ad contributes to the meaning of the candidate, although the overall change in the meaning of a candidate contributed by any *single* element may be subtle when we consider the many sociosemiotic forces (i.e., press commentary, passing comments by family and friends, etc.) that come to bear on the voter's emerging mental model of the candidate.

The Sound of Codes: The Audio Track in Political Commercials

The audio track of the political ad has its own codes. "Politics is largely a word game," according to Graber (1986, p. 24). In any commercial the audio track will carry a significant proportion of the meaning of a commercial. This is true not only because of the spoken rhetoric but also because of the texture of the aural environment created. As in film (Burch, 1973; Bordwell & Thompson, 1986), the properties of the sound, such as pitch, rhythm, and timbre, are codes that convey meaning. The careful editing of voice, sound, and music can influence the activation of semantic and emotional links in the mind of the viewer.

Some elements of the sound mix can be orchestrated by the political consultant, whereas some resist orchestration. The candidate is not only a "pretty face" but a set of sounds. The qualities of the candidate's voice are not totally controllable by the political consultant, but carry information (through paralinguistic codes) that the viewer uses to project general attributes onto the candidate. The semantic information contained in that voice is sometimes excluded from the ad precisely because it has *meaning:*

> Candidates often do not even appear, much less speak at length, in their campaign advertisements—especially if their voices are raspy or their features unappealing. (Sabato, 1981, p. 119)

The mental imagery we have of candidates is often based on aural memories of the paralinguistic qualities of their voices. Those of us who follow American politics can easily replay the audio mental images of past presidents: the southern accent and misplaced emphases of Jimmy Carter, the agitated shuffling quality of Nixon's voice, the boyish, high-pitched enthusiasm and malapropisms of George Bush.

The relationship of paralinguistic qualities to presidential communication skills has long been noted and can be seen in ancient discussion of political rhetoric (Aristotle, 1926), in discussion of Roosevelt's fireside chats (Burns, 1956), and in modern studies of presidential rhetoric (e.g., Corcoran, 1979; Graber, 1986; Windt & Ingold, 1987). The qualities of the voice can affect its persuasiveness (Hall, 1980). The absence of hedges (Lind & O'Barr, 1979) and the speech rate (Miller, Marugama, Beaber, & Valone, 1976) can affect the viewer's perception of the power and knowledge of the candidate. Even whole parties can be characterized in ads by the sounds they use. According to Sabato (1981), a Canadian political commercial used the difference between parliamentary hand clapping and desk thumping to signify a number of contrasting properties between the major parties.

Musical codes are often used because they evoke memories or, more precisely, because they provide intertextual references that open up the ad to constellations of connotations evoked by the recall of another text. According to Kern (1989), music can evoke earlier emotions and attitudes developed when the listener was being politically socialized.

There are some interesting sociosemiotic dimensions to the musical codes and genres. According to Robert Goodman, a political consultant, opposing camps purposely try to set contrasting musical identities for their campaigns (Kern, 1989).

Again, this is a little explored dimension of the coded interaction between the political commercial and the viewer. It has received a little more treatment in film theory (Belton & Weis, 1985; Bordwell & Thompson, 1986). It is most advanced in studies of the perception and psychoesthetics of music (Dowling, 1985; Handel, 1989).

Iconology and Mythology in the Political Ads

There is a tradition in the political symbolism literature that analyzes the political use of significant symbols. This means different things for different writers. In some cases, it is a study of *iconology* and *mythology*. There is a long tradition of iconographic studies in anthropology and religious studies (Ferguson, 1954; Frazer, 1950; see also the bibliography in Cirlot, 1962) and in Jungian psychology (Savickas, 1979). These studies have sometimes attempted to create dictionaries containing the meanings of key symbols, usually visual icons (e.g., Cirlot, 1962). We see similar tendencies in some studies within the political communication literature, which seek to analyze the meaning of static icons, such as the flag and faces of key figures.

There is also a fuzzy line between iconology and the study of myth. This occurs because semantically pregnant icons are treated not only as signs, but as texts as well. Myths have a narrative quality that icons, in and of themselves, do not possess other than through intertextual reference. In this way, the differences between signs, codes, and discourses are often confounded. For example, it is this capacity for narrative reference that Elder and Cobb (1983) confuse when they consider the concept and measurement of "symbolic weight" to capture the power of certain images.

Icons and myths can be analyzed historically. For example, a study of symbolism in political advertising might consider sociosemiotic issues dealing with the use, diffusion, and changing meaning of significant symbols over time. In a way, such a study would also become a diachronic study of discourse—discourse about a particular icon or myth.

This is a valid study in political communication, but it is more of an anthropological study than a psychological[5] one. The ad is read to provide insight into the communicator, the culture, and, to a lesser degree, the viewer. The analysis of political commercials can provide insights into the changing meaning of continuing references to recurring symbols and motifs, such as the American flag, a piece of political music, or complete political myths surrounding historical figures, institutions, and emblems. Pieces of such discussions can be found in Edelman (1964), Elder and Cobb (1983), Nimmo (1974), Nimmo and Combs (1980), and Nimmo and Felsberg (1986).

Such broad historical or cultural studies may be predictive of how a group of voters at a specific point in time uses and interprets certain representations. But this insight is only possible to the degree that the analyst understands what Marx called "the dust of history" and how it settles on the mind of the viewer in the layers of ideological schema. To the degree that certain political myths might actually contain schema or rules for interpreting certain types of information, they can potentially inform our understanding of how information is filled in using schema built around a particular myth.

SYNTACTIC CONSTRUCTION OF THE POLITICAL COMMERCIAL

Most developed codes, like language, have a syntax that guides the usage of signs within the code and, to some degree, the usage of signs with other codes. The study of the syntax of individual codes is a matter of general semiotics or the field specializing in that code, for example, the syntax of musical composition. Insights from such basic studies can be imported by the analyst to pick apart the usage of codes in the political commercial.

As noted earlier, video is said to possess a grammar (Carroll, 1980;

---

[5]Here I am using the word *psychological* in its restricted sense of *cognitive* psychology, as opposed to Jungian or Freudian psychology.

Metz, 1974), although there is some debate as to the strength and stability of its syntactic rules. Video syntax incorporates various codes. For the political analyst, knowledge of the syntactic rules of video is essential to understanding the structures of the political commercial, especially the way it semantically frames codes and discourses. Furthermore, video syntax is a cue of the style of the political advertising and, therefore, is essential to the analysis of the genres of political commercials.

The political commercial is a construction or, more precisely, a *montage.* The shots of the scene are constructed to invoke semantic relations between scenes. Specific sequences of shots assembled in scenes have been called *syntagmas* in the film literature (e.g., Metz, 1974; Monaco, 1977). Graphic, rhythmic, and content relations of shots in the syntagma guide and activate patterns of semantic priming and semantic relation in the viewer. This is part of the code of television, one that is consciously articulated by the director and video editor. Viewers have consciously or unconsciously learned some of its rules and use them to assemble the meaning of the commercial.

A general syntax of film has been attempted by Metz (1974) and other writers who have built on his work. For example, John Carroll (1980) presents a more psycholinguistic approach to film syntax. The consideration of the codes of montage lends itself to strict formal analysis. Using this generalized discussion of film and television grammar, the political analyst can assume, temporarily at least, that political advertising exhibits few, if any, variations on the general grammar of film and television. In the purely formal sense, the analyst of political commercials might consider, for example, codes associated with different types of transitions from shot to shot. This can be of value if the analyst wants to find syntactic patterns that are generalizable across genres of ads.

Syntax is also important when the analyst considers specific ads. The types and forms of connections made between scenes and elements in the ad suggest part of the strategy of the communicator. Syntax reveals attempts to forge semantic links. When we consider syntax in its *specific* application in an ad, we are entering the realm of semantic framing, the act of telling a narrative, the juxtaposition of the texts and sentences of a political commercial. Some examples of how syntactic relations can structure meaning are considered in the chapter on semantic framing (see chapter 6, this volume).

SOME CAUTIONS ABOUT THE ANALYSIS OF CODES

At this point, it is worthwhile to consider the advantages and disadvantages of this level of analysis. The analysis of the codes of political commercials can provide tremendous insights into the structure of the commercials and, indirectly, into the possible relationships between structure and the psychological processing of viewers. But it is not without its disadvantages.

The analysis of codes within and outside political communication is often driven by two sets of goals: (a) the analysis of a specific message and (b) the generalization of patterns of coding and psychological responses across message categories. The former is the more common goal for analysts in literature, film, art, and—yes—political advertising. All hurriedly seek some magic formulas to unlock the secret of a *particular* text.

In the analyses of individual messages, the codes are often considered informally. The analyst tends to rely on his or her own "speaker's" knowledge of the code to provide haphazard collections of the "readings" of individual ads. Too often political analysts refer to various codes narrowly as a means of manipulating "emotions and moods" (e.g., Kern, 1989). The analysis of meaning of the codes is neglected. The form of the commercial is part of its meaning.

In analyses of individual ads, the meaning of the ad is proclaimed in a hurried fashion, whereas more considered analysis of the *mechanisms* for the creation of that meaning and the likely *variations* in the derived meaning across groups of individuals are neglected. The assumption is that an ad has *a* meaning. Failure to identify possible sources of variation immediately triggers validity problems for the analysis.

The analysis of codes in a political ad is often used to unmask the ideology of the commercial. The goal of ideological unmasking is common in the semiotic literature (Biocca, 1990b). Studies of advertising and political communication that specialize in unmasking the ideology of the text (Dyer, 1982; Fiske & Harteley, 1978; Williamson, 1978) provide insights into the ads, but they are often hounded by challenges to their validity.

The analysis of codes calls for systematic specification of how a code carves up some sematic field (Eco, 1976). This is slow, tedious work, as anyone who has read the work on semantics or sociolinguistics can attest. It must be empirically based, or it cannot report patterns of usage and be "sociological." But the problems that confront the sociolinguists are only increased when we consider the systematic analysis of other codes, such as those used in television.

Much basic work into the codes of television remains to be done. Codes, even strong ones, are in a constant state of flux. Codes of television are weak codes; the rules that divide up the semantic field with the separation of expression units and semic units is weak and not highly formalized, especially across communities of viewers.

Analysts often fail to describe codes as sets of probabilities; likewise, they often fail to describe encoding and decoding as probabilistic functions. Attempts to generalize theories about specific codes should lead to probablilistic statements rather than statements of semiotic "laws" (although the rhetoric of certainty is more common). Rarely found are formal methods of theory validation or empirical methods attempting to link a hypothesized structure with the encoding activity of communicators or the decoding activity of viewers.

Any systematic analysis of codes assumes that the code is somewhat formalized, as is language. But when one studies language and its relation to meaning, one is immediately struck by how much context or the pragmatics of usage influences both form and function. Individual codes are not processed in isolation, but interact with all the codes of television. The interaction of television codes during semantic processing is not well studied; the systematic analysis of individual codes is still in its infancy. We have not reached a stage where understanding of the process yields predictable results.

The preponderance of interpretive analyses of the codes of specific ads can hamper our ability to generalize across genres of political ads. Although content-analytic studies are well suited to such generalizations, the very methodology of content analysis can lead to banal generalities about signs that have only limited connection to the interpretive context.

Nonetheless, while acknowledging some of the limitations, there are a number of reasons why an analysis of codes is worthwhile. People have internalized the codes and use them to process video. A rigorous analysis of the codes provides a theoretical means to a systematic analysis of political advertising. A rigorous use of knowledge about the structure of specific codes provides some constraints on the loose, intuitive analyses of specific ads while connecting such analyses to the larger body of literature, film, and television research. Systematic analysis can be fed into more empirically based approaches to the relationship between ad structure and the cognitive processes of the viewer (Biocca, in press).

REFERENCES

Aristotle (1926). *The art of rhetoric* (J. Freese, Ed.). London: William Heineman.

Arnheim, R. (1982). *The power of the center: A study of composition in the visual arts.* Berkeley, CA: University of California Press.

Baggaley, J. (1980). *Psychology of the TV image.* Farnborough, U.K.: Gower.

Belton, J., & Weis, E. (1985). *Film sound: Theory and practice.* New York: Columbia University Press.

Beverly, R. E., & Young, T. J. (1978). *The effect of mediated camera angle on receiver* evaluations of source credibility, dominance, attraction, homophily. Paper presented at the International Communication Association, Chicago.

Biocca, F. (1989a). *"Reading" the video screen: Psychological measurement of spatial attention and perceptual biases within television, video, and computer monitors.* Unpublished doctoral dissertation, University of Wisconsin-Madison, Madison, WI.

Biocca, F. (1989b). *The effect of literacy training on spatial attention to video monitors.* Paper presented to the International Communication Association, Montreal.

Biocca, F. (1990a). *How camera distance affects the perception of candidates during a presidential debate.* Unpublished paper, Center for Research in Journalism and Mass Communication, University of North Carolina at Chapel Hill.

Biocca, F. (1990b). Semiotics and mass communication: Points of intersection. In T. Sebeok & J. Umiker-Sebeok (Eds.), *Semiotic web 1990.* The Hague: Mouton Press.

Biocca, F. (in press). Viewer's mental models of political commercials: Towards a theory of the semantic processing of television. F. Biocca (Ed.), *Television and political advertising, Vol. 1: Psychological processes.* Hillsdale, NJ: Lawrence Erlbaum Associates.

Birdwhistell, R. (1970). *Kinesics and context: Essays on body motion communication.* Philadelphia, PA: University of Pennsylvania Press.

Bordwell, D., & Thompson, K. (1986). *Film art.* New York: Alfred A. Knopf.

Branigan, E. (1984). *Point of view in the cinema.* New York: Mouton Press.

Burch, N. (1973). *Theory of film practice.* New York: Praeger Publishers.

Burgoon, J. K. (1989). *Nonverbal communication: The Unspoken Dialogue.* New York: Harper & Row.

Burns, J. M. (1956). *Roosevelt: The lion and the fox.* New York: Harcourt, Brace, & World.

Carroll, J. M. (1980). *Toward a structural psychology of cinema.* The Hague: Mouton Publishers.

Cirlot, J. (1962). *A dictionary of symbols.* New York: Philosophical Library.

Corcoran, D. (1979). *Political language and rhetoric.* Austin, TX: University of Texas.

Diamond, E., & Bates, S. (1984). *The spot: The rise of political advertising on television.* Cambridge, MA: The MIT Press.

Dowling, W. J. (1985). *Music cognition.* Orlando, FL: Academic Press.

"Dukakis speech barks at '88 sound bites." (1990, April 22) *Raleigh News and Observer,* NC.

Dyer, G. (1982). *Advertising as communication.* London: Metheun.

Eco, U. (1976). *A theory of semiotics.* Bloomington, IN: Indiana University Press.

Edelman, M. (1964). *The symbolic uses of politics.* Urbana, IL: University of Illinois Press.

Ekman, P. (1982). *Emotion in the human face.* New York: Cambridge University Press.

Ekman, P. (1985). *Telling lies: Clues to deceit in the marketplace, politics, and marriage.* New York: Norton.

Elder, C. & Cobb, R. (1983). *The political uses of symbols.* New York: Longman.

Ferguson, G. W. (1954). *Signs and symbols in Christian art.* New York: Oxford University Press.

Fiske, J. (1987). *Television culture.* London: Methuen.

Fiske, J., & Hartley, J. (1978). *Reading television.* London: Methuen.

Fodor, J. (1975). *The language of thought.* New York: Thomas Y. Crowell.

Frazer, J. G. (1950). *The golden bough.* New York: Macmillan.

Gibson, J. J. (1966). *The senses considered as perceptual systems.* Boston: Houghton-Mifflin.

Gibson, J. J. (1979). *The ecological approach to visual perception.* Boston: Houghton Mifflin.

Gibson, J. J., Olum, P., & Rosenblatt, F. (1955). Parallax and perspective during aircraft landings. *American Journal of Psychology, 4,* 27–35.

42

Biocca

Graber, D. (1986). Political languages. In D. Nimmo & K. Sanders (Eds.) *Handbook of political communication*. Beverly Hills, CA: Sage.
Hall, E. (1974). *Handbook for proxemic research*. Washington, DC: Studies in the Anthropology of Visual Communication.
Hall, J. (1980). Voice tone and persuasion. *Journal of Personality and Social Psychology, 38*, 924–934.
Handel, S. (1989). *Listening: An introduction to the perception of auditory events*. Cambridge, MA: The MIT Press.
Hecker, S. (1986). *Non-verbal measurement of response to advertising*. Paper presented to the Advertising Research Foundation, New York.
Hemsley, G., & Doob, A. (1978). The effect of looking behavior on perceptions of a communicator's credibility. *Journal of Applied Social Psychology, 8*, 136–144.
Herbner, G., Van Tubergen, G. N., & Whitlow, S. S. (1979). Dynamics of the frame in visual composition. *ECTJ, 27*(2), 83–88.
Hervey, S. (1981). *Semiotic perspectives*. London: George Allen & Unwin.
Hochberg, J. (1986). Representation of motion and space in video and cinematic displays. In K. Boff, L. Kaufmann, & J. Thomas (Eds.), *Handbook of perception and human performance* (vol. 2, pp. 21-1–21-64). New York: Wiley.
Kaid, L., & Davidson, L. (1986). Elements of videostyle. In L. Kaid, D. Nimmo, & K. R. Sanders (Eds.), *New perspectives in political advertising*. Carbondale, IL: Southern Illinois University Press.
Kepplinger, H. M. (in press). The impact of presentation techniques: Theoretical aspects and empirical findings. In F. Biocca (Ed.), *Television and political advertising, Vol. 1: Psychological processes*. Hillsdale, NJ: Lawrence Erlbaum Associates.
Kepplinger, H. M., & Donsbach, W. (1986). *The influence of changes in camera perspective on the perception of the speaker*. Paper presented at the meeting of the International Communication Association, Chicago.
Kern, M. (1989). *30-second politics: Political advertising in the eighties*. New York: Praeger.
Key, M. R. (1977). *Nonverbal communication: A research guide and bibliography*. Metuchen, NJ: Scarecrow Press.
Kipper, P. (1986). Television camera movement as a source of perceptual information. *Journal of Broadcasting and Electronic Media, 30*, 395–307.
Lind, E., & O'Barr, W. (1979). The social significance of speech in the courtroom. In H. Giles & R. St. Clair (Eds.), *Language and social psychology* (pp. 145–179). Oxford, UK: Blackswells.
Lyons, J. (1977). *Semantics, Vol. 1*. Cambridge, UK: Cambridge University Press.
Mandell, L., & Shaw, D. (1973). Judging people in the news unconsiously: Effect of camera angle and bodily activity. *Journal of Broadcasting, 17*, 353–362.
McCain, T. A., Chilberg, J., & Wakshlag, J. (1977). The effect of camera angle on source credibility and attraction. *Journal of Broadcasting, 21*, 35–46.
Metz, C. (1974). *Film language: A semiotics of cinema*. New York: Oxford.
Miller, N., Maruyama, G., Beaber, R., & Valone, K. (1976). Speed of speech and persuasion. *Journal of Personality and Social Psychology, 34*, 615–625.
Monaco, J. (1977). *How to read a film*. New York: Oxford University Press.
Nimmo, D. (1974). *Popular images of politics*. Englewood Cliffs, NJ: Prentice-Hall.
Nimmo, D., & Combs, J. E. (1980). *Sublminal politics: Myths & mythmakers in America*. Englewood Cliffs, NJ: Prentice-Hall.
Nimmo, D., & Felsberg, A. J. (1986). Hidden myths in televised political advertising. In L. Kaid, D. Nimmo, & K. R. Sanders (Eds.), *New perspectives in political advertising* (pp. 249–267). Carbondale, IL: Southern Illinois University Press.

Osgood, C., Suci, G., & Tannenbaum, P. (1957). *The measurement of meaning*. Urbana, IL: University of Illinois Press.

Pryluck, C. (1976). *Sources of meaning in motion pictures and television*. New York: Arno Press.

Sabato, L. J. (1981). *The rise of political consultants*. New York: Basic Books.

Savickas, A. (1979). *The concept of symbol in the psychology of C. G. Jung*. Innsbruck: Resch.

Sebeok, T. (Ed). (1986). *Encyclopedic dictionary of semiotics,* Vols. 1–3. Berlin: Mouton de Gruyter.

Tiemens, R. (1970). Some relationship of camera angle to communicator credibility. *Journal of Broadcasting, 14,* 483–490.

Williamson, J. (1978). *Decoding advertisements: Ideology and meaning in advertising*. London: Marion Boyars.

Windt, T., & Ingold, B. (Eds.). (1987). *Essays in presidential rhetoric*. Dubuque, IA: Kendall/Hunt.

Zettl, H. (1973). *Sight, sound, motion: Applied media aesthetics*. Belmont, CA: Wadsworth.

Zettl, H. (1976). *Television production handbook*. Belmont, CA: Wadsworth Publications.

5

The Analysis of Discourses Within the Political Ad

Frank Biocca
University of North Carolina at Chapel Hill

> Politics is talk.
>
> —Bell (1975)

WHAT IS A DISCOURSE?

A discourse between two people seems clear enough. It is a conversation between two people, over some specified period of time, and the words and gestures they use. Such a discourse between two or more people is open to study. In fact, a great deal can be learned about unspoken social rules from the observation of discourse (Stubbs, 1983; Van Dijk, 1980).

But the term *discourse* has been given wide currency in the humanities and, to a lesser degree, in the social sciences. The scope of the word has been expanded and the meaning generalized to the study of many types of communication exchange. Through metaphoric usage, it has come to mean a host of social and communication phenomena whose study is tentatively organized under the interdisciplinary project of discourse analysis (Van Dijk, 1985a, 1985b, 1985c, 1985d).

What are political discourses? How do ads refer to, combine, or participate in discourses? Let's begin by using the following definition as a starting point:

> A discourse is a thematically and ideologically structured, self-referring progression of communications (messages, texts) circulating within a definable community of communicators and receivers over a specified period of time.

45

Although the general field of discourse analysis tends to concentrate on the study of verbal and written language, the analysis of discourse is not necessarily restricted to linguistic codes. A discourse is the visible evidence of communication exchanges. The exchange is accessible through artifacts, such as recorded discussions, articles, books, films, and even physical objects, such as products—all artifacts that serve to express meaning in the discourse. The boundaries of the discourse are commonly defined by the community of speakers—for example, the "discourse of medical experts" (e.g., Foucault, 1965)—or by the dominant themes or preoccupations that characterize the discourse—for example, the "discourse of science."

A discourse is about something. It refers to some part of our experience. It defines it. In the act of defining it, it influences our experience of it, and limits our thought about that segment of experience.

Political ads are part of a discourse. For example, an ad can be defined as part of the discourse of the candidate. It can also be part of a larger discourse. It might be connected to social discourses, for example, the discourse on incarceration and the death penalty. In a very real way, the ad is one sentence in an ongoing discussion about some segment of social experience. By struggling to define that segment of social experience, the discourse influences our understanding and behavior in or toward that part of constructed reality.

A discourse is cumulative. The very act of naming, of using one word before another, sets in motion a discourse. The selection of one word influences the words and phrases that follow. Similarly, in a campaign, each ad, each speech act, influences the others that follow. If the campaign is well organized, the ads are seen as a unified speech, a discursive act directed at the electorate. Even if they are not well organized, the universe of ads presented by a candidate or in a campaign is treated as some unified discourse by the press and many informed segments of the electorate. The collection of ads is interpreted as symptomatic of some electoral trend (e.g., "this is a negative campaign!").

An ad is the product of a discourse. The meaning of a word must often be considered in the context of the sentence in which it occurs, and the sentence in the context of the paragraph or text in which it appears. In a similar way, an individual political ad cannot be considered solely as an independent unit but must be considered a part of a much larger discursive structure. It also refers to and is connected to a number of discourses. The people who produce the ad—politicians and consultants—and the voters who view the ad are interpenetrated by discourses about the world around them. They are the objects of discourses, participants in discourses, and taken up by discourses.

Ads interact with each other. A negative ad, for example, is often responded to immediately. The ads speak with and about each other. They are, in a literal sense, a discourse.

Discourses are the exercise of power. The power to speak and name in a mass-mediated society is the power to define. Some "speakers" speak more than others. The "speakers" have varying relationships to the "listeners," the audience of the discourse. A discourse may also be penetrated by certain recurring themes or patterns of speech. It is clear that in electoral politics, the power to control the discourse, to define the meaning of terms such as *liberal* and *conservative* is the power to win.

Discourses have patterns.

> Much like sentences, discourse may exhibit structures that have a systematic, rule-governed nature. . . . It is further understood that text of discourse may have general, abstract, or content-free properties, which might be accounted for by some kind of discourse grammar and properties that are variable across different contexts (situations, speakers, etc.) in the same culture. (Van Dijk, 1988a, p. 23)

In a phrase, discourses exhibit a *discursive structure*. The discursive structure can be influenced by the power relations of the actors and by a set of ideas that organizes the discourses. The ideas exhibit an internal logic; they are *ideo-logies.*

The ads in an election as a whole constitute a discourse. They frame the discussion (discourse) of politics in many elections, especially in the final weeks. Looking at a group of ads as "speech acts," the discourse of a community of speakers, for example, Republicans, may be characterized by different patterns in the use of codes, thema, references to other discourses, and so on, than discourse of some other community, for example, Democrats. Each ad or group of ads can be characterized as possessing a pattern in its use and framing of other discourses. In other words, each ad or group of ads can be analyzed to determine its discursive structure. By considering an ad as a unit, we can analyze the discourse of the ad and attempt to identify the discourses that the ad refers to, that is, current issue debates, other ads, and other media products (intertextual references).

STRATEGIES FOR ANALYZING THE DISCURSIVE STRUCTURES OF POLITICAL ADS

For the purpose of analysis of the discursive structure of an ad or set of ads, the ads can be treated as "speech acts." An analysis of the discursive structure can look for larger, more obvious macrostructural features. In some cases these can be studied using content-analytic techniques. More microstructural analyses of discourses necessitate video analytical skills similar to those used by a linguist or psycholinguist (see Van Dijk, 1988a, 1988b; Van Dijk & Kintsch, 1983).

MACROSTRUCTURAL ANALYSES

Genre Analysis

Science starts by naming. In our attempt to understand political messages, we might first attempt to classify them. The very act of naming reflects the taxonomic urge, an urge at least as old as Aristotle and as obsessively systematic as Linnaeus.

Practitioners refer to schools of political consulting. The profession of political consulting has terms that attempt to classify *types* of ads as a way of identifying some overarching structure that is common to all of them. These working genres include such expressive names for ads as "video-newspaper" ads or "walk-me-talk-me political advertising" (Kern, 1989, p. 35).

On an intuitive level, it is clear that genre analysis can provide a useful tool for dissecting and analyzing our area of study, the political ad. A quick view of the literature of political advertising reveals the use of a number of classificatory schemes (e.g., Devlin, 1986; Kern, 1989; Sabato, 1981; Shyles, 1986), but many appear to possess not only arbitrary boundaries but arbitrary criteria for classification. Furthermore, we see a preoccupation—one might say an obsession—with the distinction between "issue" and "image" ads.

If we are to use genre analysis as an analytical tool, then we must first ask two fundamental sets of questions before haphazardly generating yet another typology of genres: (a) Why bother with identifying a set of genres? Is this just another useless academic exercise? (b) If we are to analyze genres in other than an arbitrary content-analytic fashion, what criteria should be used?

A genre analysis can yield powerful insights into the political communication if and only if it can be firmly tied to one of the stages of the communication processes. More specifically, maximum analytical value will be derived from criteria for genre specification that are closely tied to the *production process* within the political community or to the *sociopsychological processing* by voters. Whether genre analysis is viewed from the perspective of communicators or from the perspective of the viewer, the universe of genres is defined in relation to a set of processes. This provides a constraint on the universe of structures potentially identifiable by an analyst. It also provides the rest of us a means of assessing the relative analytical value of competing typologies and a way of validating a proposed typology. Let us briefly consider these two approaches to genre analysis.

Genre from the Perspective of the Producer

Political ads are the end product of a production process. Like all production processes, the production of political ads is simplified by the application of formulas. Formulas refer to production *rules* that lead to consistent *structures*. Viewed this way, genre analysis becomes an analytical tool in the study of the sociology of political communicators and in the sociosemiotics of the pragmatics of message construction. For example, Kaid and Davidson (1986) have attempted to define genre through content analysis and interviews with producers in order to develop a means of distinguishing the video style of incumbents and challengers.

Tying the validity of genre analysis to the production process provides a set of constraints on the existing plethora of typologies. Structures are not arbitrarily determined; they are specified in relation to some specific production processes and identifiable communities of producers (e.g., political consultants, parties, candidates). Genre analysis is also a study of *canon formation*. What determines the canon of acceptable structures? What forces help sanctify a specific set of ads or genres so that they become models for future producers and reference points for critics? Researchers in political advertising can build upon genre analysis in film studies (Altman, 1984; Feuer, 1987; Neale, 1980; Shatz, 1981) and, to a lesser degree, genre studies in literary theory (Connors, 1986).

Genre Analysis from the Perspective of the Viewer

Genres are not simply a purely "academic" activity, the product of the analyst. Genres can have life. They can reflect a pattern of psychological activity in the viewer.

Viewers may use genres differently. For example, a study by the National Republican Campaign Committee found that viewers extracted and remembered a great deal of candidate "personality" information from "talking head" commercials (Sabato, 1981).

Genre analysis can help the researcher look for discourse schematas (Van Dijk, 1988a), interpretive templates used by viewers that may include grammars (sets of procedural instructions). Some of the work on the presence of different processing strategies for so-called *issue* or *image* commercials (Geiger & Reeves, in press) may be detecting the viewer's use of such discursive schematas for that type of message.

There may be a sociosemiotic relationship between the psychological processes of specific communities of voters and certain genres of political commercials. For cultural reasons, certain interpretive communities of voters may be more attuned to certain formats of commercials. For example, the Republican study cited earlier noted that political ads using the "man-in-the-street" genre were particularly popular with liberal voters and had higher recall with this group (Sabato, 1981).

Can there be other criteria for classifying the genres of political commercials? It may be interesting to get genre distinctions that are *purely formal*[1] or *historical.* But such classifications are of limited value to the analysis of what is intended by an ad, what it means to viewers, and what its effects on an election are. Genres are part of a tacit contract between the advertising industry and its audience. If that is the case, the specification of whether a genre does or does not exist should be falsifiable by reference to the existence or nonexistence of that tacit contract (see Todorov's [1975] arguments on falsifiability). That is not to say that such genres do not reflect or make use of formal or historical categories. Where the analysis of genre engages formal or historical constructs, it tends to define genres with reference to a community of viewers, either a historical community or a subcultural interpretive community, specifiable for the purposes of identification by demographic, psychographic, or other cultural variables.

Interdiscursive and Thematic References

As an utterance—a speech act—the political ad is not a completely self-contained discourse. It is an act of political engagement. It engages existing discourses, provides a retort to previous discourses, or suggests reinterpretation of existing discourses or specific texts. For example, ads often refer to the discourse of other ads, especially in negative campaigns (see discussion of the Graham campaign in Sabato, 1981).

Reference to an issue in an ad is an interdiscursive reference. When the ad refers to an issue, it makes reference not to some state in the world, but to our sociopolitical *discussion* of some state of the world. Something is an issue because it is being discussed; it is a discourse that has developed around a certain theme or existential referent (e.g., the

---

[1]By *purely formal,* I am referring to analyses where the specification and description of form is an end in itself. The analyst is uninterested, or unwilling at that point of the analysis, to specify whether the formal distinctions he or she specifies relate in any way to either production or reception processes.

environment). The reference might be to a discourse in general, or to discursive acts of a specific actant (e.g., the Democrat's position on the environment).

This structural feature has psychological import because it refers to knowledge presumably possessed by the viewer. A large part of the meaning of the ad is contained not in the ad itself, but in its relationship to the viewer's knowledge of other texts and to the discourses to which it refers. When the discursive reference is central to the message,[2] the communicator is often signaling the listener that the message is a sentence in an existing discourse. Its meaning is to be interpreted within the *context* of that existing discourse. Therefore, it is a claim also on the discursive competence of the listener, that is, the degree of knowledge he or she possesses about that discourse.

Interdiscursive references should not be interpreted too narrowly to refer only to "issue" references. Through the techniques of montage, narrative, and well-known personages, the ad makes reference not only to issues and other ads, but to other texts or expressions. The political ads might mimic the codes or structure of a popular movie (e.g., Senator Glenn and *The Right Stuff*), or a genre of films (e.g., crime films). For example, one early Eisenhower political ad used the familial genre of the Disney-like cartoon to represent the "bandwagon" for the avuncular "Ike." Another ad adopted the style of the popular "March of Time" newsreel series to provide an interpretive frame for an Eisenhower commercial about "The Man from Abilene" (see Sabato, 1981). This active or passive reference to other texts or genres is often referred to as *intertextuality* in the literature on semiotics and literary theory (Jardine, 1986). Here we consider intertextual references to be only a subcategory of interdiscursive references.

What do such references presume about the communication act, or more importantly, about the viewer? To establish the presumed semiotic competence of the model viewer of this message, the analyst might consider a diagram of all the interdiscursive references of a particular ad. The interdiscursive references may sometimes be inferred by cues given by the use of music, actors, backdrops, and so on. To generalize about patterns of interdiscursive references for whole groups of ads (e.g., ads from the Democratic parties), traditional content-analytic strategies may be used. Examples of the tallying of one kind of discursive reference— the issues in the set of political ads—are common (e.g., Boiney & Paletz, 1990; Kern, 1989; Patterson & McClure, 1976; Shyles, chapter 9, this

---

[2]Centrality might be communicated by its position in the message. It might occur at the beginning, suggesting the topic of the ad. Repeated reference within the ad to an ongoing discourse can also be used to signal centrality.

volume). Kern (1989), for example, provides a content analysis of the universe of issues in the 1984 election, as well as the "frequency of reference" to specific issues. He breaks this down according to categories of communicators, the party issuing the ads, and whether the politician is running for congress, the senate, or the presidency. The implicit assumption is that the ads for a party or a type of politician constitute a kind of discourse whose structure is analyzable. Of course, simple content analytic strategies may not capture the full range of interdiscursive references, especially subtle ones, but it can provide some insight into the structural dynamics of a large universe of ads. A thorough understanding of the interdiscursive references involves the next level of analysis, the semantic framing of the ad (see chapter 6, this volume).

Actantial Universe of the Ad(s)

Ads make references to social actors. The commercial represents social actors, such as demographic groups, certain professions, classes, and so on. For example, single shots of the commercial are used to evoke references to "the poor," "blue collar workers," "farmers," and so on. Over and over in the 1988 presidential commercials we see candidates speaking to or shaking the hands of represented "farmers" and "blue collar workers" denoted by their dress through baseball caps, overalls, and hard hats.

But ads will also refer to nonhuman "actors," such as corporations, the environment, and so on. A commercial from candidate Gore used a corporate building to represent unspecified "polluters."

Actors are the subjects or objects of propositions in political commercials. They are often portrayed as the causes or effects of represented actions. They are, therefore, central to the viewer's mental representations of the commercial. Keeping with a terminology that links the structure of the message with psychological processes, I refer to these represented social actors as *actants* (see discussion in Biocca, in press-a). The semiotic concept of actant (Eco, 1976; Greimas, 1986; Greimas & Courtes, 1982) is useful here for a number of reasons. First, it clearly distinguishes references to social actors from the actors (players) in the commercial. Second, the concept allows nonhuman forces, such as "the economy" and "China," to be actors in the propositions that constitute the commercial.

An analysis of the political commercial can establish a conceptual diagram of the actantial universe of the commercial. At a higher level, the analysis of the semantic framing of the commercial suggests the manner in which the actants of the commercial are related in the video propositions of the commercial. The commercial intends to alter the represented semantic structure of these actants, the most prominent of which is the candidate. For example, the semantic framing of a commercial may attempt to transfer semantic markers (properties) of one actant to another (see Biocca, in press-b, for an example).

In some cases, the analyst might be interested in characterizing the actantial universe of a group of commercials. In such cases, the analysis of the actants may be more of an end in itself, one in which the analyst is attempting to establish referential patterns similar to global analyses of interdiscursive references.

For example, some actants may be over- or underrepresented. In the universe of political advertising the world of voters is only made up of workers, farmers, housewives, senior citizens, and babies. Any cursory review of presidential commercials shows that candidates are rarely shown shaking the hands of businessmen and white collar workers. Yet in reality it is the hands of the powerful that politicians most often shake; this is not the case in the world of political commercials.

Patterns of reference include not only frequency of reference but also the location of the actant in propositions. For example, an analyst might be interested in when and how minority members are represented in political commercials. Are the actants subjects or objects or propositions? Are they portrayed as causal agents or as part of the consequences of actions?

Such analysis says something about how power relations are portrayed in the ad. In many ads, the representatives of various groups are merely part of a passive audience for the politician. The candidate acts upon them, or they are portrayed as the causes of the candidate's actions. In some populist ads, such as the series developed by the Gore and Jackson campaigns in the 1988 election, the people represented in the ad are not just part of the scenery, but are represented as initiators of social actions. An analysis of the locations of actants in propositional structures tends to lead the analyst toward a more microstructural analysis of the ad.

Such analyses are not common in the present study of political advertising. A good example of a discourse-analytic analysis using a wide range of news stories as well as more fine grained analyses of specific news stories can be found in Van Dijk (1988b) and Van Dijk and Kintsch (1983).

Analyzing the Represented Speaker of the Ad

How does the ad address its viewer? Does it speak directly to the viewer as an equal, as when the politician looks out of the screen in a heart-to-heart conversation with the voter? Is the viewer a voyeur watching the candidate from afar, like a member of a crowd watching a motorcade? With each speech act there is a represented speaker and an implied listener, a kind of *model viewer* (Biocca, in press-a). A relationship is offered to the viewer, a kind of semiotic contract. The viewer may accept, decline, or take an alternative strategy relative to the message.

The viewer creates a mental model of the speaker and calculates the implied listener for the message. Psychologically, the interpretive process would appear to require it (Biocca, in press-a). The viewer must construct a model of the speaker to infer the intent and knowledge base of the communicator. This assessment is essential to the viewer's understanding of the message. The speaker of the political ad can be perceived to be an individual or a collective of speakers (i.e., a company, a political party, an institution, etc.). Looking at it from the psychological perspective of the viewer, the represented speaker/voice can affect the *point of view* (Biocca, in press-a; Branigan, 1984) adopted by the viewer and, therefore, the way the meaning of the ad is organized in the mind of the viewer.

Because we are emphasizing the structure of the political message rather than the mental processes of the viewer, let us consider how the represented speaker is constructed in the political ad. Although all ads are objectively the speech of the candidate's organization, the represented speaker may vary greatly from ad to ad. Political ads are constructed to appear to be alternatively the utterance of the candidate, the party, some objective disembodied voice, public opinion, or "the people."

Political commercials, like all television messages, make use of a variety of devices for representing the speaker. The speaker of the political commercial is an actant of the commercial. The key formal elements that may contribute to the viewer's representation of the speaker and the structure and meaning of the ad are: (a) the represented *social and class position* of the speaker; (b) the presence of a *unified or diffused* voice; (c) the *presence or absence of the speaker(s)* in the diegetical space of the ad; and (d) the speaker's *direct or indirect address* of the viewer.

Because viewers automatically classify people according to their own particular classification of social types, speakers will often be chosen carefully to represent some shared social type. In a political commercial, classification by social class and position is particularly marked. Individual actors or voters may speak on camera to represent social communities (e.g., farmers, women) or, indirectly, to represent the targeted viewer.

> If one's polling results indicate that black women over forty years of age
> are a swing group, for example, then such an individual saying just the
> right thing is included in the commercial, giving the targeted viewer
> someone with whom to identify. (Sabato, 1981, p. 123)

The long history of research into the effects of the source of a message
on persuasion (Petty & Cacioppo, 1981; Reardon, 1981) shows that the
represented speaker will in many cases influence the perceived value of
what is spoken, depending on the viewer's evaluative criteria (Chronkite
& Liska, 1980) of the source within the context of the message and
viewing situation.

Unlike film, which may have a diffuse and ambiguous voice, political
commercials are often organized around the voice of a single narrator to
more firmly organize the propositional logic of the commercial.
Speakers may be part of or absent from the possible world depicted in
the commercials. Narrators/speakers may be represented on camera
speaking from the possible world (diegetical space) represented in the
commercial. For example, a number of the 1988 presidential commercials show the candidate speaking to groups of voters. The candidate is
the narrator of the commercial and is also presented in the represented
world of the commercial, be it a farm, political rally, and so on. More
commonly, the speaker is a disembodied voice (nondiegetical) commenting on the images that constitute the commercial. In this latter case,
the viewer is more likely to adopt a more passive, voyeuristic point of
view (see section on point-of-view in Biocca, in press-a).

The commercial may directly address the viewer, either grammati-
cally (imperative statements about what "you" should do) or visually
(through eye contact with the viewer). In the political ad, the speaker
may be embodied as a talking head directly addressing the viewer in the
role of "the candidate," "a concerned citizen," and so on. The use of
pronouns in the text of the ad suggest the linguistic point of view and
the relationship of the speaker to what is spoken (e.g., "I come to you
today . . .", "You will make a difference in this election . . .", "They
have damaged this country . . ."). Filmic conventions, such as the use of
subjective camera angles (a shot of a scene through the "eyes" of the
speaker), can provide vivid representations of first-person point of
view. The use of verbal and film language establish the level of
communicative tension between the communicator and viewer, as well
as the force of the communicator's requests and statements.

In negative ads the candidate is rarely the speaker. Consultant wisdom
suggests that the candidate should not even be represented (Kern, 1989).
On the contrary, accusations and innuendo are spoken by calm, rational
male voices to offer authoritative or objective commentary, a third-

person device clearly borrowed from the documentary genre. Accusation may also be voiced by irate and "innocent" citizens (see description of negative ads from the 1986 Hunt-Helms race in Sabato, 1981).

In summary, adopting a voice is more than just a stylistic device; it establishes a set of assumed relationships between the speaker (communicator) and the listener (viewer) regarding shared knowledge, shared social roles, and other pragmatic factors that influence not only what is said but what is assumed about the relationship of the speaker to the listener. The viewer infers and fills in values regarding his or her expectations about the speaker's knowledge, intentions, and the relationship of that inferred knowledge to the themes of the message. How the message is visually and verbally enunciated gives some hints to the viewer not only of how to infer and construct the model communicator of the ad—the speaking subject behind the propositions—but also the model viewer of the ad, the role offered to the viewer.

MICROSTRUCTURAL ANALYSES

The viewer's psychological experience of a commercial is a moment-to-moment interpretive process (Biocca, in press-a). Very subtle semantic and syntactic procedures are executed in response to the structural features of the message. Viewers must determine and make judgments about the propositions within an ad. They must relate concepts presented on the audio track to the images and establish the local semantic coherence of shots and scenes. Viewers must make all kinds of inferences, some of them entailed by the propositions of the video, some necessary for bridging sequences in a narrative.

Some progress has been made on the microstructural analysis of written and oral texts (e.g., Clark & Clark, 1977; van Dijk & Kintsh, 1983). But what about video and its many multilayered codes, even the layers of meaning within a single shot? We are faced with problems when trying to systematically analyze video discourses at the microstructural level.

First, we are faced with some fundamental theoretical problems. If the analysis of written discourse involves the analysis of propositions, what constitutes a proposition in video? How does the viewer distill the proposition? Can a single shot contain multiple propositions? Probably, yes. But how might they be interrelated? What are the rules that establish relations of local semantic coherence in video? What are the linguistic devices present on the audio track and what are the pictorial devices?

As the reader can see, there may be more questions than answers. In the companion article in volume 1 of this series, I suggested the kinds of inferences and calculations that a viewer most likely must make in the process of decoding television in general, and political commercials in particular (Biocca, in press-a).

But little empirically validated work on the structure of video has been done at this level. There does exist some very fine grained analyses in the area of film studies (e.g., see references in Bordwell & Thompson, 1986; Nichols, 1981). These can provide a rich theoretical storehouse from which to draw. But whereas the in-depth analyses of the structures of individual films suggest relationships between form and cognition, they are not centrally guided by what is known about psychological processes (with the exception of neo-Freudian Lacanism), nor are the insights well integrated into the cognitive science literature. Of course, integration with cognitive theories is not the goal of many of these writers. On the other hand, such integration is valuable if we are to use this literature to guide our understanding of how structure relates to psychological processes. Holding to strict criteria of psychological validity, it is difficult to sort out those competing claims that do not have psychological validity; it is also difficult to define the generalizability of such claims and their scope conditions.

There are some bright spots in this kind of analysis. For example, Geis (1982) has done interesting work on the psycholingustics of commercial advertising, specifically the kinds of inferences likely to be made on the basis of the kind of inflated language common in commercial advertising. But the conditions of the field of research into television and political advertising are such as to place real limitations on our ability to specify some of these microstructures. I refer the reader to the companion chapter (Biocca, in press-a) for the kinds of processes that might be related to such structures, to Van Dijk & Kintsch (1983) for an example of the analysis of texts, and to traditional film theory and film semiotics for structural features that have been identified (Colin, 1985; Metz, 1974; Nichols, 1981).

REFERENCES

Altman, R. (1984). A semantic/syntactic approach to film genres. *Cinema Journal, 23*(3), 14–15.

Bell, D. (1975). *Power, influence, and authority: An essay in Political Linguistics.* New York: Oxford University Press.

Biocca, F. (in press-a). Viewer's mental models of political commercials: Towards a theory of the semantic processing of television. In F. Biocca (Ed.), *Television and political advertising, Vol. 1: Psychological processes.* Hillsdale, NJ: Lawrence Erlbaum Associates.

Biocca, F. (in press-b). Models of a successful and an unsuccessful ad: An exploratory analysis. In F. Biocca (Ed.), *Television and political advertising, Vol. 1: Psychological processes.* Hillsdale, NJ: Lawrence Erlbaum Associates.

Boiney, J., & Paletz, D. (1990). In search of the model model: Political science vs political advertising perspectives on voter decision making. In F. Biocca (Ed.), *Television and political advertising, Vol. 1: Psychological Processes.* Hillsdale: Lawrence Erlbaum Associates.

Bordwell, D., & Thompson, K. (1986). *Film art.* New York: Alfred A. Knopf.

Branigan, E. (1984). *Point of view in the cinema.* New York: Mouton.

Chronkite, G., & Liska, J. R. (1980). The judgment of communicator acceptability in the process of persuasion. In M. Roloff & G. Miller (Eds.), *Persuasion: New directions in theory and research* (pp. 101–139), Beverly Hills, CA: Sage.

Colin, M. (1985). *Langue, film, discours: Prolegomenes a une semiologie generative du film.* Paris: Klincksieck.

Connors, R. J. (1986). *Genre theory in literature. Form, genre, and the study of political discourse.* Columbia, SC: University of South Carolina Press.

Devlin, L. P. (1986). An analysis of presidential television commercials, 1952–1984. In L. Kaid, D. Nimmo, & K. R. Sanders (Eds.), *New perspectives on political advertising* (pp. 21–54). Carbondale, IL: Southern Illinois University Press.

Eco, U. (1976). *A theory of semiotics.* Bloomington, IN: Indiana University Press.

Feuer, J. (1987). Genre study and television. In R. Allen (Ed.), *Channels of discourse* (pp. 113–134). Chapel Hill, NC: University of North Carolina Press.

Foucault, M. (1965). *Madness and civilization: A history of insanity in the age of reason.* New York: Pantheon Books.

Geiger, S. F., & Reeves, B. (in press). The effects of visual structure and content emphasis on the evaluation and memory for political candidates. In F. Biocca (Ed.), *Television and political advertising, Vol. 1: Psychological processes.* Hillsdale: Lawrence Erlbaum Associates.

Geis, M. L. (1982). *The language of television advertising.* New York: Academic Press.

Greimas, A. (1986). Actant. In T. Sebeok (Ed.), *Encyclopedic dictionary of semiotics, Vol. 1* (p. 7). Berlin: Mouton de Gruyter.

Greimas, A., & Courtes, J. (1982). *Semiotics and language: An analytical dictionary.* Bloomington, IN: Indiana University Press.

Jardine, A. (1986). Intertextuality. In T. Sebeok (Ed.), *Encyclopedic dictionary of semiotics* (pp. 387–389). Berlin: Mouton de Gruyter.

Kaid, L., & Davidson, L. (1986). Elements of videostyle. In L. Kaid, D. Nimmo, & K. R. Sanders (Eds.), *New perspectives in political advertising.* Carbondale, IL: Southern Illinois University Press.

Kern, M. (1989). *30-second politics: Political advertising in the eighties.* New York: Praeger.

Metz, C. (1974). *Film language: A semiotics of cinema.* New York: Oxford University Press.

Neale, S. (1980). *Genre.* London: British Film Institute.

Nichols, B. (1981). *Ideology and the image: Social representation in cinema and other media.* Bloomington, In: Indiana University Press.

Patterson, T. & McClure, R. D. (1976). *The unseeing eye.* New York: Putnam.

Petty, R. E., & Cacioppo, J. T. (1981). *Attitudes and persuasion: Classic and contemporary approaches.* Dubuque, IA: Brown.

Reardon, K. (1981). *Persuasion: Theory and context.* Beverly Hills, CA: Sage.

Sabato, L. J. (1981). *The rise of political consultants.* New York: Basic Books.

Shatz, T. (1981). *Hollywood Genres.* New York: Random House.

Shyles, L. (1986). The televised political spot advertisement: Its structure, content, and role in the political system. In L. Kaid, D. Nemmo, & K. Sanders (Eds.), *New perspectives in political advertising*. Carbondale: Southern Illinois University Press.

Stubbs, M. (1983). *Discourse analysis: The sociolinguistic analysis of natural language*. Oxford, England: Basil Blackwell.

Todaraov, T. (1975). *The fantastic: A structural approach to a literary genre*. Cleveland: Case Western Reserve University Press.

Van Dijk, T. (1980). *Macrostructures*. Hillsdale, NJ: Lawrence Erlbaum Associates.

Van Dijk, T. (Ed.) (1985a). *Handbook of discourse analysis, Vol. 1: Disciplines of discourse*. London: Academic Press.

Van Dijk, T. (Ed.) (1985b). *Handbook of discourse analysis, Vol. 2: Dimensions of discourse*. London: Academic Press.

Van Dijk, T. (Ed.) (1985c). *Handbook of discourse analysis, Vol. 3: Discourse and dialogue*. London: Academic Press.

Van Dijk, T. (Ed.) (1985d). *Handbook of discourse analysis, Vol. 4: Discourse analysis in society*. London: Academic Press.

Van Dijk, T. (1988a). *News as discourse*. Hillsdale, NJ: Lawrence Erlbaum Associates.

Van Dijk, T. (1988b). *News analysis: Case studies of international and national news in the press*. Hillsdale, NJ: Lawrence Erlbaum Associates.

Van Dijk, T., & Kintsch, W. (1983). *Strategies of discourse comprehension*. New York: Academic Press.

6

The Orchestration of Codes and Discourses: Analysis of Semantic Framing

Frank Biocca
University of North Carolina at Chapel Hill

> MACHIAVELLI: "... I arouse or lull minds, I reassure or disturb them, I plead for and against, true and false. I have a fact announced and I have it refuted, according to the circumstances; in this way I plumb the public thought, I gather the impression produced. I try combinations, projects, sudden decisions. ... I fight my enemies as I please. ..."
>
> —Joly (1864)

At the beginning of chapter 1, the political ad was described as a product of semiotic engineering. In the major races we can safely assume that the engineers of the campaign—consultants, copywriters, directors, cameramen—are highly trained craftsmen skilled in the manipulation of their particular medium—be it rhetoric, make up, camera movements, or set design.

> In the hands of a media master, a political commercial can become a work of art—impressive, effective, enthralling, and, in afterthought, disturbing. (Sabato, 1981, p. 112)

The purpose of the semiotic construction is clear; it is an intervention in the discourse surrounding a particular election. The ad attempts to reshape the discursive space surrounding the candidate.

But how is this accomplished? To answer how this is accomplished is not easy. The answer would have to be tied to the empirical study of individual cases. On the other hand, it is possible to address *how it is*

61

attempted. Using this information, we could investigate the actual effect through empirical investigations of cognitive processing and public opinion. In experimental or field settings we could estimate the manner in which a semiotic construction influences the semantic processing of a particular community of voters (e.g., Biocca, in press-b).

DEFINING "SEMANTIC FRAME"

In this section, we turn to the concept of *semantic framing* to describe mechanisms by which codes and discourses are combined. A semantic frame is a macrostructural feature of a message. It may combine a variety of codes and discourses. It is called a semantic frame because it frames the meaning of the message; it orients and directs the semantic processing of the viewer. Semantic frames define the topic of the message, the context in which the messages' propositions are to be understood, and the way of thinking about the message.

The great dramatist Kenneth Burke (1959) used a similar concept to describe the structure of stories (see also Smith & Johnston, chapter 8, this volume). Frames provide the means of "building the mental equipment" used to structure the reality that surrounds us. In a similar fashion, a message's semantic frames are most like a message's blueprints. The semantic frames are plans to erect the *model viewer* inside the mind of the empirical viewer (see discussion of the model and empirical viewers in Biocca, in press-a). These blueprints are embedded in the message as a textual or message strategy. The viewers use the blueprints to construct their meaning of the message.

Psychologically, the semantic frame can influence the meaning of a political ad by selectively activating a viewer's schemata. More specifically, semantic frames influence semantic processing by selectively *priming* (Carr, McCauley, Sperber, & Parmelee, 1982; Meyer & Schvaneveldt, 1976) semantic networks of desired concepts. Semantic frames provide cues for the instantiation of "appropriate" schema (Rumelhart, 1980; see related discussion in Biocca, in press-a).

Any image or word can semantically prime a wide range of meanings. The semantic frames organize the contexts within which the codes and discourses will be processed so that the *desired subset* of possible meanings will be activated in the mind of the viewer of the political message. For example, a close-up shot of an old man can mean a great many things on its own. Extensionally, the shot of the old man can refer to a specific man at some point in time. Its intensional meaning will be influenced by its context, how it is framed in the message. In a political commercial the picture of the old man might be positioned in the script so that it refers to "old people on social security," "traditional American values," "conservative forces," "a candidate's father," "victims of crime," and so on. As the famous Kuleshov editing experiments demonstrated (Pudovkin, 1954), a shot, like a word, can be made to mean a variety of things depending on how it is semantically framed. Even our perception of the unchanging facial expression of the old man can change when influenced by the context of the message.

Semantic framing is certainly not unique to political ads; it is a fundamental property of communication. When we communicate we are attempting to paint an image in the mind of the receiver, but we do not have full control over the paint brush. In fact, we only provide instructions to the receiver on how to paint the image. In a psychological sense, it is the receiver who inevitably does the painting, even as he or she responds to our instructions. In this way the received message is jointly created.

THE GOAL OF THE POLITICAL AD: ALTERING AND DISPLACING SEMANTIC LINKS

An ad is framed to increase the chances of attaining a political subgoal. The overall goal, of course, is to be elected. But a number of subgoals must be achieved along the way. Many have to do with creating and managing the meaning of the candidate. These are semantic subgoals.

At the beginning of a campaign, the candidate's organization starts with an assessment of the public's perception of the candidate. The consultant determines the "bench mark" position of the candidate against which the campaign team can measure changes in opinion. This is most commonly determined using a benchmark opinion poll (Sabato, 1981), focus groups, and other traditional marketing and social science techniques. The purpose of this public opinion research is to determine the candidate's so-called *strengths* and *weaknesses*. The campaign team attempts to get a sense of who the candidate is in the mind of the voter at the beginning of the campaign. The varying perceptions of the candidate are determined for various demographic, psychographic, and ideological groups. The goal of the ad campaign is to manage that image by creating, accentuating, diminishing, or changing various voter perceptions.

Looking at this same problem psychosemiotically, we are able to define some of these subgoals a little better. *Persuasion* is the rearrangement of connections between the semantic features that constitute a concept or *attitude object*. In effect, the benchmark studies are a formal, empirical attempt to measure the semantic properties of a supersign, the candidate. In some ways, this is often only a study of the meaning of the candidate's name, and only indirectly a study of the "flesh and blood" candidate.[1] A measure is made of the aggregate semantic links attached to the sign (node) stimulated by the expression of the candidate's name.

The benchmark poll also attempts to measure the discursive space of the election, at least that which is in the foreground. What are people "talking" about? Political consultants also attempt to measure the discursive structure of each discourse, determining how, for example, issue positions are inflected and framed by various groups.

Sometimes the discursive space is represented by multidimensional measurement techniques (Romney, Shepard, & Nerlove, 1972; Woelfel & Fink, 1980). These are commonly used in marketing research (Green & Rao, 1972). In the case of these statistical models, the notion of a semantic space is literally projected onto a computer screen. The "meaning"[2] of the candidate and the issues can be plotted and represented as a position in a multidimensional representation of the semantic space (see Barnett, Serota, & Taylor, 1976; Sabato, 1981). Implicitly, a multidimensional model of the candidate's attributes is an unarticulated form of structural semantics.

Alternatively, the candidate/concept can be represented in a crude semantic network. The *connections* to other nodes can be termed the *semantic features or links* of the expression, "candidate X." Typically, in most semantic models these features are represented by lexemes that act as tokens for the general meaning (set of connections) represented by the lexeme. It is not the presence or absence of a node itself (e.g., "leader") that is important, but the strength of the connection to the cluster of features represented by the lexeme (e.g., verbal label "leader"). Such a semantic network model is closer to the intent of the ad than a multidimensional model because the semiotic engineering goal of the political ad is to either introduce new links to semantic features or to

---

[1]Telephone public opinion polling is normally used as well as some focus groups. The sign used to stimulate retrieval of semantic associations is normally the verbally spoken name of the candidate. There is a difference between reactions to a name and the moving, talking video image, a distinction that is sometimes forgotten by political consultants. Different semantic processes (meanings, associations) of the candidate might be accessed if the memory retrieval cue is a picture or a videotape of the candidate.

[2]A clear distinction must be made between the representation of the aggregate (socio-semiotic) meaning of the candidate and the representational structure of the candidate in an individual mind. Even though the two structures are correlated—we are social beings, after all—the theoretical discussion of the individual representation must address more complex issues dealing with the context in which the representation is accessed by a specific voter and patterns of semantic processing within the voter.

rearrange the semantic structure of the candidate by creating, strengthening, weakening, or obfuscating links to various features.

Let us take a general example from the 1988 presidential campaign. The candidate/concept "Bush" was semantically associated with the attribute "wimpy" in the minds of many voters at the beginning of the 1988 campaign. The attribute captured by the lexeme "wimpy" was a set of perceived behaviors and traits stored in the semantic memory of voters. This "problem in perception" needed to be addressed in the behavior of the candidate, "news bites," and in political ads. These semiotic projects sought to weaken the semantic connection to the attribute "wimpy" by reorganizing the voter's representation of the behaviors of the candidate. Not surprisingly, Bush started appearing in political ads or in news bites talking "tough" and engaging in rugged, outdoor sports—Bush at the helm of the speed boat, Bush the jogger, Bush "kicking the ass" of Dan Rather in their infamous live news confrontation. Ads depicted Bush "the oilman" and Bush "the young fighter pilot." A *frame* was constructed around the candidate/concept "Bush." These represented images and behaviors that were negatively marked in relation to the concept "wimpy." The strength of viewer's memory traces of these images helped determine the degree to which new perceived traits were connected to the sign "Bush" and the degree to which the semantic connection to the concept "wimpy" was attenuated by the presence of these new links.

The semiotic engineering of the candidate becomes more complex when the campaign staff wishes to have the candidate mean different things to different groups of voters, in effect to sociosemiotically guide and control the polysemic dimensions of the candidate supersign. It is true that voters may selectively attend to different aspects of the representation of the candidate, and that ads can be targeted to support these various representations. By the judicious use of signs and discursive references, the candidate attempts to be or to mean "different things to different people" (different sociosemiotic communities) by accentuating different connections between the candidate concept and various semantic features.[3] In any case, it is part of the postmodernist condition that candidates and other public phenomena (personalities, products, movements, issues, etc.) must constantly remake and renew their meaning. During the course of the 1988 campaign, there were a

---

[3]This process ("blue smoke and mirrors") can get candidates elected or can "fabricate" the appearance of political consensus. But it can also generate the kind of meaningless (normless) discourse voters have come to distrust and disdain in the modern political campaign.

number of new "Bushes." Richard Nixon has made a career out of recreating his public persona.

BASIC MECHANISMS OF SEMANTIC FRAMING

To construct a message, one must frame it. The consultant's goal is to alter the semantic features of the candidate or some issue/concept. In some cases the ad may seek to reinforce voters' concepts about an issue or candidate, including, unfortunately, the viewer's prejudices (see Sabato, 1981).

What is it about the message that accomplishes this? If we adopted the perspective of the rhetorician, we could probably identify a large artillery of figures and tropes used to rearrange the semantic features of the candidate. Guided by the insights of the ancient field of rhetoric, the oldest study of semantic framing, I opt for a different approach and strive for a more parsimonious typology.

Instead of identifying semantic frames simply from properties of the message, it is better to identify them according to the *kinds of semantic links* they are attempting to forge. A semantic link is a cognitive operation that connects two concepts. The assumption is that the purpose of a semantic frame is to establish new semantic *links* between the key conceptual node (candidate/opponent/issue) and some other nodes or clusters (i.e., attributes, schema). With this simple assumption we can distill some fundamental operations of semantic linkage from the universe of semantic frames, including rhetorical devices.

There are five types of semantic links attempted by semantic frames in political messages. Some can be subdivided, as our analyses require. These five kinds of semantic links capture most of the kinds of semantic operations attempted in the semantic framing of political ads.

Contextual Links

There is a body of well-supported research that indicates that perceptual and semantic judgments are influenced by context. The study of the subtle influence of message context on semantic processing is discussed in the perception of fundamental units such as phonemes (Lieberman, 1967), the identification and meaning of lexemes (Marcel, 1983a, 1983b; Meyer & Schvaneveldt, 1976), sentence context and word recognition (Morton & Long, 1976), the recognition of items in a visual scene (Biederman, 1987; Biederman, Glass, & Stacy, 1973), and the under-standing of whole paragraphs (Rumelhart, 1980). The viewer's mental model of the political ad and of various elements within the ad is a product of a whole set of contextual computations.

Each item in a commercial has certain semantic features. The viewer's identification of an item, such as an object or word, results in the activation of semantic links (feature sets) through a process known as *semantic priming.* In network models of semantic memory, semantic priming is often represented as a kind of excitatory impulse fanning out from the concept and variously activating links to whole networks of related concepts.

When a viewer decodes a scene in a political commercial, it involves the simultaneous activation of semantic features generated by the viewer's identification of individual signs among the many codes present in the scene. For example, the *momentary* meaning of the candidate may be affected by meanings generated from the decoding of signs of clothing, nonverbal gestures, colors, backgrounds, and so on. Processing is somewhat holistic (parallel). The semantic priming from the identification of these various signs "contaminates" the meanings of other codes *at that moment.*

People make judgments of scenes based on the co-occurrence of items. Semantic features linked to one object may be transferred to another simply through their co-occurrence. In classic semiotic terms, the transfer is a kind of indexical meaning of the sign (Eco, 1976). The semantic frame attempts to influence judgments by simply putting two things *within the same frame,* that is, establishing semantic interrelationships through co-occurrence.

Semantic links used to process that instance may be *strengthened* and *alter* the long-term connections between the concepts in the viewer's semantic memory. The contextual connection that influences meaning in the moment (i.e., the momentary perception of the candidate) can strengthen the links between two nodes (e.g., candidate and the concept of "leadership") or alter whole networks of semantic links.

Classificatory Links

There is evidence that individuals continuously make classificatory judgments or judgments of similarity. To identify is to classify. Computations are initiated to ascertain the set membership of an object on the basis of the possession of certain semantic features (Tversky, 1977) or on the basis of the similarity with some prototype (Rosch, 1978). To understand something is often to classify it: "This is this *kind* of thing." We also use prototypes to classify people (Cantor & Mischel, 1979; Taylor & Crocker, 1981), including those presented on television.

Thinking and, by extension, the understanding of television involve the establishment of a set membership of an object, scene, or person. The viewer searches for the prototype representing a class of objects. For example, most television narratives would not be understandable if viewers were not making heavy use of character and scene genres, stereotypes, and so on.

The attempt to shape the processing of set membership is addressed in classic rhetoric by analysis of some enthyemes, that is, those rhetorical syllogisms that deduce semantic features and set membership. For example (my apologies, of course, to the residents of Boston):

Proposition 1: All Boston politicians are crooked (classification and assignment of semantic feature).
Proposition 2: Candidate X is a Boston politician (classification).
Proposition 3: Therefore, candidate X is crooked (deduction and transfer of semantic feature).

Political ads are often structured to influence the classificatory processing of viewers. The item in question is framed in the ad by suggesting a classificatory link to some prototype. The most obvious kinds of classificatory semantic framing are manipulations of codes and discourses that attempt to classify the candidate as a certain *type* of politician, or his opponent as some *type*. The same is true of issues.

This can be a subtle process based on the use of nonverbal, iconic codes. For example, in the 1988 election there was discussion of Gary Hart's mimicry of Kennedy's gestures and hair style to attempt a closer match to the Kennedy presidential prototype.

Oppositional Links

Nodes or concepts can be linked by opposition. In many ways oppositional links are simply the absolute negation of contextual links and classificatory links. For example, when two concepts are linked by opposition, it normally follows that two *cannot co-occur,* for example, night versus day. In a similar fashion, oppositional links establish that two nodes or concepts do not share properties in common, for example, life versus death. The two items cannot be classified as part of the same set, because they do not share features. Note, too, that in pure oppositional linkage the very existence of one concept (e.g., death) logically necessitates the negation of its opposite (e.g., life).

In the semantic framing of political discourse, as well as other forms of discourse, oppositional semantic links are frequently used to frame arguments and concepts. But here the oppositional semantic linkage may not be *necessitated* by the very logic of the concept (e.g., life vs.

death). Rather, an opposition is rhetorically framed *as if* one concept logically necessitated the negation of the other (e.g., communism vs. democracy).

Causal and Narrative Links

Political ads and viewers share a common property, the tendency to use narratives. Narratives are stories, sequences of states, actions, and consequences. Stories are often about changes and the effect of some person or thing on a situation or another person. One can argue that, in some ways, narrative thought is just a subclass of *causal* reasoning.

Rumelhart (1977) has suggested that a fundamental property of narratives is a causal connection between states of the world exhibiting the following story grammar: State → Event (Agent) → Change of state → (Reaction)[4] (see related discussion in Biocca, in press-a). Politicians are often shown as "agents" that take a "state" (both meanings of the word *state*) and through some event bring about change.[5] Many semantic frames in political ads structure codes and discourses to influence the causal inferences constructed in the viewer's mental model of a represented event. In references to states of the world, candidates are most often represented as causal agents of positive states; opponents are represented as the agents of negative states.

Time sequence is also an important part of narrative modeling. Viewers are likely to reconstruct a time-based order of events, even when the events are syntactically presented out of order (Mandler, 1978; Mandler & Johnson, 1977), as is often the case in film and video.

When watching a political ad, viewers are highly likely to generate a mental model of the commercial that includes narrative or causal inferences. A number of semantic framing devices use film editing and other syntactic devices to manipulate the viewer's mental modeling of causal sequences.

Metaphoric and Hierarchial Links among Codes, Discourses, and Schema

A number of theories claim that semantic memory appears to be encyclopedic (Clark and Clark, 1977; Eco, 1976; Fodor, 1975). By this they mean that memory is organized into hierarchies of interrelated and

---

[4]The items in parentheses are not as essential, and are sometimes deleted in the narratives or people's summarized memory for a narrative.

[5]Whether that change is marked positive or negative depends on whether the commercial is a pro-candidate or negative-attack commercial.

cross-referenced clusters of concepts (e.g., Collins & Loftus, 1975; Quillian, 1968). At each level a cluster of semantic features is attached to a key concept. The key concepts may be organized hierarchically in memory. For example, one classic study of semantic memory suggests that it takes longer to process the statement "Robins have skin" than "Robins have feathers." The concept *robin* is situated in a semantic hierarchy that is linked by a kind of "is a" connection in the following fashion: robin → "isa" → bird, bird → "isa" → animal . . . and so on (Quillian, 1968). Differences in answering yes to whether robins have skin or robins have feathers result because the concept *skin* is stored with the concept *animal,* which is higher and more distant in the semantic hierarchy than the concept *bird.* Whereas theorists may argue as to the degree to which hierarchies exist (e.g., Collins & Loftus, 1975), many agree that concepts appear to be organized in clusters. Clusters are linked through well-traveled connections (those most often activated) between related concepts.

If semantic memory is organized into these clusters of concepts and features, then meaning can be transferred by linking one cluster of features to another through some sort of plausible link, one based on similarity, for example. Metaphors do precisely this. Metaphors create links between verbal or video phrases through a process of substitution of a sign from one domain of the semantic encyclopedia with a sign from another. Philosophers, logicians, and psychologists since the days of Aristotle have tried to define the actual mechanisms and functions of the metaphor (Goodman, 1968; Niklas, 1986; Ortony, 1979; Ricoeur, 1977).[6]

Metaphors can provide powerful devices for semantic framing in a political commercial. A metaphorical statement has two distinct subjects, a principal subject and a subsidiary subject, where the focus of the connection lies. The commonplace feature of the subsidiary subject—a feature that is strongly implicated (connected)—is linked to the principal subject through the semantic transference of the metaphor. The mention or reference of the subsidiary subject activates the implicated semantic feature. When the actual subject (principal subject) has been substituted by the subsidiary subject, the context of the video or phrase suggests what the principal subject should be. The implicated features of the subsidiary subject become attached to the retrieved principal subject. Metaphorical constructions exist in a variety of syntactic structures,

---

[6]For Black (1979), metaphorical connections must be understood not at the level of the individual sign but at the level of the verbal or video phrase, and that context plays an important part in the ease with which a metaphor is interpreted (Ortony, 1979).

including nominal, predicative, sentential, and narrative structures within the audio and video tracks of the televised message.

Let's use this metaphorical phrase as an example: "At the Press conference, the President was *hit with a barrage* from reporters." In our example, the whole metaphorical phrase, "hit with a barrage," is an imagistic subsidiary subject, whereas the phrase, "asked a set of questions," is the principal subject. The semantic properties of the former, the image of battle and damage, which is strongly implicated in the subsidiary subject, is transferred to the principal subject, "asked a set of questions." Note, too, that the metaphor alters not just the meaning of the action but the inferred relationship between the press and the president. It gives the press the actantial role of aggressor and the president the actantial role of victim.

The key feature in the area of the political communication is the theoretical assertion found in Goodman (1968) and, in a different fashion, in Freud, that semantic features are transferred from one subject to another (see also Metz, 1982).

TYPICAL USAGE OF SEMANTIC FRAMES IN POLITICAL ADS

Now that we have identified five basic types of semantic links, we can look for semantic frames in political ads that manipulate such links, and we can identify some broad classes of semantic frames that are frequently used in political ads, especially those that attempt to shape the *meaning* of the candidate.

The classes of semantic frames are by no means exhaustive, nor are the categories mutually exclusive. But the examples identify some of the key video rhetorical structures within political messages.

Semantic Framing of the "Possible World" of the Commercial

Semantic framing begins with the opening shot, the very composition of the mise-en-scene. There appears to be a coded rule that the perception of the candidate is influenced by the environment in which he or she is portrayed. Consultants appear to be responding to an intuitive sense that the environment of the shot provides a rich field of contextual links that influence the viewer's perception of the candidate.

Let us take an example of a concrete set of codes that is part of all shots, the popular codes attached to architecture and outdoor scenes. The candidate must be portrayed against some backdrop. This could be a relatively neutral studio backdrop. For example, a number of the 1988 Dukakis commercials show Dukakis giving a speech or talking into the camera against a backdrop of "presidential blue." But in most cases these architectural backdrops are not semantically neutral. Most are able, and often intended, to activate semantic features that might prime favorable meanings linked to the candidate. For example, candidates, especially those for lower office, are often shot on the backdrop of stone and marble, the architecture of institutions and governments. Part of this semantic framing might be intended to activate a *classificatory link* "the candidate is part of government-history-authority" (indexical relation).

Similarly, backdrops provide a variety of other semantic links. The candidate may be portrayed against the backdrop of farms, urban streets, and so on. Such backdrops become part of the semantic identity of the candidate. It places him or her in a possible world with distinct properties that are transferable to the candidate. These are *contextual links*. For example, in the 1988 presidential primaries, Republican candidate Dole was frequently portrayed speaking against a backdrop of rich, green, corn fields and in rural settings. A whole series of commercials for Republican candidate Jack Kemp show him walking within a mythical "small town" America. Bush, on the other hand, was often represented moving within institutional and governmental settings, especially those that appeared "presidential" (e.g., reviewing the troops, in foreign settings, and so on.)

In many of the scenes in these commercials, the candidate is shown moving, interacting with people, and active. He is the active force in each scene; he seems to be influencing the world around him. For example, in the 1988 Bush primary commercials, the candidate is frenetic, always active, moving, talking, shaking hands. The semantic frame suggests a *causal linkage,* expressed propositionally, "The candidate is taking action in these areas, be it farming, urban decay, and so on." In the activity of the possible world depicted by the commercial, the candidate is *causing* things to happen.

The context of the backdrop also suggests the kinds of people that inhabit that possible world. Depending on how a scene is structured, the candidate may be portrayed in some actantial role in the unfolding narrative of the commercial (see scripted example of a Bush commercial in Biocca, in press-b) or affiliated with some social group that inhabits the world (e.g., member of.government, people of the streets, etc.). This can also be used negatively. The political consultant Robert Squier cast a governorship in a militaristic frame by emphasizing the role of the governor as "commander-in-chief of the National Guard." The governorship was cast as a militaristic world and, indirectly, as a world where *men* dominate. The candidate's opponent was a woman. By framing the selected classificatory links of the semantic concept of *governor,* and the possible world surrounding the governorship, the commercials classified the woman *out* of the job (Sabato, 1981). In the full pejorative sense, she was semantically "framed."

Clothing is like a backdrop; it has its codes (Barthes, 1983). The framing of the codes of dress provide both contextual and classificatory semantic framing of the candidate. For example, one producer discusses this part of his work with a candidate:

> One thing we did while shooting was make him look dignified, experienced, a little older than he was. We put him in a traditional blue suit and tie. (Kaid & Davidson, 1986, p. 201)

It is also a time-honored ritual in speeches before various organizations that the candidate wear some item of clothing related to the group he or she is addressing. For example, when addressing Mexican Americans, more than one candidate will wear a sombrero; when addressing teamsters, a jacket with the name of the union local, ad nauseam. The candidate is framing a classificatory judgment, expressed propositionally as "he is one of us" (viewed from the perspective of the group in question).

Similarly, populist semantic framing often manipulates the codes of dress, showing the candidate in the "dress of the people." For example, there were pictures and ads featuring Jimmy Carter dressed as a farmer, Gary Hart in a lumber jack shirt, Michael Dukakis in a hastily borrowed leather jacket sitting on a bale of hay. There appears to be a convention in political commercials that when the candidate is to be portrayed as "talking honest" and "straight," he is often informally dressed. Primary commercials for presidential candidates Gore, Babbitt, Hart, and Jackson show them informally dressed and "talking straight" to the "people." It is perhaps telling that Dukakis, the Democratic candidate who the voters came to see as stiff and formal, was rarely represented in anything but a suit. It seemed as if it were an extension of his skin.

Artifacts such as books, flags, pictures of a family, and so on have meaning and are used to attach meaning to a candidate. Objects and products have functions in our society, but more importantly are significant vehicles for conveying meaning (Mick, 1988). In commercials, the candidate is often surrounded by objects that are used as semiotic vehicles.

Books, for example, are sometimes used to contextually link to a candidate the semantic features dealing with learning and seriousness. In one campaign a whole series of ads was built around a book "manufactured" for use in the commercials.

"The idea behind it . . . was a serious project, so serious that [the candidate] wrote a book about it," says Squier, adding tongue-in-cheek, "And everybody knows books are serious." (Kern, 1989, p. 37)

Squier implicitly states the assumption of his semantic framing device, a kind of contextual enytheme:

Books are serious.
Candidate X wrote a book.
Therefore, candidate X is serious.

The most commonly represented artifact in the presidential political commercials is the American flag. In the 1988 presidential commercials it showed up in one form or another in over 50% of the commercials. Candidate Dukakis did his share of flag waving and had more than one commercial where the flag was the complete backdrop. Gephardt was silhouetted by a furled flag as he passionately delivered his stump speech. Flags waved in the foreground as candidates spoke, flags stood in their offices, and flags provided the motif for their campaign logos. In commercial after commercial, flags shouted "nation," "people," "political process," or simply "patriotism." Semantically speaking, all candidates wrapped themselves in the flag.

Artifacts are also used as metaphors for policies. Those who watched the 1988 Democratic nomination convention may recall how Michael Dukakis's old snow blower was conspicuously used as a metaphorical device for Dukakis's pragmatic economic policies to emphasize his frugality. In a Dukakis commercial titled, "The Bowl," all of Massachusetts is metaphorically represented by a tarnished silver bowl. A pair of hands progressively works on it during the commercial until it is restored to its original luster.

In the world of video, as elsewhere, there are no fixed realities, no "America"—only represented Americas. When the codes of dress, architecture, and artifacts are manipulated in a political commercial, the candidate is semantically projected into a possible world. Candidates are projected into the worlds of the family, the farm, "small town America," "the halls of government," "overseas," and so on. These are worlds of myth, geography, or subculture. These worlds have meaning—certain people inhabit them and certain things are possible. Each world comes with some semantic and evaluative properties. The semantic framing occurs from an attempt to transfer the semantic properties of the world, its artifacts, its features, or its actantial roles to the candidate. These devices can provide the elements for many kinds of semantic links, including contextual, classificatory, causal, and metaphorical.

Semantic Framing through the Juxtaposition of Shots and Codes

Semantic framing using juxtaposition operates by a very simple principle: put any two images, codes, or discourses side by side and they will semantically interact. I call this the *Mondrian approach,* after the great painter who explored composition and color by simply putting differently painted rectangles side by side.

A political commercial is a vehicle similar to a Mondrian painting; it is a collage, a loose assemblage of images. This collage of shots can nonetheless generate all sorts of semantic connections in the mind of the viewer. Often, the goal of the consultant is to simply generate positive ones when the representation involves the candidate, and to produce negative semantic links when the represented candidate is the opponent.

The difference between the commercials in a campaign is less a matter of mechanism than it is of craft. Certain juxtapositions of images, sounds, and rhetorical devices pack more power; they are semantically richer and they more readily activate the voter's emotions. For example, Schwartz's now-famous Daisy commercial for the Johnson 1964 campaign gains much of its power from the way it constructs its semantic frames and activates contrasting emotions. The commercial uses the contrast between the innocent play of a child and the horrifically grim game of nuclear war. A number of analogical relations cement the link between the two parallel discourses. The commercial is knitted together by a sequence of visual metaphors that substitute the fuzzy yellow ball of a daisy with the child's eye and, finally, the fireball of a nuclear cloud. In a peaceful, pastoral setting, a golden-haired child ritualistically counts as she pulls the petals off a daisy. She looks up as her counting is substituted by the male voice, monotonically counting down. The camera slowly zooms into an extreme close-up of her eye as the countdown progresses, until the eye dissolves into the flash of a nuclear explosion. The surprise and horror of the opposition, which is held together by the semantic continuity provided by the metaphorical devices in the audio and visual track, help to create their own meltdown, the meltdown of Barry Goldwater's campaign.

Syntactic manipulations are obviously conscious editorial decisions. They can clearly signal the framing intent of the communicators. To put two pieces of video side by side is to suggest a connection, both semantic and syntactic, between the two shots. Film syntax provides a powerful vehicle for the semantic framing of the message.

Let us consider two types of syntagmas from Metz's (1974) "grand syntagmatique." Chronological syntagmas that advance a narrative are called *narrative syntagmas*. These forms are intuitive and are commonly used to establish causal links between a candidate and a set of actions. When complete enough to constitute a scene, the syntagma might contain the essential elements of narrative—(State), action, (change of state). For example, a commercial opens with shots of a social problem; we see a shot of the candidate enacting legislation; the commercial ends with shots of the solution to the problem (i.e., smiling voters). Abbreviations and variations of this formula are common. In most cases, a causal semantic link is intended.

A second type of syntagma, a nonchronological syntagma, Metz calls a *parallel syntagma*. The latter represents the kind of sequence common in associational films (Bordwell & Thompson, 1986). Let us consider an example of a kind of parallel syntagma. In a parallel syntagma, a sequence of shots is assembled, most often to link two motifs or two possible worlds. The semantic link between the two sequences can be varied and open, but often some form of classificatory and metaphorical connection is intended. For example, a commercial sequence might intersperse pictures of a senator working in his office with shots of ordinary Americans happily working in various walks of life. The composition of the juxtaposed shots might be structured so that the bodily actions of the senator are echoed by the workers. Visually, a contextual or classificatory link is established.

For example, a Bush attack ad titled "New Jersey at Risk," a sequence of images of polluted water representing Boston harbor, is interspliced with a sequence of beautiful beaches and bathers, representing New Jersey shorelines. A contrastive link is intended. The announcer activates causal links by ominously suggesting that in a Dukakis presidency the images of pollution would overtake the latter.

Contrastive juxtaposition of code can be produced by manipulating the audio and video track. For example, excerpts of a politician's speech about his accomplishments in eliminating poverty might be overlayed on pictures of more poor and homeless. Similarly, the picture of a smiling opposing candidate might be shown as the announcer lists a series of woes in the state or nation. The smiling face suggests that the candidate is uncaring.

The 1988 campaign provides an example of a particularly devastating attack ad, created by the Bush campaign, titled "Tank Ride." Here footage from a Dukakis "photo opportunity" showing the candidate riding in a tank was used against him. The footage of Dukakis looking self-conscious and foolish, rolling about aimlessly playing tank commander, is overlayed by a serious male voice listing all the military items that Dukakis had opposed. An additional layer of meaning was provided by the sound of a tank engine noisily shifting gears and sputtering. In this case, the interaction between the codes of the audio and video track provides contrast and irony. The ad also makes skillful use of the audience's stereotype that politicians are insincere.

Semantic Framing of the Discursive Propositions

The political ad is an intervention, a sentence uttered in the context of a discourse. Political ads refer to ongoing discourses; they always refer to communication processes outside themselves. References to the discourses surrounding issues are the most common and obvious discursive references found in this genre of persuasive messages.

Referenced discourses can often be summarized by a few simple propositions (at some cost, of course). Gross oversimplification is often how issues are communicated to, through, and by mass media practitioners. For example, a 1988 Gephardt commercial summarizes trade imbalances with a set of simple propositions, including one that argued that trade barriers made a $10,000 Chrysler car cost $48,000 in Korea.

Even the simplest proposition rarely stands on its own. In the mind of the viewer, many propositions are but one statement in a hierarchy of related propositions. Ideologies structure propositions so that each can be embedded in some other proposition stated at a higher level of abstraction (a general principle) or specified at a lower level by its instantiation in some more restricted case or example. The ad constructs a guided tour of the viewer's own discursive space. The ad can overturn the implications of a proposition by changing its connections to other propositions. This is the essence of the rhetorical struggle that is at the heart of many ads.

Eco (1976) provides a good example of how propositions are embedded in each other and how the implications of propositions are overturned (see Fig. 6.1). He diagrams the rhetoric that circulated the public debate about cyclamates, a popular artificial sweetener that was linked to cancer and finally removed from the market place. Eco contrasts the rhetoric surrounding (a) the introduction of the product/concept with (b) the rhetoric surrounding the removal of cyclamates. In Fig. 6.1 we see how the opposition of "sugar versus cyclamates" is connected through causal links to propositions at higher levels of generality. In semantic frame 1, the highest level of generality presented indicates that the connotative interpretation of "sugar versus cyclamates" is governed by the rhetorical frame "death versus life." In the rhetorical frame surrounding the introduction of the product, sugar implies death and cyclamates implies life.

Example of Semantic Framing
Through Embedded Propositions

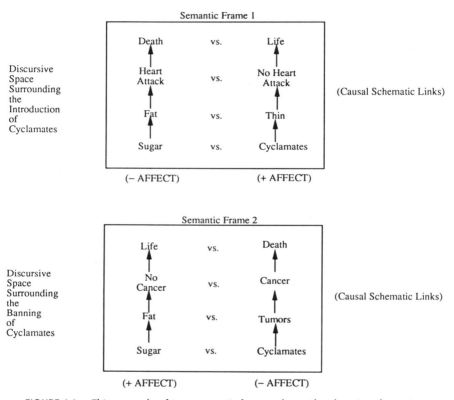

FIGURE 6.1.   This example of two semantic frames shows the changing discursive space surrounding the introduction and, finally, the banning of a product, the artificial sweetener, cyclamate (based on Eco, 1976; Helbo, 1983). Similar discursive spaces surround candidates and issues. In the pressure of the campaign these structures can evolve in a similar way, leading to dramatic reversals of the affective charge associated with an issue or candidate.

Note how the semantic framing of propositions can lead to the reversal of conclusions at the higher levels of semantic opposition. In the rhetoric surrounding the removal of the product diagramed in semantic frame 2, the structure "sugar versus cyclamates" is framed so that the implications are reversed. The causal connections are restructured to connote that sugar implies life (possible life) and that cyclamates implies death (certain death).

Note, too, that the altered semantic frame is not composed of simple negations of the earlier propositions. Semantic frame 1 contrasts positively marked concepts with negative affective markers. Semantic frame 2, on the other hand, is not just a simple inversion of affective polarities but an independent structure. The structure contrasts concepts that are neutral or mildly positive with negatively marked concepts.

This illustrates a point regarding how rhetoric best overturns existing semantic frames or those advanced by opponents: Simple negation of lower level semantic links and the associated propositions will normally not be effective; it tends to reinforce the existing structure. The best rhetorical strategy establishes different semantic links at lower levels to *lead* to reversals of propositions (connotations, conclusions) at higher levels.

The new semantic links that result from the semantic framing of propositions are influenced by how the discourse/issue is framed. *Framing,* both in the popular sense and in the sense we use it here, means phrasing the discursive/ideological/issue proposition at a level of generality or specificity that will activate more pro-propositional semantic links than negative ones. Of course, in negative advertising the opposite rule applies: the level of generality/specificity is chosen to maximize negative inferences and linkages. For example, a debate about a foreign policy alternative is framed as a battle between freedom and oppression (a higher-level proposition).

This has been the traditional concern of many studies of rhetoric (for example, see Baird, 1964). In fact, the embedding of propositions into higher levels of generalization or the application of higher-level propositions to specific instances is part of the essence of syllogistic reasoning. It reflects the use of logical deduction and induction. But it must be pointed out that in the political ad, as elsewhere, deduction and induction do not necessarily contribute to the truth value of the propositions. They are merely common modes of reasoning and argumentation. In political ads, as in everyday life, persuasion means the framing of intended messages in their best or worst light.

Semantic Framing by Manipulating Actantial Links

In the political commercial, more than in many other genres, the people and forces presented are a central focus for creating new meanings. Actants play the role of heroes, villains and supporters. All play important roles on the commercial's small stage. The actants are linked in various ways, and together they form the actantial universe of the ad. This universe is an ideological one.

Each commercial has some obvious semantic manipulation of actantial roles. Many work with prototypical representation of various types of supporters: workers, farmers, retirees, and so on. Videotaped endorsements also focus on actantial roles. They attempt to transfer the positive associations of the endorser to the endorsee. There are also more manipulative attempts to use actantial links to convey meaning.

One semantic framing mechanism involving the manipulation of actantial links is "guilt by association," a standby of the negative attack ad. A good example is the infamous Willy Horton ad from the 1988 Bush campaign. The ad shows two faces, one of Willy Horton, rapist and murderer, and one of Michael Dukakis, Democratic candidate. An announcer discusses Dukakis's furlough program. The faces of Horton and Dukakis are both shown in the center of the screen. The shots of both men are somber, black and white photographs. Both photos are cropped in a similar way: they are mug shots. Horton and Dukakis have similar, dour expressions. The ad continuously flips back and forth between the photos, as if they were flip sides of each other, while the announcer tells a story linking the two men. This is a classic case of guilt by association. The semantic framing of the ad is well crafted, down to its use of graphic devices to transfer some of the negative semantic features of the picture of Willy Horton to Michael Dukakis. On the audio track a causal link is formed: the horror of a Willy Horton is the product of Dukakis's decisions. On the video track a classificatory link is established: Willy Horton is just the flip side of Michael Dukakis himself.

As an individual, a candidate has no fixed set of features. Rather, the candidate takes on features that depend on which actantial roles are developed for him in public discourse, in the ads, and in the minds of the voters themselves. Political ads can manipulate the perceived actantial roles of the candidate or an opponent by not only juxtaposing one actant with another, as in the Willy Horton ad mentioned earlier, but also by accentuating the classificatory links of a candidate.

Through a political ad's passing reference or anecdote, the candidate can be given some stereotypical actantial role. The lack of detail allows the viewer to fill in the default values attached to that role. Biographical campaign spots are most likely to use these devices. For example, in the 1988 presidential primary spots, Dole, Bush, and Dukakis are portrayed in the role of military hero. One may argue about the degree to which these men played the role in real life. But numerous campaigns, such as those for Joe McCarthy and Lyndon Johnson, have used photos of the candidates in uniform to suggest (instantiate) a stereotypical role that may not have been justified by the much duller facts. This recalls Machiavelli's observation that "men generally are as much affected by what things seem as what they are. . . ."

Almost every male candidate who can, plays the role of faithful husband and father in his commercials. In the family series of Bush commercials that aired in the 1988 election, George Bush is metaphorically portrayed in a patriarchial role in parallel narratives that link him metaphorically as father of a large family and father of the land (see in-depth analysis of this ad in Biocca, in press-b).

Many candidates are represented as leaders among their politician peers. Pictures showing other politicians listening to the candidate are common. Because of the egalitarian sentiments of Americans, candidates must be both exceptional and people "just like you and me." A quirky 15-second spot for former general Alexander Haig, Republican presidential primary candidate in 1988, shows him waiting for and clumsily eating a piece of pizza. It ends with him smiling and winking his eye at the camera. The inhuman Haig is humanized in 15 seconds.

One of the most prominent examples in the 1988 campaign of classificatory semantic framing through manipulation of actantial links comes not from an ad, but from a Bush speech in which he accuses Michael Dukakis of being a card-carrying member of the American Civil Liberties Union (ACLU). It is simultaneously an artfully constructed and destructively ugly piece of political rhetoric, a good example of the semantic framing through negative classificatory links. In this one phrase, Dukakis is classified as a "card carrying member," strongly implicating and priming the oft repeated phrase "card carrying communist." He is further classified negatively as a "supporter of the ACLU." The ACLU, as an actant, had highly negative semantic features with swing voters, such as the so-called *Reagan Democrats.* These key voters believed the organization was soft on crime and coddled criminals. The phrase blatantly attempts to dredge up devastating connotations (that is, a set of negative semantic features) and attach them to an actantial role of the concept/node, Michael Dukakis.

Framing the Perceived "Share of Voice"

The listener/viewer assesses not only who is speaking, but *how many* are speaking. To put it another way, the listener/viewer probably makes an evaluation of the social representativeness of a discursive position. Some examples are: "He's speaking for himself." "He's speaking for the party." "He's speaking for the silent majority of Americans." "Most people believe that."

As a mechanism of social survival, it is likely that individuals use information to evaluate the relative strength of sentiments in the social environment. It is a primordial reflex, one that is political in the purest sense of the term. The power of the crowd, of group opinion, is political power in its brute sense. Psychological research on prototype extraction, heuristics, and risk assessment (Kahneman, Slovic, & Tversky, 1982; Rosch, 1978) and the mass communication work on the spiral of silence (Noelle-Neumann, 1974) as well as cultivation theory (Gerbner, Gross & Signorelli, 1980) suggest a mechanism by which the individual automatically calculates the representativeness of a phenomenon, opinion, or discursive position. In the context of our interest, we can consider this a mechanism for assessing the perceived *share of voice*[7] of a discourse (i.e., an issue or social problem) or discursive position (i.e., a sentiment, attitude, policy position, or social behavior).

Framing devices in the televised political ad speak to this process of social monitoring. Through the use of visual or verbal codes, the political ad suggests the social extent of the discourse or the distribution of discursive positions. Traditional studies of propaganda refer to the *band wagon effect* (Lee & Lee, 1979), where people listening to a set of arguments are told that the position advanced is widely held or gaining adherents and that they'd better "climb on board." Exaggerating the extent of a discourse or a favored discursive position is probably one of the most common framing devices in political advertising and everyday attempts at persuasion (e.g., a child arguing with a parent, "Everybody is doing it!").

A number of rhetorical devices for framing the perceived extent of a discourse or discursive position can be found in the audio track of an ad. The voice over is a common source. Typically, a voice, often a disembodied announcer, rhetorically states the social extent of a discursive position: "Most people believe . . . ," "Americans have long thought . . . ," "We feel that. . . ." Note that the framing mechanism simply utilizes an all-encompassing collective noun to describe the discursive community: "Americans," "people," "we," and so on. In the 1988 election, for example, a Bush ad used a twist on this typical device by having Bush's wife describe Bush's support in terms of friendship by saying, "He has thousands of friends." In the warm glow of that particular ad, the political power of the crowd was softened by its portrayal as an extended family (see transcript in Biocca, in press-b).

But the use of language is certainly not the only way in which the audio track frames the perceived discursive share of voice. The presence of applause, cheering, and so on acts as a sign for a large unseen

---

[7]This concept is borrowed from the advertising profession's (media planning) concept of share of voice. In media planning it refers to the relative amount of advertising among competing companies. In our case, the share of voice is the individual's perception of the distribution of public opinion, the relative strength and militancy of various issues or political positions.

community. Television itself is still based on primitive notions of the crowd and the "canonical audience" (Biocca, 1988). In physical gatherings, the movement, murmur, and rumbling of the crowd are how we experience *directly* the discursive share of voice. In the politics of the street, the share of voice embodied in the crowd can literally be a matter of survival.[8]

Similar codes and signs are used on the video track to guide the viewer's calculations of the share of voice. The representation of supportive crowds is one device.[9] The candidate is represented speaking to a throng or shaking the hands of many voters in a variety of settings.

Another device used in ads represents the extent of a discourse by quite literally using large numbers of speakers. For example, a 1988 Bush attack ad features a sequence of representative voters uttering quick negative swipes at Dukakis and the economic health of the state of Massachusetts (e.g., one renames the state "Taxachusetts"). Each appears selected to represent the "speech" of different social strata: blacks, blue collar workers, female executives, small business people, and so on.

It is true that the dissemination of scientific public opinion polls prevents the wholesale misrepresentation of the discursive map of an election. But readership of poll data among more apathetic swing voters is likely to be much lower than that of ideologically committed voters. Swing voters are often the target of political advertising. But the construction of the perceived social reality is composed of many kinds of judgments, and the manipulation of perceived share of voice can be much more subtle than a simple tally of pro and counter attitudinal voices.

We use television to determine the structure of social reality, one that we cannot experience directly. Political ads are distorted windows on our social reality, but our habits of viewing often make us look through them as if they were true. This may be due to our tendency to automatically calculate the position of the model viewer constructed by the message. Part of this viewing may include the assessment of the relative distribution of the share of voice.

---

[8]In the jaded, antiseptic, and televised politics of the American elections, we often forget that electoral politics is still a matter of crowds and street rallies. In democracies such as India, Haiti, and South Africa, for example, the politics of the crowd is not only a symbol of power but the very exercise of power, including the doling out of political punishment for opponents in the form of raw violence.

[9]Power has often been represented by the "crowd." For example, the film masterpiece, *The Triumph of Will,* makes full use of the crowd in its representation of the chanting throngs at the Nazi Nuremberg rally.

The Question of Intentionality: How Much Is the Communicator Aware of the Semantic Framing of the Message?

Does the consultant and copywriter of the ad know that he or she is using a semantic frame and attempting to create a causally or contexually linked mental model in the mind of the viewer? To what degree are the possible communication effects intended? This is a version of the classic question of intentionality put in the context of political communication: To what degree is the communicator aware of all the signs and signals he or she is communicating? When looking at the message from the point of view of the receiver, the question of *true* intentionality is unimportant; all that matters is the receiver's *model* of the message and the receiver's calculation of the intentionality of the communicator in that model.

But the notion of semantic framing of the message implies conscious design—or does it? I am not implying that a semantic framing decision by the copy writer or media consultant is a conscious one in all cases, but selection and editing by their very nature involve purposeful decisions. In some cases structural decisions are made on the basis of highly calculated hypotheses of communication effects (see political consultant's discussions in Kern, 1989; Sabato, 1981). In other cases, selection of a semantic frame, a code, or approach is based on an intuitive semantic insight that "it looks right." In either case, the amount of self-consciousness of the communicator or the degree to which a communicator can articulate the mental model under which he or she makes decisions does not in any way lessen the structural role played by the semantic frame within a political commercial.

SUMMARY AND CONCLUDING NOTES

It can be argued that all communication has a persuasive or political component to the degree that it assumes a specific world view or attempts to reconstruct one. The political ad offers us a particularly valuable text to explore. The persuasive intent is not disguised. This naked persuasive purpose puts the political and ideological character of semantic framing in high relief. The goals of the ad are clear. Its mechanisms can be put under a glass and analyzed.

I have sketched out various levels of analysis of the symbolic or semiotic study of political advertising. More narrowly, I have addressed only those issues in the analysis of political ads that might bear on the possible relationships between the structure of the ad and the viewer's mental representations of those ads.

The study of political advertising could be greatly improved by becoming more systematic and synthesized. I have suggested that a kind of psychosemiotics and sociosemiotics of political advertising might help us to generalize about the structures of these ads and, ultimately, about the influence of codes, categories, and genres of ads on specific viewers. With well-developed theories we could zero in on the relationship between specific ads and specific groups of voters.

Figure 6.2 summarizes the approach outlined in the past few chapters. If we look at the various types of analyses of the structure and content of political ads, we find that most of the work is done at one or more levels of analysis: signs, codes, discourses, and semantic frames. The choice of the level depends on the question that interests the researcher. Some analyses consider only the semantic frames of the ads, whereas

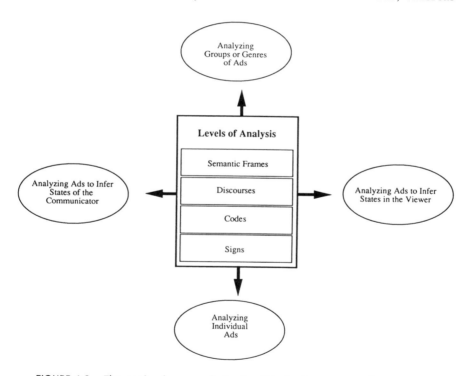

FIGURE 6.2. The goals of any analysis of political advertising tend to gravitate around two axes. For any level of analysis, the analyst will tend to make inferences about the communicator (e.g., intentions, strategies, biases, etc.) or about the viewer (e.g., attention, meanings, opinion change, etc.). Analyses will also vary as to the degree to which they seek to generalize; some analyses, like those conducted by political consultants in the heat of battle, are only interested in understanding the structure of a particular ad, whereas others are pushed to generalize about the structure of groups or genres of ads.

others operate with more fine-grained and exhaustive analyses of specific signs and discourses in the ads. Most move up and down the scale from signs to semantic frames, adjusting their analytical lens to suit their purpose.

Much of the literature can also be divided according to the degree to which the analyst seeks to generalize. In the day-to-day practice of political consulting, the analyst is interested in one ad only, the ad being developed for his or her candidate. Generalization is not an issue; immediate, pragmatic considerations are paramount. The question is whether this particular execution of an ad, its specific set of structures, will work well at this moment in time for this specific community of voters.

On the other hand, the discussion of the processes of political advertising involves generalizations across genres of ads. The role of signs, codes, discourses, and semantic frames must be discussed, not only in the analysis of specific ads, but in the generalizations for groups of ads such as those for challengers versus incumbents, negative ads, or ads in one election or another.

Similarly, the analysis of the structure of the ads is rarely conducted as an end in itself. Any discussion of form, be it the esthetic or rhetoric of a political ad, seeks to make some inference about the communicator and the production process (i.e., incumbent ads, 15-second commercials, etc.) or about the receiver and the reception process (i.e., negative ads and voter apathy, camera angles and the perception of candidates, etc.). In some broad cultural studies, the structure of the ad is studied to make inferences about the environment that bonds both the communicator and the viewer. The researcher is concerned with the organizational, social, and cultural environment that gives rise to a particular pattern of semiotic activity.

The study of political advertising as a communication genre holds particular interest for a number of reasons. The peculiar style of electoral politics patterned after the American model is reproducing itself globally, including parts of Eastern Europe. Central to American-style political discourse is the televised political message, whether it is called a paid political announcement, an educational message from the party, or a "free" news bite.

The 30-second spot has become the haiku of political thought. Quick references to codes and discourses are the shorthand of political communication. All issues, no matter how complex, must be uttered and considered in these short bursts of signs. The televised political ad is a product of a sociopolitical system in which the video and computer screen constitute both the window and the fence around social thought. In an information-cluttered environment, a minute of the voter's attention is at a high premium. When a significant part of voter decisions about who will control the future is made on the basis of the "information" contained in carefully structured messages, the analyst must come to understand the structures through which much political thought will be increasingly articulated, be it for good or bad. Michael Dukakis did not understand television in 1988 and admitted that the medium contributed to his defeat ("Dukakis speech," 1990). Like politicians, voters are boxed in by the frame of the video screen, but also by something more subtle—the semantic frames of the political ad.

REFERENCES

Baird, C. (1964). *Rhetoric: A philosophical inquiry.* New York: The Ronald Press.

Barnett, F., Serota, K., & Taylor, J. (1976). Campaign communication and attitude change: A multidimensional analysis. *Human Communication Research, 2*(3), 227–244.

Barthos, R. (1983). *The Fashion System,* New York: Hill & Wang.

Biederman, I. (1987). Recognition by components: A theory of human image understanding. *Psychological Review, 94,* 115–147.

Biederman, I., Glass, A. L., & Stacy, E. (1973). Searching for objects in real world scenes. *Journal of Experimental Psychology, 97,* 22–27.

Biocca, F. (1988). The breakdown of the canonical audience: Comments on the Linolof and Gunther articles. *Communication Yearbook* (Vol. 11, pp. 127–130). Beverly Hills, CA: Sage.

Biocca, F. (in press-a). Viewer's mental models of political commercials: Towards a theory of the semantic processing of television. In F. Biocca (Ed.), *Television and political advertising, Vol. 1: Psychological processes.* Hillsdale, NJ: Lawrence Erlbaum Associates.

Biocca, F. (in press-b). Models of a successful and an unsuccessful ad: An exploratory analysis. In F. Biocca (Ed.), *Television and political advertising, Vol. 1: Psychological processes.* Hillsdale, NJ: Lawrence Erlbaum Associates.

Bordwell, D., & Thompson, K. (1986). *Film art.* New York: Alfred A. Knopf.

Burke, K. (1959). *Attitudes towards history.* Los Altos Ca: Hermes Publications.

Cantor, N., & Mischel, W. (1979). Prototypes in person perception. In L. Berkowitz (Ed.), *Advances in experimental psychology,* (pp. 43–64). New York: Academic Press.

Carr, T. H., McCauley, C., Sperber, R. D., & Parmelee, C. (1982). Words, pictures, and priming: On semantic activation, conscious identification, and the automaticity of information processing. *Journal of Experimental Psychology: Human Perception and Performance, 8*(6), 757–777.

Clark, H. H., & Clark, E. (1977). *Psychology and language.* Chicago: Harcourt Brace Jovanovich.

Collins, A., & Loftus, E. F. A. (1975). A spreading activation theory of semantic processing. *Psychological Review, 82,* 407–428.

Dukakis speech barks at 88's sound bites. (1990, April 12). *The News and Observer* (Raleigh), p. 6a.

Eco, U. (1976). *A theory of semiotics.* Bloomington, IN: Indiana University Press.

Fodor, J. (1975). *The language of thought.* New York: Thomas Y. Crowell.

Gerbner, G., Gross, L., & Signorelli, N. (1980). The "Mainstreaming" of America: Violence Profile No. 11. *Journal of Communication, 30,* 10–27.

Goodman, N. (1968). *Languages of art: An approach to a theory of symbols.* Indianapolis, IN: Bobbs-Merrill.

Green, P., & Rao, V. (1972). *Applied multidimensional scaling: A comparison of approaches and algorithms.* New York: Hold, Rinehart and Winston.

Helbo, A. (1983). *Semiologie des messages sociaux: Du texte a l'image.* Paris: Edilig.

Joly, M. (1864). *Dialogue aux Enfers entre Machiavel et Montesquieu.* Paris: Edition.

Kahneman, D., Slovic, P., & Tversky, A. (Eds.). (1982). *Judgement under uncertainty: Heuristics and biases.* Cambridge, UK: Cambridge University Press.

Kern, M. (1989). *30-second politics: Political advertising in the eighties.* New York: Praeger.

Lee, A., & Lee, E. (1979). *The fine art of propaganda.* San Francisco, CA: International Institute for General Semantics.

Lieberman, P. (1967). *Intonation, perception, and language.* Cambridge, MA: MIT Press.

Mandler, J., & Johnson, N. (1977). Remembrance of things parsed: Story structure and recall. *Cognitive Psychology, 9,* 11–151.

Mandler, J. (1978). A code in the mode: The use of story scheme in retrieval. *Discourse Processes, 2,* 11–35.

Metz, C. (1982). *The imaginary signifier.* Bloomington, IN: Indiana University Press.

Meyer, D., & Schvaneveldt, R. (1976). Meaning, memory structure, and mental processes. In C. Cofer (Ed.), *Structure of human memory* (pp. 46–64). San Francisco, CA: Freeman.

Mick, D. (1988). Schema-theoretics and semiotics: Towards a more holistic, programmatic research on marketing communications. *Semiotica, 70*(1/2), 1–26.

Morton, J., & Long, J. (1976). Effect of word transition probability on phoneme identification. *Journal of Verbal Learning and Verbal Behavior, 15,* 43–51.

Niklas, U. (1986). Metaphor. In T. A. Sebeok (Ed.), *Encyclopedic dictionary of semiotics, Vol. 1* (pp. 549–551). Berlin: Mouton Press.

Noelle-Neumann, E. (1974). The spiral of silence: A theory of public opinion. *Journal of Communication, 10,* 43–51.

Ortony, A. (Ed). (1979). *Metaphor and thought.* Cambridge: Cambridge University Press.

Pudovkin, V. (1954). *Film technique and film acting.* London: Vision.

Quillian, R. (1968). Semantic memory. In M. Minsky (Ed.), *Semantic information processing* (pp. 328–339). Cambridge, MA: MIT Press.

Ricoeur, P. (1977). *The rule of metaphor.* Toronto: University of Toronto Press.

Romney, A. K., Shepard, R. N., & Nerlove, S. B. (1972). *Multidimensional scaling, Vol. 1: Theory and applications in the behavioral sciences.* New York: Seminar Press.

Rosch, E. (1978). Principles of Categorization. In E. Rosch & B. Lloyd (Eds.), *Cognition and categorization* (pp. 27–48). Hillsdale, NJ: Lawrence Erlbaum Associates.

Rumelhart, D. (1977). Understanding and summarizing brief stories. In D. Laberge & M. Collins (Eds.), *Basic processes in reading: Perception and comprehension* (pp. 265–304). Hillsdale, NJ: Lawrence Erlbaum.

Rumelhart, D. (1980). Schemata: The building blocks of cognition. In R. J. Spiro, B. J. Bruce, & W. F. Brewer (Eds.), *Theoretical issues in reading comprehension: Perspectives from cognitive psychology, linguistics, artificial intelligence, and education* (pp. 33–58). Hillsdale, NJ: Lawrence Erlbaum Associates.

Sabato, L. J. (1981). *The rise of political consultants.* New York: Basic Books.

Shyles, L. (1986). The televised political spot advertisement: Its structure, content, and role in the political system. In L. L. Kaid, D. Nimmo, & K. R. Sanders (Eds.), *New perspectives in political advertising* (pp. 107–138). Carbondale, IL: Southern Illinois University Press.

Taylor, S., & Crocker, J. (1981). Schematic basis for social information processing. In T.

Higgins, C. P. Herman, & M. P. Zanna (Eds.), *Social cognition, The Ontario symposium.* Hillsdale, NJ: Lawrence Erlbaum Associates.

Windt, T., & Ingold, B. (Eds.). (1987). *Essays in presidential rhetoric.* Dubuque, IA: Kendall/Hunt.

Woelfel, J., & Fink, E. (1980). *The measurement of communication processes: Galileo theory and method.* New York: Academic Press.

II

Analyses of the Meaning of Political Ads

7

Bad Signs and Cryptic Codes in a Postmodern World: A Semiotic Analysis of the Dukakis Advertising

David Descutner
DeLysa Burnier
Algis Mickunas
Richard Letteri
Ohio University

The television advertising of Michael Dukakis was judged a failure on nearly every count both by campaign insiders and by members of the popular press. McCabe (1988), briefly a member of the Dukakis advertising team, claimed that the campaign's advertising "was perhaps the greatest single marketing and communications disaster of the twentieth century, of far greater and more lasting significance than the fiascoes of 'new Coke' and the Edsel combined" (p. 33). Drew (1988) assailed the poor timing and blurred message of the Dukakis advertising, and Edwin Diamond (1988) observed the advertising failed "to add up to a coherent whole." Moreover, he noted that it "[was] isolated and unrelated to what the candidate [was] saying at his news events" (p. 36). Some of the harshest criticism of the candidate's advertising originated within state party organizations, where dissatisfaction grew so pronounced that some organizations began to produce their own spots. Furthermore, Rothenberg (1988) reported that near the end of the campaign, "Dukakis ads [were] subjected to a barrage of criticism in the advertising and political communities" (p. 43).

Providing some answers to the key question of why the Dukakis advertising failed so decisively is the chief intent of this study. Many answers already have been given to this question, ranging from the disorganization of the advertising team, to the failure to understand important national symbols, to Dukakis's unwillingness to run negative advertisements. Our answer follows from a yearlong analysis of the

Dukakis campaign, its television advertising, and the coverage that advertising received in the popular media.[1]

Driving the research was our primary purpose to build and extend theory as it applies to the study of political advertising. Specifically, we wanted to explore the theoretical issues associated with the postmodern turn in contemporary culture, particularly as those issues relate to political advertising. Synthesizing the work of Fredric Jameson (1983), Andreas Huyssen (1986), Calvin Schrag (1988), Arthur Kroker and David Cook (1986), and Stuart Ewen (1988), all of whom discuss aspects of postmodernism, we took some first steps toward constructing a preliminary theory of postmodern political advertising.

With our preliminary theory as a point of departure, we then looked for a way to track the influence of the postmodern turn on advertising. We chose semiotic theory and method to guide our inquiry, and our corollary purpose was to extend semiotic research to the study of political advertising and thereby contribute to its refinement and development. The core principles of semiotic theory, as a later section establishes, are consonant with the assumptions of the postmodern turn, and semiotic method offers a rigorous set of procedures for analyzing how meaning is produced in advertising. Ultimately, we expect that semiotic analysis will help to answer the key question raised earlier by illuminating the interior reasons why the Dukakis advertising did not succeed.

THE POSTMODERN TURN

Precisely defining *postmodernism* or what constitutes *postmodern culture* is a difficult assignment because the terms are used variously by different fields and disciplines. At first glance, postmodern architecture seems to have little in common with what passes as postmodern literature, just as postmodern film seems to bear little resemblance to postmodern art. All of these expressive forms figure prominently in what is called *postmodern culture,* but superficial inspection yields few clues about where they might overlap. Closer inspection, however,

---

[1]We sought a broad and detailed understanding of Dukakis and his campaign. Specifically, the candidate and the campaign were tracked in *The New York Times, The Christian Science Monitor,* and *The Washington Post Weekly. Newsweek, Time,* and *U.S. News and World Report* were examined as well. In addition, we followed television news coverage of the campaign closely by watching regularly several network and cable news shows. We also maintained contact with the media director for the Dukakis Ohio organization and a Boston headquarters staff member. Through these contacts we were given access to the candidate's national and Ohio television advertising, including both approved and unapproved spots.

reveals that these and other postmodern forms of expression, including political advertising, do share a certain orientation to culture and, moreover, operate from common assumptions.

The Postmodern Orientation

The postmodern orientation to culture insists on erasing traditional distinctions in levels of culture. Jameson (1983) has observed that central to postmodernism is "the effacement . . . of some key boundaries or separations, most notably the erosion of the older distinction between high culture and so-called mass or popular culture" (p. 112). Jameson notes as well that with no clear demarcations in place between high culture and low culture, postmodernism makes legitimate the serious study of low-culture forms such as gothic and detective novels, B-rated films, television shows, and even the "whole landscape of advertising" (p. 112). Indeed, Jameson explicitly links postmodernism and advertising with the assertion that "our advertising, for example, is fed by postmodernism in all the arts and inconceivable without it" (p. 124). With this observation Jameson lends support to our thesis that contemporary advertising is fundamentally influenced by the postmodern orientation, but what still remain unclear are the nature of this orientation and the assumptions on which it rests.

Perhaps the most useful way to conceive of the postmodern orientation is as a turn in thinking, a change in perspective and sensibility. That such a turn is closely tied to advertising was one proposition advanced by Huyssen (1986):

> What appears on one level as the latest fad, advertising pitch, and hollow spectacle is part of a slowly emerging cultural transformation in Western societies, a change in sensibility for which the term "postmodernism" is actually, at least for now, wholly adequate. The nature and depth of that transformation are debatable, but transformation it is. (p. 181)

Huyssen's proposition fits with an evolving line of research seeking to describe the development and consequences of postmodernism. Schrag (1988) has contributed to that research, and he captured well the principal features of the postmodern turn:

> Obviously, to attempt a universal definition of postmodernity would be sheer folly. It is not a unified system of beliefs; nor is it the designation of a chronological period of history (although admittedly it draws heavily on post-World War II intellectual and social currents). It is more an attitude,

a frame of mind, an assemblage of social practices, a way of seeing the world and acting in it. (p. 2)

Schrag's account begs the questions of what kind of attitude, what frame of mind, and what way of seeing the world may be called postmodern. Answering these questions will require considering some of the assumptions of postmodernism.

The Assumptions of Postmodernism

Postmodernism typically is described as an "anti-esthetic," as an oppositional turn in thought. In Schrag's terms, postmodernism adopts an adversarial attitude and oppositional frame of mind toward conventional values and practices. It sees the world as a place where images are produced like commodities to be sold to willing mass publics, and it sees culture not as a series of esthetic monuments consecrated by tradition but instead as a "corpus of codes and myths" (Foster, 1983, p. x) designed to produce assent and quiescence. We have already noted its opposition to the standard division between high culture and mass culture. Similarly, postmodernism stands against the realist tradition of accepting claims to truth and against conventional acceptance of humanism as a conceptual foundation.

Postmodernism assumes that claims to truth deserve to be met with what Jean-François Lyotard (1984) calls *incredulity* (p. xxiv). It repudiates truth in the realist sense of an adequate and accurate representation of the world. Messages in the postmodern view stand as true not because they reflect accurately the world, but only because they gain adherence from an audience. Christopher Norris (1988) cogently made this point:

> We are now living in a postmodern epoch where all claims to truth have been finally discredited, where language games circulate without any epistemological warrant, and where "performativity"—the power of those language games to get themselves accepted on a short-term, provisional basis—becomes the sole criterion for deciding what is rational in any given context of debate. (p. 77)

An advertising example of this incredulity toward truth claims may be found in the *Joe Isuzu* spots, where the main character unabashedly lies about the advantages of Isuzu vehicles. The subtext here is that truth is irrelevant to advertising and, moreover, that the Isuzu spots are honest in any case because they make no pretense to telling the truth.

Related to its derogation of truth, postmodernism also rejects humanism as a legitimate foundation. Humanism assumes, according to

Catherine Belsey (1980), that individuals are "the origin and source of meaning" (p. 7). Likewise, Richard Kearney (1987) points out that humanism "establishes man as sovereign source of truth" (p. 40). In contrast, postmodernism assumes that language and other expressive forms like the image—all of which fall under the semiotic heading of signification—are themselves the source of meaning. Meaning resides not in subjects' minds but rather with the signifying practices themselves. What postmodernism sees, according to Kearney, is a culture "increasingly governed by images which the human subject no longer controls or creates" (p. 39).

The Ralph Lauren print advertising exemplifies the antihumanist view that images alone produce meaning. The Lauren advertising, as Debora Silverman (1986) has shown, portrays an upper-class world of beautiful people, elite sports, and sumptuous clothes and furnishings. Contrary to humanism's view, the images themselves are the source of meaning in the Lauren advertisements, not the individual readers' perceptions or cognitions. The images in the advertisements succeed by depicting what Silverman calls a "way of living" that provokes interest, then recognition, and finally belief by supplying pleasure through an evocation of memory and desire. They remind readers of a bygone era when products supposedly bore the stamps of tradition and quality (memory), and they whet our appetites for contemporary products with the same stamps (desire). As successful as these Lauren print advertisements may be, no medium is better suited to the imagistic signification of the postmodern turn than television, and no form illustrates better than advertising this kind of signification.

Television, Advertising, and Postmodernism

Kroker and Cook (1986) contend that television is a "pure image-system" (p. 268), and they insist that "TV is the real world of postmodernism" (p. 267). Denouncing the older realist view that television reflects society, Kroker and Cook take exactly the opposite tack: "In a postmodernist culture, it's not TV as a mirror of society, but just the reverse: it's society as a mirror of television" (p. 268). Television has little to do with truth, as any number of critics have shown, and its advertising exemplifies the antihumanism of the postmodern turn. On the latter point, Judith Williamson (1983) asserts that "advertising seems to have a life of its own; it exists in and out of other media and speaks to us in a language we can recognize but a voice we can never identify. This is because advertising has no 'subject' " (pp. 13–14).

Television images are produced in order to be consumed for entertainment and information, and to satisfy our need for spectacle and drama. Speaking of television news, one place where we might expect some concern for truth, Ewen (1988) made this observation: "The operative words here—entertaining, thrilling, drama—are a giveaway as to what is meant by 'truth.' In the ratings game, the news—out of economic necessity—must be transformed into a drama, a thriller, entertainment. Within such a context, the truth is defined as that which sells" (p. 265). Ewen, moreover, asserted that watching television reduces to the two activities of "spectatorship and consumption" (p. 268).

Murray Edelman (1988) indicted television news on the same grounds as Ewen, and his key term of *spectacle* closely resembles Ewen's key terms of *drama* and *spectatorship:*

> The spectacle constituted by news reporting continuously constructs and reconstructs social problems, crises, enemies, and leaders and so creates a succession of threats and reassurances. These constructed problems and personalities furnish the content of political journalism and . . . also play a central role in winning support and opposition for political causes and policies. (p. 1)

Edelman's indictment of television news is the pretext for his broader charge that television is responsible for turning politics into a "political spectacle" where history and inequalities are erased, plural interpretations are discouraged, and dramatic characters and conflict are imperative. The political spectacle displaces attention from the ideologically constructed political world and urges citizens to take the attitudes of "bemusement and obliviousness" (p. 120) toward serious issues and problems.

We are drawn to compelling images as spectators are to spectacle, and we consume those images and that which they signify because they create "structures of meaning." Williamson (1983) stated that these structures of meaning are coextensive with the techniques of advertising, the means by which "images, ideas, or feelings . . . become attached to certain products" (p. 30). Williamson used a semiotic method to identify and analyze these structures of meaning, much as we use semiotic method to investigate critically the political advertising of the Dukakis campaign.

Summary

So we have seen that the postmodern turn effaces traditional distinctions between levels of culture and represents an antiposition on the matters of truth and humanism. The primary focus of the postmodern turn is on the production of meaning through images, and it emphasizes the power of spectacle and the activity of consuming "commodified images." The interrelations between postmodernism and advertising have been established, as is the case that television is the exemplary medium of postmodernism. Finally, the possibilities of using semiotics to tease out these interrelations have been suggested. With this background on the postmodern turn in mind, we now move to explaining the semiotic theory and method we use in our critical analysis of the Dukakis advertising.

SEMIOTIC THEORY AND METHOD

For the last 20 years semiotics, the study of signs and sign systems, has been much discussed in both Europe and the United States. During that time, rival semiotic theories and methods have proliferated. At the root of nearly all current theories and methods are the seminal works of one European structural linguist, Ferdinand de Saussure, and one American philosopher, Charles Sanders Peirce. Our aim here is not to describe comprehensively the respective contributions of Saussure and Peirce, but rather to define those elements of each that play some part in our later analysis. In an effort to make our account of semiotics clear, we use examples borrowed from our later analysis of the Dukakis advertising.

Saussure and Peirce

Saussure discovered that a sign has two elements: the signifier is the "sound-image," and the signified is the idea being conveyed. Saussure (1959) maintained that the "bond between the sound and the idea is radically arbitrary" (p. 113), which is to say a sign's meaning has nothing to do with any natural or necessary connection between its signifier and signified. Forging a connection between signifier and signified produces a semantic structure, or "structure of meaning," for the sign. Our analysis of the Dukakis advertising, for example, found that such a structure was rarely established. Neither Dukakis's personal identity nor his political identity was ever effectively clarified. Consequently, the signifier of Dukakis as he appeared in the spots lacked semantic depth, and that made it difficult for the spots to associate him with images of desirable values and goals.

Like Saussure, Peirce (1958) held that the relation between the sign and its object was arbitrary. Unlike Saussure, Peirce claimed that signs consist of three parts: the object, or that which the sign represents; the ground, or what can be conveyed about a given object; and the interpretant, or the meaning created by the sign, which in turn becomes another sign. Peirce believed that signs are constituted as meaningful through a logical process of interpretation in which error, change, and correction are inevitable. He conceived of signs as concrete, communicative phenomena interpreted by and through critical self-reflection.

Peirce and Saussure concurred on one other essential proposition, namely, that human reality is fundamentally a product of sign systems. Our experience is interpenetrated with signs, so much so that signs literally produce what we call reality. Signs, therefore, are not names or labels reflecting what we encounter in experience. On the contrary, semiotics agrees with the postmodern turn that signs produce meaning through and by their relationships with one another. As Graeme Turner (1988) stated: "Semiotics sees social meaning as the product of the relationships constructed between 'signs.' The 'sign' is the basic unit of communication and it can be a photograph, a traffic signal, a work, a sound, an object, a smell, whatever the culture finds significant" (p. 45).

Peirce's emphasis on context and concrete instances of communication fits neatly with our interest in analyzing specific instances of political advertising. That same emphasis of Peirce also inspired the semiotic theory and method of Umberto Eco.

Eco's Semiotic Theory and Method

Eco (1976) incorporates Peirce's triadic conception of the sign as well as his typology of signs, which he defines in terms of whether they function as icons, indexes, or symbols. Eco's *theory of settings* represents an attempt to study phenomena like "objects, images, and experiences" that arise outside the sign system but ultimately function as signs within the cultural arena. For example, nearly everything that carries a charge in political advertising—national symbols, events and figures from history, popular icons and images—arose outside the sign system of political advertising but now function as signs integral to that system. This notion of sign systems intersecting with one another in the process of signification is called *intertextuality*.

Intertextuality

Eco and other semiotic scholars have long recognized the importance of intertextuality in signification. Eco (1976) defined communicative messages as "texts," and asserted that understanding any given text requires familiarity with other texts. Our experience with and prior knowledge of political advertising texts allows us to understand the particular piece of advertising before us at the moment. Political advertising "cannibalizes" earlier texts' forms, stories, and design in order to produce seamless messages that remind us of these other texts and simultaneously ask us to believe what they present. One crucial shortcoming of the Dukakis advertising is the absence of intertextual richness. Borrowing scarcely at all from plenary cultural texts, such as contemporary music, film, and television, the Dukakis advertising comes across as one-dimensional and visually impoverished. Most important, what permits us both to understand the text before us and to recognize its link to other texts is our awareness of its operative codes.

Codes

Within the multiple systems of signs, the interaction of which may be called *intertextuality,* are rules that establish transitory correlations between and among signs. Eco (1976) labeled the rules that establish such transitory correlations as *codes,* and argued that communication is possible only to the extent that a writer and reader share knowledge of the operating code. Semiotic's notion of codes proves quite useful for analyzing images, as Turner (1988) documented:

> When we deal with images it is especially apparent that we are not only dealing with the object or the concept they represent, but we are also dealing with the way in which they are represented. There is a 'language' for visual representation, too, sets of codes and conventions used by the audience to make sense of what they see. Images reach us as already 'encoded' messages, already represented as meaningful in particular ways. (p. 45)

Viewers can decode advertising images in the ways intended by advertisers only if they grasp the code being employed.

Turner (1988) proceeded to point out that semiotics has been applied fruitfully to the study of advertising: "Semiotics has enquired into advertising to show how the selection of signifiers with positive connotations (water-skiing, relaxing by a pool) is used to transpose those associations on to an accompanying advertised product, such as cigarettes" (p. 46). Perhaps the most controversial spots aired by the Dukakis campaign—those centering on a team of Bush "handlers" discussing how best to package Bush—failed precisely because viewers did not share the code implied within the advertising texts.

Narrative Structure

Another category of semiotic analysis for Eco (1976) is a text's narrative structure. Simply put, narrative structure refers to the sequence of events through which all texts communicate their themes and values. Eco and other writers, like W. B. Gallie, have said that "the notion of understanding can be explained in terms of following a story, perceiving a narrative pattern" (Culler, 1981, p. 215). John Fiske (1987) noted the importance of narrative, especially in relation to television:

> Narrative and language are two of the main cultural processes shared by all societies: they are 'simply there, like life itself.' Like language, narrative is a basic way of making sense of our experience of the real. . . . Given that narrative is such a fundamental cultural process, it is not surprising that television is predominantly narrational in its mode. (p. 128)

Understanding a television narrative, including those characteristic of advertising texts, depends on being familiar with its intertextual references and its implicit codes. As we illustrate later, the Dukakis advertising had little success in fulfilling these requirements of narrative structure.

Semiotic Analysis of the Dukakis Advertising

From the above account of semiotic theory and method, it should be clear that semiotic analysis is a systematic interpretive practice that may be used to illuminate the interior of political advertising. In what follows, we report the conclusions we draw from our analysis of the Dukakis advertising, which is informed by the above semiotic concepts (Eco, 1976).[2] We begin by identifying three problems that recurred throughout the Dukakis advertising. These problems are: (a) a failure to take full advantage of intertextuality; (b) a lack of compelling images, especially those that evoke emotion and memory; and (c) an inability to present Dukakis as a sign of semantic depth. We also examine how an indifference to narrative structure and an absence of shared codes conspired to limit the effectiveness of one set of Dukakis advertisements.

---

[2]The procedures we used to study the Dukakis advertising were as follows: Each of us separately watched both the approved and unapproved spots and took extensive notes. We then watched the spots together twice, and discussed each one intensively while making additional notes. After a 3-day interim, during which we worked separately to cast our observations into semiotic terms sensitive to the postmodern influence, we met again to compare findings. The initial concurrence across our findings was surprising, and more discussion only further reinforced our conviction that we had considerable intersubjective agreement about the particular spots and the advertising as a whole.

Constrained Intertextuality in the Dukakis Advertising

All advertising exploits intertextuality to some degree to communicate its messages. What makes intertextuality work is the code of the familiar: audiences understand and respond to advertisements if they are familiar with the music, the narrative, and the styles borrowed from other cultural texts. Better and worse use can be made of intertextuality, however, and the Dukakis advertising used it in a restricted and unimaginative manner. Television audiences in the postmodern age expect a sophisticated mix of high and low culture, different and competing styles, and various forms of media. This mixing of cultures, styles, and media represents a postmodern form that Jameson (1983) calls "pastiche" (p. 114). Opera now is used to sell both cars and champagne, cartoon characters sell serious products like vitamins, and the concept of revolution in conjunction with the Beatles' song on that same theme is used to sell athletic shoes.

Given the limitless possibilities of intertextuality and the fact that postmodern audiences are accustomed to pastiche advertising, the textual sparseness of the Dukakis spots seems all the more curious. It almost appears a decision was made to keep the advertisements as straightforward and simple as possible, perhaps to present Dukakis as an "unpackaged" candidate relying on substance more than selling. That such a strategy would be anachronistic in the postmodern world of advertising is all too obvious. Whatever the strategy may have been, the unfortunate result was a series of advertisements defined by an uninteresting and flat textual landscape. Indeed, the texts missing from his advertisements are as interesting as the relatively few included.

First, neither recognizable rock, country, classical, or patriotic music was used in the Dukakis advertising. Instead, unfamiliar muzak-like music accompanied several of the spots. Familiar music can add significantly to the effectiveness of a candidate's spots, as the 1984 Reagan advertising team understood with their use of Lee Greenwood's patriotic country anthem. The Dukakis spots, however, ignored this advertising convention, and they seem flat as a result.

Second, photographic texts from Dukakis' past that would have delineated his personal history and would have made him a signifier with semantic depth were never used, except in a convincing spot that was never approved. Why that spot was never approved remains a mystery, for it effectively wove together the Dukakis family text with the personal text of the candidate. The spot included vivid pictures of his parents, and pictures of him playing sports, debating in college, serving in the military, and beginning a career in politics. All these images were placed into a familiar, yet stirring, narrative of a family emigrating to America and fully participating in the American dream.

Beyond its narrative use of family photographs, this advertisement also worked because it evoked a past that is part of our collective memory. In the advertisement the past became a text with which we are all familiar, and it was even represented to us in a form most people value, family photographs. Williamson (1983) semiotically explored the bond between memory and advertising, and gave this account of that bond:

> Advertisements rely to a great extent on this property of memory; and since it is impossible for them to invoke the actual, individual past of each of their spectators—the past that does go to make up personality—they invoke either an *aura* of the past, or a common undefined past. . . . We are shown a hazy, nostalgic picture and asked to 'remember' it as our past, and simultaneously, to construct it through buying/consuming the product. (p. 158)

The "common, undefined past" the Dukakis photographic narrative signifies is that of the immigrant experience, an experience remote now to most Americans but one they readily consume in popular novels, television miniseries, and films.

Third, obvious political texts, like those signifying the legacy of the Democratic Party and its presidents, were missing from the Dukakis advertising. With the exception of one unapproved spot, little or no attempt was made to link the Dukakis candidacy to popular presidents like Franklin Roosevelt, Harry Truman, and John Kennedy. The omission of the Kennedy's image is especially puzzling given Dukakis's frequent stump references to a second "Boston-Austin" Democratic presidential ticket. Even the text embodied by Lloyd Bentsen, who was viewed favorably by voters and the press, was largely absent from Dukakis advertising. Bentsen signified both federal government experience and the traditional Democratic party, two associations Dukakis needed to boost his own candidacy.

In sum, the many complaints about the flatness of the Dukakis advertising may be attributed partly to its constrained use of intertextuality. Outside of some unapproved spots, the Dukakis advertising overlooked the intertextual possibilities of music, nostalgia, and the Democratic Party.

The Absence of Compelling Images in the Dukakis Advertising

Nearly every writer who addresses the postmodern turn agrees that images are the currency of contemporary culture. Especially powerful are images of color, spectacle, and drama because they are visually compelling. Few of the Dukakis advertisements contained such images, which means again that the postmodern audience's expectations were not fulfilled. Few of the spots had images of the sort found in the Bush advertisements on Boston Harbor and on the Massachusetts prison furlough program. Those images had a visceral impact; the first achieved its effects with a color scheme emphasizing the greenish cast of filthy and polluted water, and the second achieved its effects with a combination of grainy film and blatant fear appeals leavened with a twist of racism.

By contrast, the Dukakis advertisements relied extensively on close-ups of the candidate speaking directly to the camera. These head shots dramatized his short stature and exaggerated the already outsized features of his face: his thick hair, bushy eyebrows, small and barely open eyes, and determined but unhappy smile. Moreover, no unusual camera angles or lighting were used to stimulate the audience's visual interest. The color scheme of nearly all the spots was a deep, clinical blue that seemed to wash out rather than heighten the already unexceptional images.

Furthermore, the advertisements filmed at the Democratic Convention failed to take full advantage of the spectacle evident in such mass gatherings. Regularly showing the crowd's reaction to passages from his speech would have maximized the image of the spectacle; Bush's convention advertisements included many crowd reaction shots, but Dukakis's advertisements rarely used such shots and therefore failed to exploit the imagistic possibilities of such a scene.

Also missing from the Dukakis spots were images of the candidate's family, which are a staple of political advertising. The Bush advertisements were replete with vivid images, including the famous shot of him hoisting his granddaughter, but the Dukakis family was featured only in unapproved spots and those approved ones solely aimed at the Hispanic vote. What makes this absence mysterious is that the Dukakis family was used with good effect during the convention. Moreover, the Dukakis family is quite telegenic, more so even than he is, and their presence would have supplied attractive images to be associated with the candidate. Indeed, such images would have lent visual support to Dukakis's claim that education is a ''father's concern'' in the advertisement ''Family Education.''

The few negative advertisements the Dukakis campaign eventually ran also were rendered ineffective by weak images or by tension between the image and the verbal script. Regularly aired were the images of Bush sitting with Manuel Noriega and of Bush caught in a ''silly'' pose, smiling and waving while the voiceover recounted his record on pollution, drugs, education, and Social Security. Neither image of Bush was believable because both resembled the kind of laughable photographs tabloids routinely print that are cropped to make the person look guilty of some crime. Having sacrificed credibility with these ill-chosen images, the semantic associations these advertisements tried to make between those images and Bush's record were doomed to fail.

Similarly, one negative advertisement playing to voter worry about "President Quayle" ends effectively with Quayle himself speaking in a halting monotone that confirms every received opinion about his being unqualified for high office. After building an effective message out of anti-Quayle images, however, the advertisement vitiated its effect with a terrible closing line printed on the screen: "Hopefully, we'll never know how great a lapse of judgment that really was." Such writing would not pass muster in a freshman composition class, and its lack of force seems all too much like a description of the entire Dukakis campaign.

Dukakis as Empty Sign

The final problem with the Dukakis advertising was its inability to present the candidate as a sign with semantic depth. If we follow Eco's lead and imagine Dukakis as a "semantic tree," then we would see a tree off which few "semantic markers" branch (Eco, 1984). Conspicuous in their absence from the advertising were positive semantic markers representing qualities such as vitality, emotion, presence, and patriotism. Eco (1984) contended that semantic markers permit distinctions between things and between persons, which means they allow us to recognize the identity of one person as distinct from another. In advertising terms, Dukakis's "product identity" was never well defined, and semiotics helps to explain this problem.

Advertising operates by associating a signifier without meaning to the mass audience—a new "product" like Dukakis—with a signified of well-established meaning, such as economic prosperity (Williamson, 1983). Such advertising promises that in "buying" Dukakis by supporting his candidacy, the audience is also buying economic prosperity for itself. The logic here is that economic prosperity already carries an affirmative meaning for the mass audience, and the individuals within that audience will transpose that meaning to Dukakis. The goal, then, is to have audiences connect the signifier of Dukakis with the affirmative signified of economic prosperity, thereby producing a sign of considerable power for the campaign.

The only requirement with this logic is that the candidate must have some persuasive claim to the associative signified and must also be linked to policies that transcend the obvious and carry some emotional force. With respect to the above example, Dukakis had little claim to the signified of economic prosperity because the mass audience associated the departing President Reagan with their perception of improved economic conditions in the country. Moreover, associating Dukakis, as many spots did, with the obvious signifieds of opposition to drugs, pollution, and crime did not supply him with a political identity by differentiating him from his opponent. Neither did attempts to associate him with unemotional values, such as competence and leadership; those values may well be appealing but not for emotional reasons of the sort optimally exploited in the Bush advertising. Product differentiation is indispensable to successful advertising, something the Bush campaign understood very well.

The purpose of the Bush spots on the "Pledge of Allegiance," gun control, and prison furloughs was not to address major issues, but instead to differentiate him from Dukakis on a set of emotional issues, and thereby supply Bush with a clear political identity. A corollary result of the Bush spots was to connect Dukakis with negative semantic markers on the values of patriotism, citizen rights, and toughness on crime. Even when the Dukakis campaign did produce a spot aimed at differentiation that was dependent on an emotional signified—the charged issue of plant-closing notification—political circumstances arose that limited its effectiveness. By the time the spot aired, President Reagan had reversed his opposition to the plant-closing bill and signed it into law. The president's reversal defused the emotional impact of the Dukakis spot and subverted its goal. Not until late in the campaign, when Dukakis mistakenly used the word *liberal* to describe his views, did he discover a signified with affirmative and emotional semantic associations (Drew, 1988). Although it was too late to gain many votes by incorporating the liberal signified into his advertising, Dukakis did wrap himself in the liberal mantle for the remainder of the campaign. Given the wide recognition that Bush probably had won the election, the Dukakis campaign may have decided to celebrate the liberal signified in order to boost party morale and promote voter turn-out in congressional, state, and local elections.

Problematic Codes in the Dukakis Advertising

We now turn to a more intensive semiotic analysis of one series of five spots on the "packaging" of the Republican ticket. The first four pertain to the "packaging of George Bush" and the fifth to the "packaging of Dan Quayle." All are complex advertising texts traversed by many different codes, the understanding of which is central to the success of the spots. Writing in *Ad Week* about the first spot in this series, Barbara Lippert called it "one of the most denounced ads in American history" (Rothenberg, 1988, p. 43). Lippert's statement is perhaps hyperbolic, but her criticism is warranted because there are defects in the spots.

The "packaging of George Bush" spots (see Appendix) all are in the style of documentary realism, as they all commence with a date and time printed on the screen that seem to correspond to actual events in the campaign. In keeping with this style, viewers are given the impression they are eavesdropping on a group of men, apparently political consultants, devising strategy for the Bush campaign. Their job is to sell the candidate as they would any other product. The setting and images signify that this is a new kind of campaign run by white-collar professionals with neither party ties nor personal loyalty to Bush. They are ensconced in a state-of-the art boiler room and surrounded by signs of advanced technology, such as multiple and flashing television and computer screens.

Each spot shows the consultants discussing how Bush might respond to campaign events or to certain issues raised by Dukakis. Among the issues addressed are drugs and Noriega, middle-class health insurance, crime and the federal prison furlough program, and the arguable wisdom behind the choice to put Dan Quayle on the national ticket.

Narrative Structure

The narrative of these advertising texts unfolds through a series of binary oppositions that define "the lines of conflict which will determine or motivate the events and actions of the story" (Turner, 1988, p. 74). These texts attempt to draw "lines of conflict" between the legitimate tactics and values of the Dukakis campaign and the illegitimate tactics and values of the Bush campaign. The intended contrast may be seen in the printed message that closes each spot: "They want to sell you a package. Wouldn't you rather choose a President?"

Translating this closing message into oppositions yields this structure:

Bush	*Dukakis*
They (Bush consultants) want to	Wouldn't you (Informed voters)
Sell (Manipulate into buying)	Rather choose (Make a rational de-
You (Gullible voters)	cision unswayed by
A Package (Bush)	manipulation)
	A President (Dukakis)

Underlying these oppositions are further "lines of conflict" running through the spots, and in this case they are expressed in terms of contrasting values.

Eco's (1979) analysis of Ian Fleming's novels used the aforementioned method of identifying oppositions between the values of James Bond and those of his enemies. The oppositions between Bond and his enemies, like those the advertisements express between Dukakis and Bush, are not "vague" but rather " 'simple' ones that are immediate and universal" (p. 147). Consider the following "simple" and "immediate" oppositions highlighted in the Dukakis advertisements:

Bush	*Dukakis*
Candidate of Images/Perceptions	Candidate of Real Issues/Facts
Insincere	Authentic
Amoral	Moral
Vacillation/Compromise	Leadership/Strength
Corporate/Wealthy	Working People/Middle Class

Eco argued that drawing sound inferences from texts requires "inter-textual competence" (p. 21). In the case of the Dukakis advertising, intertextual competence may be defined as familiarity with the genre code, the class code, the insider code, and the truth code, all of which intersect in these spots to produce meaning. If these spots are to produce meaning for viewers, that is, to make possible inferences coextensive with what they intend to signify, then viewers must be familiar with their predominant codes. Presuming familiarity by the mass audience with such diverse codes constitutes the critical flaw in these advertising texts.

Genre Code

These spots are intertextual to the extent that the mass audience, if it is to understand and appreciate them fully, must have knowledge of the genre of advertising texts to which they belong. That genre is known informally as "real life, real people" advertising, and it makes use of hand-held cameras and naturalistic settings and dialogue. Apple Computer, AT&T, and Nissan are three companies whose products exploit this genre of advertising, but John Hancock Insurance pioneered in its use. The John Hancock spots were created by David D'Allesandro, who also produced the "Bush Consultants" spots under scrutiny here.

Even assuming that the audience makes the intertextual link required, reliance on this code poses another problem. The earlier spots in this genre refer to concrete work experiences and personal worries common to many Americans, such as buying business equipment and making personal decisions about financial planning. In these spots the experiences presented are everyday ones and the settings are familiar. In contrast, the Dukakis spots presuppose wide knowledge of and interest in contemporary campaign practices, and that seems questionable given that fewer than half of the electorate actually votes. Indeed, there is little evidence the electorate closely follows any national campaign, much less worries about how one is being conducted. Moreover, the experiences and settings presented in the Dukakis spots are hardly the sort that most Americans encounter each day at their jobs. Finally, whereas the other spots in the genre direct viewers' attention pointedly to their products that will reduce/facilitate work and take away personal worry, the Dukakis spots do not effectively direct attention to their product. In fact, the picture of Dukakis used at the end of the spots is so small that it is easy to miss on the first or second viewing.

Class Code

The class code is signified through the characters featured in the spots. The consultants are all white males who seem rich and bristle with the props of their privileged profession—suspenders and vests, bow ties and tie bars, expensive watches and half-glasses, legal pads and rolodexes. Clearly, viewers are supposed to interpret these characters as members of the same upper class as Bush. Speaking from their insular worlds, they express amazement at the fact that 37 million Americans have no health insurance, and they are likewise shocked that Bush has a "problem" with the middle class.

These spots use the class code to vilify these consultants. When the spots close with the line, "They want to sell you a package," it is plain that the individuals (they) with such ominous intentions are the consultants themselves. They are depicted as cynical and enjoying more material advantages than most Americans, in the hope that their expressed attitudes and signs of wealth will make voters suspicious of Bush. The flaw with relying on this code is simple: In the postmodern age where once traditional distinctions and boundaries no longer obtain, the traditional boundaries between classes likewise have been blurred. Americans, poor and middle class alike, aspire to elite jobs and material advantages, and they are cued by popular media, such as television and films, to hold the upper class in high regard. Even Americans well outside the domain of the upper class are able to buy objects representing elite tradition and image, and these same Americans prefer the "quality" of Ralph Lauren to the bargains at Filene's basement.

Insider Code

Related to the class code is the insider code that signifies the kinds of issues and people of interest only to those viewers with a fascination for inside Washington politics. That few voters hold such a fascination for

"Beltway" stories is an article of faith in Washington itself. Only intensive familiarity with the insider code would allow viewers to see the consultants in the spots as representing the actual Bush campaign team of Roger Ailes, James Baker III, Lee Atwater, and Craig Fuller. Specifically, knowledge of the controversy swirling around this team's use of negative advertising and heavy-handed use of symbols like the flag is a precondition for understanding what the consultants so cynically discuss in the spots.

Similarly, understanding two of the cleverest lines in the spots also requires knowledge of the insider code. When one consultant suggests that Bush should say "I don't remember" to charges about his meeting with Noriega, the recommendation has an ironic twist, for it also evokes for insiders the memory of Bush saying the same words to extricate himself from the Iran-Contra scandal. Furthermore, when the Roger Ailes look-alike calls to check on the possibility of removing Dan Quayle from the ticket, he refers to his secretary as "Rosemary." Seeing the humor in that choice of name depends on viewers using the insider code to recall Rosemary Woods, Richard Nixon's famous secretary who erased eighteen minutes from a Watergate tape.

Truth Code

The master code implicit in these spots and all of the Dukakis advertising may well be the truth code. Certainly, the "Bush Consultants" spots turn fundamentally on this code. Bush is portrayed as a candidate who will say anything, however misleading or false, in order to gain votes. His consultants also are portrayed as contemptuous of the truth, amoral experts who laugh cynically when one member of the team momentarily questions a proposed strategy on ethical grounds.

Contrasted with this unappealing picture of Bush in the hands of amoral consultants is Dukakis, and specifically the latter's record as governor of Massachusetts. Dukakis's record on crime, drugs, and pollution is reported as a collection of indubitable facts, supported by the voice of truth itself. The clear, if unbelievable, implication is that Dukakis, with truth on his side, does not need consultants or strategies to win the election.

The drawback to relying on the code of truth is that audiences in the postmodern age do not necessarily subscribe to or even expect such a code to be employed. This pervasive incredulity toward truth claims in the postmodern age perversely makes the Bush consultants appear more honest simply because they admit their dishonesty and do not claim to have truth in their possession. In effect, the critical message of the "Bush consultants" spots turns back on itself and ends up becoming an endorsement of the postmodern "honesty" of the Bush team.

By contrast, Dukakis almost seems quaint if not anachronistic in his insistence that truth sanctions his candidacy. He appears to be clinging to a moral style of campaigning that seems obsolete in the postmodern age. Furthermore, the Dukakis spots are predicated upon the viewers recognizing that they have been manipulated and even misled by the Bush campaign. If those spots were to have any effect, viewers would have had to concede they had been duped, which seems unlikely given the prevailing skepticism of the postmodern age.

CONCLUSION

Working from the complementary perspectives of the postmodern turn and semiotics, we have examined the key question of why the Dukakis advertising failed in its mission. We began by sketching a preliminary theory of the postmodern turn. We then proposed using semiotics to track the influence of the postmodern turn upon political advertising. Against the backdrop of the postmodern turn, we then used semiotics to analyze the Dukakis advertising in order to determine why it failed.

Using concepts defined semiotically—intertextuality, image, and sign—we located some general problems with the Dukakis advertising. We noted that the constrained intertextuality and absence of compelling images characteristic of the Dukakis advertising limited its suasory effect. We also observed how the advertising as a whole failed to establish semantic depth for the sign of Dukakis appearing in the particular spots. Finally, we used the semiotic concept of code to analyze a controversial series of Dukakis spots. We showed how the codes implicit in those spots either required specialized knowledge or interests (genre code and insider code), or appealed to beliefs and norms no longer widely held in the postmodern age (class code and truth code).

Informing our analyses of the Dukakis advertising was a concomitant aim to build theory and extend it through application to the phenomenon of political advertising. We grounded our analyses in a theoretical account of the postmodern turn, and we demonstrated that the assumptions of semiotic theory fit well with the assumptions of the postmodern turn. Furthermore, we showed in the analyses themselves how semiotic method illuminates the interior of political advertising and thereby helps to explain why that advertising failed.

ACKNOWLEDGMENTS

Preparation of this chapter was supported by a grant from the National Political Advertising Research Project (NPARP). We thank Professor Frank Biocca of the

University of North Carolina at Chapel Hill, Project Director of NPARP, for his encouragement and patience. We gratefully acknowledge the judicious editorial comments of the anonymous reviewer(s) for NPARP and of Professor Walter R. Fisher of the University of Southern California.

REFERENCES

Belsey, C. (1980). *Critical practice.* New York: Methuen.
Culler, J. (1981). *The pursuit of signs.* London: Routledge & Kegan Paul.
Diamond, E. (1988, October 10). The lite hurrah. *New York,* pp. 34–37.
Drew, E. (1988, December 12). Letter from Washington. *The New Yorker,* pp. 119–138.
Eco, U. (1976). *A theory of semiotics.* Bloomington, IN: Indiana University Press.
Eco, U. (1979). *The role of the reader.* London: Hutchinson.
Eco, U. (1984). *Semiotics and the philosophy of language.* Bloomington, IN: Indiana University Press.
Edelman, M. (1988). *Constructing the political spectacle.* Chicago: The University of Chicago Press.
Ewen, S. (1988). *All consuming images.* New York: Basic Books.
Fiske, J. (1987). *Television culture.* New York: Methuen.
Foster, H. (Ed.). (1983). *The anti-aesthetic.* Port Townsend, WA: Bay Press.
Huyssen, A. (1986). *After the great divide.* Bloomington, IN: Indiana University Press.
Jameson, F. (1983). Postmodernism and consumer society. In H. Foster (Ed.), *The anti-aesthetic* (pp. 111–125). Port Townsend, WA: Bay Press.
Kearney, R. (1987). Ethics and the postmodern imagination. *Thought, 62*(244), 39–58.
Kroker, A., & Cook, D. (1986). *The postmodern scene.* New York: St. Martin's Press.
Lyotard, J. (1984). *The postmodern condition: A report on knowledge.* Minneapolis, MN: University of Minnesota Press.
McCabe, E. (1988, December 12). The campaign you never saw. *New York,* pp. 33–48.
Norris, C. (1988). *Paul De Man.* New York: Routledge.
Peirce, C. S. (1932). In C. Hartshorne and P. Weiss (Eds.), *The Collected Papers of Charles Sanders Peirce* (Vol. II). "Ground, Object, and Interpretant". Cambridge, MA: Harvard University Press, (pp. 134–155).
Rothenberg, R. (1988, October 20). The disarray in Dukakis's ad team. *The New York Times,* p. 43.
Saussure de, F. (1959). *Course in general linguistics.* New York: Philosophical Library.
Schrag, C. (1988, Autumn). Liberal learning in the postmodern world. *The Key Reporter,* pp. 1–4.
Silverman, D. (1986). *Selling culture.* New York: Pantheon Books.
Turner, G. (1988). *Film as social practice.* New York: Routledge.
Williamson, J. (1983). *Decoding advertisements.* New York: Marion Boyars.

APPENDIX

Dukakis Advertisement Titles

The following are the official titles for advertisements referred to in this paper. They appear in the order they are discussed. Unapproved advertisements are identified as such.

1. *Anything Possible* (unapproved) and *Leadership* (unapproved)
2. *Pledge* (unapproved)
3. *Chairman, Failed, Crunch,* and *Blackboard*
4. *New Era*
5. *Dos Cartas* and *Immigrant*
6. *Family Education*
7. *Chairman, Failed, Crunch,* and *Blackboard*
8. *Oval Office*
9. *Plant Closing*
10. The *Packaging of George Bush* series: *Remember, Say It, Flag, How Many More,* and *Crazy*

8

Burke's Sociological Criticism Applied to Political Advertising: An Anecdotal Taxonomy of Presidential Commercials

Larry D. Smith
Purdue University

Anne Johnston
University of North Carolina at Chapel Hill

For a moment, return to the fall of 1984 and imagine a family in "Hometown, U.S.A." sitting together watching television when, during a station break, an advertisement appears. This ad features several faceless businessmen walking down the steps of an official building on their way to their chauffeured limousines. As this scene unfolds, an announcer relates how these nameless people have victimized millions of Americans through their domination of the nation's financial markets. The commercial closes with a plea for an end to this victimization through the election of Walter Mondale as President of the United States.

A bit later the family witnesses another advertisement. This ad offers a bear—a huge, fierce-looking beast with menacing claws and demeanor—moving through a wooded area. An announcer identifies the animal and observes how some fear the bear, whereas others say it doesn't exist. After several close-ups, the bear confronts a silhouette of a person on a hillside. The commercial ends with a shot of Ronald Reagan framed against an American flag with a graphic that states: "President Reagan—Prepared for Peace."

To some viewers in "Hometown," these scenes were merely trite displays of partisanship that deserved little attention. To others, these spots offered information to be used in the construction of their personal realities regarding the fall elections, providing what Burke (1973) termed "medicine" or "equipment for living" (p. 293).

Burke (1973) maintained that discourse offers equipment for living through its capacity to present knowledge of the "typical, recurrent

115

situations'' (p. 293) of life. That is, as people *identify* with public messages, they learn of strategies (their medicine) for the negotiation of daily events. Whether a teen learns courting behavior from a soap opera, a child grasps social relations from a comic book, or a family gains political insights through a television ad, people discover ways to encounter their world through the contents of these portrayals. Hence, Burke advanced his "sociological criticism," through which critics may pursue the medicine in "works of art" (movies, music, print media, etc.) and "social situations outside of art" (ceremonial activities, public assemblies, etc.).

We apply this perspective to those strategically conceived "works of art" that are political advertisements. Returning to our aforementioned examples, notice how the Mondale ad portrayed the business community in a villainous role as it implied how "big business" had abused millions of Americans. In contrast, the Reagan spot advocated strength in the face of an uncertain future as it cast the President in a heroic role.

Although conceived through partisan pens, both narratives provided knowledge of the 1984 election. Yet, this information was not expressed in a random fashion; to the contrary, each spot was a carefully crafted story offered through a strategically selected structure. Burke (1959) referred to these structures as story "frames" that stress "peculiar ways of building the mental equipment (meanings, attitudes, character) by which one handles the significant factors of his time" (p. 34). Thus, if our family in "Hometown" gained anything through the Mondale and Reagan ads, they gathered that knowledge through *identification* with those *types* of commercials. [1]

The significance of this form of political communication may be observed in the literature of a variety of disciplines. [2] We complement those works through a Burkean interpretation of the subject matter. In so doing, we fashion a taxonomy of narrative strategies based on Burke's sociological criticism and apply that framework to a sample of presidential spots. [3] Subsequently, we pursue one objective: to generate knowl-

---

[1] For more on identification and the fundamental elements of Burkean theory, see Burke's works (Burke, 1965, 1966, 1967, 1969b). Burke presented eight story frames: the epic, comedy, tragedy, elegy, satire, burlesque, grotesque, and didactic.

[2] The literature associated with political advertising is very extensive; however, several recent works are: Diamond & Bates (1984); Jamieson (1984); and Kaid, Nimmo, & Sanders (1986).

[3] The sample assembled for this study was provided by the Political Communication Center of The University of Oklahoma. A sample of 209 spots was randomly selected from a population of 806 presidential commercials. The authors offer their deep appreciation to Mr. Joseph Magrini, the Political Communication Archives, and the Oklahoma faculty for their assistance in this effort.

edge as to how a commercial's narrative structure contributes to the interpretation of its "mental equipment."

BURKE'S SOCIOLOGICAL CRITICISM APPLIED TO POLITICAL ADVERTISING

Concerns over the processes through which people use media to construct realities have clearly captured the attention of the scholarly community.[4] One recent example involved Barker's (1988) use of Fiske and Hartley's notion of "verisimilitude" to pursue the "realness" (p. 44) of television. Barker concluded that television programs—and media in general—have no "realness" until they "engage the viewer during the process of decoding" (p. 51).

Barker also cited Hall's view that "each message in the television text not only suggests a 'preferred reading,' " but also "simultaneously prescribes the parameters for a range" (p. 52) of interpretations. In other words, "encoders" (writers, directors, technicians, etc.) use strategies that establish the boundaries of possible "decodings" by audiences. Although Barker focused on the technical facets of the "encoding process" (e.g., camera shots, lighting, etc.), attention must be extended to the narrative aspects as well.[5]

The notion that encoders establish parameters of interpretation through specific strategies appears consistent with Burke's claim that certain story frames provide distinct forms of mental equipment. To that end, Brummett (1984c) suggested that Burke's frames are "rhythms of symbolic action" into which "we cast discourses to help us to accept our trials and triumphs in life" (p. 217). As we shall see, certain "trials and triumphs" lend themselves to specific forms of expression. If a narrator wishes to portray the pain and humiliation suffered by some audience, the frame used to convey those sentiments would no doubt be distinct from one designed to generate feelings of joy and celebration. The selection of a story's "rhythm" may be the most important decision made by the encoder.

To observe how these rhythms apply to political ads, we must first define those "works of art." Kaid (1981) stated that political advertising is a "communication process by which a source . . . purchases the

---

[4]See, Andrew (1984); Corcoran (1984); Fiske & Hartley (1978); Hall (1980); Hartley (1982); and Nimmo & Combs (1983).

[5]Chatman's (1978) work divided the internal workings of a narrative into two parts: story and manifestation. To Chatman, "the story is the *what* in a narrative," whereas the "discourse" or manifestation represents "the *how*" (pp. 19–22). Barker's work addressed Chatman's "how," whereas we emphasize the story's content—Chatman's "what."

opportunity to expose receivers through mass channels to political messages with the intended effect of influencing their political attitudes, beliefs, and/or behaviors" (p. 250). Kaid claimed that the "unique element" of the process involved the "paid nature of the communication," since this "gives the source the right to control the form and content of the message" (p. 250).

This control over content allows a candidate to articulate the story lines of that candidacy. Candidates and consultants mold realities about themselves, their candidacies, their ideologies, and (perhaps most importantly) their opponents through these productions. In addition, research suggests that political advertising is not only a popular means of public communication; it also serves numerous communication functions for the campaign (Devlin, 1986; Sabato, 1981). For instance, commercials generate an awareness of issues that other campaign communications are unable to duplicate (Hofstetter & Zukin, 1979; Joslyn, 1980; Patterson, 1980; Patterson & McClure, 1976; Shyles, 1983).

Studies also have provided information on the ways in which ads employ specific rhetorical and production styles. For example, researchers have found differences in the presentational styles of issue and image ads (Shyles, 1984, 1986) and in the advertising strategies used by incumbents and challengers (Kaid & Davidson, 1986; Latimer, 1984; Payne and Baukus, 1985). Nevertheless, although political narrators may control the form and content of their messages, they are in no way able to dictate audience interpretations of ads. They can merely posit a range of possible responses to their labors. Burke's sociological criticism and his representative anecdote shed light on how storytellers establish these parameters through specific narrative strategies.[6] By developing anecdotes (i.e., plots or story lines) based on Burke's frames and applying that taxonomy to a sample of presidential ads, we may discover how narrators provide medicine regarding candidates for the nation's highest elective office.

THE TELEVISION COMMERCIAL AS PURVEYOR OF POLITICAL MEDICINE: AN ANECDOTAL TAXONOMY

Hall (1965) and Holman (1980) concurred with Burke's (1959) observation that no poetic category "can be isolated in its chemical purity" as these categories "overlap upon one another" (Burke, 1959, p. 57). Consequently, as one constructs a taxonomy of frames, one must respect

---

[6]The anecdote was introduced in Burke, 1969a. See also B. Brummett (1984a, 1984b, 1985); Smith & Golden (1988); and Scodari (1987).

the distinctiveness of each story form as well as acknowledge the potential for overlapping categories to emerge.

Burke offered three basic types of stories: positive, negative, and transitional. He designated the epic, tragedy, and comedy as positive frames; the elegy, satire, and burlesque as negative stories; and the grotesque and didactic as transitional narratives.[7]

The Positive Frames: The Epic

Burke (1959) described epics as story lines that emphasize the activities of heroes through a magnification of that role. This magnification serves two purposes: "It lends dignity to the necessities of existence, 'advertising' courage and individual sacrifice . . . and it enables the humble man to share the worth of the hero by the process of 'identification' " (pp. 35–36). Holman (1980) added that an epic presents a central character of "imposing stature" in a setting "vast in scope" involved in "deeds of great valor or requiring superhuman courage" (p. 161).

The epic provides medicine for audiences via an identification with the activities of the central character, the hero. The setting in this story line is downplayed in favor of an emphasis on the hero's actions; therefore, the plot follows the deeds of the hero in a fashion that *always* places that character in a superior position to the surroundings in which those activities take place. If the scene is extravagant, the hero's actions are even more fantastic. In the epic, the scene *never* overcomes the central character's actions.

Although this anecdote always features a hero (a person, institution, or cause) in a setting of significance doing great things, the story may choose to place the ad's sponsor in a supporting role. That is, the sponsor may be an agent exercising the hero's will or a product of the hero's labors (e.g., the product is "made in America" with America serving as the hero, and the sponsor is an agent and/or product of that hero). Epics may also address the humorous nature of the hero's labors or, as Holman implied, employ fantasy as a means to portray heroism.

Table 8.1 indicates the popularity of the epic strategy in our sample of ads. Beginning with Eisenhower's "The Man from Abilene" series and its newsreel-like format, commercials have used celebrities, causes, and

---

[7]Since the primary objective of any taxonomy involves the exclusiveness of its categories, we confine our categories to Burke's positive and negative frames. Although the transitional frames—the grotesque and didactic—are meaningful, their portrayals of "mystical principles" and "sentimental heroes" are troublesome with regard to the integrity of the categories. In fact, the primary distinction between the didactic frame and an epic involves the tale's *manifestation;* therefore, adaptations of Burke's first six frames appear to preserve the exclusiveness necessary for the taxonomy to function.

Table 8.1 Frequnecy of Appearance

	N	Percent
Epic	123	59
Comedy	0	0
Tragedy	2	1
Elegy	74	35
Satire	4	2
Burlesque	3	1
Other	3	1
Total	209	99

settings to establish the heroic qualities of their products. As time passed, however, the sophistication of these tales grew from rather obvious portrayals of "candidates as heroes" toward stories that featured the sponsor as an agent of an established, perhaps less controversial, hero. A recent example of this strategy appeared during the 1984 election. The Reagan "Morning in America" series (see Morreale, chapter 11, this volume; Simons and Stewart, chapter 12, this volume) magnified the situation for audiences, featured opportunities for identification with that construction, and placed the president in a heroic light (albeit as a supporting actor).

The series offered scenes of everyday people prospering in towns "not too far from where you live." The narrator emphasized that "America today is prouder and stronger and better" under the leadership of President Reagan and claimed that Reagan was "doing what he was elected to do." The ads featured wedding ceremonies, people moving into new homes, citizens of every ethnic background raising the flag or participating in parades, and a host of other "Mom, Country, and Apple Pie" scenes. The spots ended by asking, "Why would we want to return to where we were less than four short years ago?" or "Now that our country's turning around, why would we ever turn back?" as the video faded to a photo of Reagan (the only time we see the candidate).

The characters in this tale represented all walks of life. Yet they shared two important traits: patriotism and prosperity. To portray these characteristics, the situation was magnified in a manner that promoted identification across party lines. The hero was neither Republican nor Democrat, but the American people. Therefore, it was patriotic to support the heroic recovery and to maintain this prosperity. Once again, note how these ads depicted "America" in a "Land of Opportunity" leading role and the president as an agent who contributed to that cause. By placing Reagan in this role, the story established two objectives: (a) it deflected criticisms against Reagan through an emphasis on the scene (e.g., prosperity), and (b) it promoted identification across party lines via its patriotism theme. In virtually every respect, these ads represented the state-of-the-art of epic storytelling.

In sum, the epic features some heroic force that fosters positive associations with a strategically selected audience. The popularity of this anecdote no doubt lies in its simplistic structure and its ability to present products in a favorable light. Although the stories told through this anecdote vary from instance to instance, its internal workings make it a highly recognizable—and immensely popular—rhetorical strategy.

The Positive Frames: The Comedy

Burke (1959) described comedy as "essentially *humane*" as it dramatizes the "quirks and foibles" of its characters; hence, comedy "converts downward as the heroic converts upward" (pp. 42–43). This emphasis on "human error" prompted Brummett (1984c) to suggest that "comedy's revelation of error calls for the tolerant correction and reinstatement of the fool in society . . . because it also reveals error to be an unavoidable part of the human condition" (p. 220).

The comedy offers equipment for living through identification with the activities of a "fool" who is confounded by his or her situation. The setting in this story line contrasts the epic in that the scene is often the tale's most prominent feature. Thus, the plot presents the central character's ineptitude in the face of a situation of consequence. As the scene increases in significance, so does the central character's inability to handle that predicament.

Humor appears frequently in political advertising, but seldom in *comic* form. Narrators often use humor in satiric or burlesque attacks on the opposition, thereby leaving the tale with a *negative* resolution. In comedy, a correction occurs that fosters a *positive* ending. Subsequently, spots utilizing the comic anecdote are rare; in fact, no examples of this strategy emerged from our sample of presidential commercials.

In any event, consider a Federal Express spot as an example of this story line in action. This ad depicted the activities of a chaotic assembly line in a factory named "Blotto Skateboard & Co." As a group of odd-looking characters crudely assembled skateboards, a man walked up to a particularly stupid-looking character, raised a skateboard over his head as if to strike this person, and shouted: "Rollo, where's the package?" The character replied, "I have no idea" when, suddenly, an arm appeared on the screen. A narrator asserted (as the hand signaled): "Hold it! If you'd used Federal Express, you wouldn't be having this problem. Come with me." The ad moved to scenes of hard-working Federal Express employees in action as the narrator explained where the

characters had made their mistake. The spot concluded with the narrator's proclamation, "Next time, send it Federal Express," while the two
fools skated off, mumbling, "I had no idea Federal Express did that,
absolutely no idea."

This story offered the activities of two fools—albeit lovable, perhaps
sincere fools—who promoted identification through the error of their
actions. The audience's medicine is obtained through the correction of
the central characters' condition. In the Federal Express example, notice
how the "fools" in the skateboard factory overcame their situation
through the appearance of the sponsor. The ad stressed the *correction* of
the fools' condition. Through such a strategy, a positive ending is always
present since the audience is not left to ponder a negative conclusion.
This emphasis on correction separates the comic anecdote from other
uses of humor, such as those found in epics and the negative frames.
Indeed, the comedy's use of fantastic situations, foolish behaviors, and
positive endings via a correction make it a distinctive narrative form.

The Positive Frames: The Tragedy

The tragic story line also features the personal limits of characters;
however, whereas the comedy "deals with man in society," the tragedy
emphasizes "the cosmic man" (Burke, 1959, p. 42). Brummett (1984c)
associated Burke's "cosmic man" with the purpose of this frame, that is,
"to get people back in tune with the principles that have been violated"
(p. 219) in the story.

Hall (1965) claimed that the "tragic hero is neither completely good
nor completely without goodness" in that the character "is a person of
importance who has a flaw through which is brought about his down-
fall" (p. 30). Brummett (1984c) noted how the comic and tragic story
lines, as symbolic forms, "manage guilt" (p. 218) in a vicarious fashion
as audiences participate in the story's resolution. But whereas the
comedy *corrects* the fool and accepts that character once the correction
is made, the tragedy *punishes* the central character for his or her
"crime."

The tragedy provides medicine through its portrayal of the courage
and dignity of a character's efforts to cope with a difficult situation.
Thus, the tale's plot stresses the scene, the character's labors, and the
universal principle confronting that character in fairly equal terms.
These elements transact to produce a somewhat negative story that is
transformed to positive ends via the central character's sacrifice (Burke,
1959).

There are only a few examples of this strategy in our sample, but a
1968 Nixon ad demonstrates the technique. The spot, entitled "Wrong

Road," opened with video of a dirt road framed against a gray sky with Nixon's voice-over stating: "For the past five years we've been deluged by government programs for the unemployed . . . the cities . . . the poor, and we have reaped from these programs an ugly harvest of frustration, violence, and failure across the land." A pale, haunting flute accompanied Nixon's remarks as the video featured slow-moving scenes of poverty, darkness, and dispair. Nixon claimed, "Our opponents will be offering more of the same, but I say we're on the wrong road." Suddenly, the music changed pace (trumpets, etc.) as the video shifted to rapid scenes of people at work. Nixon declared, "I believe we should enlist private enterprise, which will produce progress, not promises, in solving the problems of America." The ad closed with the graphic, "This time vote like your whole world depended on it," with a "Nixon" logo following.

This story described society's failure to care for the needy—a universal principle of importance—through a tragic strategy. Note that the tale's central character was neither the sponsor, Nixon, nor the Democrats, but the American people. The American people made a mistake in their reliance on government programs; as a result, the nation was *punished* through "frustration, violence, and failure." Still, all was not lost—"happiness" could be restored—the audience's guilt could be managed through a change in administrations. Hence, the story ended positively through scenes of prosperity and Nixon's pledge. Without question, the story emphasized the punishment suffered by "good people" who fell because of a misplaced faith in "government programs."

The epic, comedy, and tragedy are unique in their positive resolutions to the situations they construct. Whereas the epic enjoys popularity through its portrayal of heroism, the comedy and tragedy appear less frequently, due to the complicated nature of their structures. Often, when narrators turn to the actions of fools or victims, they do so with an eye toward the *negative* resolution.

The Negative Frames: The Elegy

As Burke (1959) introduced the elegy, he noted its similarity to comedy, as the tale "spreads the disproportion between the weakness" of the characters and "the magnitude of the situation" (p. 44). Consequently, the elegy is fertile ground for "individual trickeries," as narrators magnify a situation to a point "where more and more good reasons for complaint are provided" (p. 44).

Holman (1980) described the elegy, plaint, and complaint as sharing similar story lines due to their emphasis on expressions of sorrow. This description is instructive, and Holman referenced three distinct applications of this strategy. The narrator either: (a) "laments the unresponsiveness of his mistress"; (b) "bemoans his unhappy lot and seeks to remedy it"; or (c) "regrets the sorry state of the world" (p. 95). The elegy provides medicine for audiences through identification with the central character's lament. In essence, this tale places its characters in a negative situation and leaves the audience to experience that condition vicariously. This strategy joins the epic as the most frequently used anecdote in our sample (see Table 8.1).

The 1952 "Eisenhower Answers America" series used the elegy with some regularity. One 20-sec spot involved a young white male who gazed up toward the heavens and asked, "General, just how bad is waste in Washington?" The scene shifted to Eisenhower (the candidate appeared to look down, as if the young man sat at his feet) as the candidate declared, "How bad? Recently just one government bureau actually lost 400 million dollars and not even the FBI can find it. It's really time for a change."

A second example appeared during the 1972 campaign in a McGovern attack on Nixon. The ad began with the sound of a teletype and video of newspaper headlines that condemned the Republicans (e.g., "Testimony Ties Top Nixon Aide to Secret Fund," "FBI Finds Nixon Aides Sabotaged Democrats," "House Study Tells of $700,000 In a Suitcase for Nixon," etc.). As the headlines flashed slowly, a male voice-over stated: "This is about the government. This is about credibility . . . spying . . . lying . . . dishonesty . . . stealing . . . deception. This is about the White House." Finally the headlines and comments stopped (there were 22 statements) as the announcer proclaimed, "And this is how you stop it. With your vote." A McGovern graphic appeared simultaneously. Obviously, this frame is in direct contrast to the previous story lines, due to its introduction of the negative without a meaningful, positive resolution (i.e., an ending that extends beyond a slide of the sponsor or an expression of a slogan). Eisenhower merely expressed his astonishment with the situation ("not even the FBI can find it"), whereas McGovern regretted the "sorry state" of the opposition. This strategy contrasts the tragedy all the more markedly in that it does *not* allocate time to discuss how the sponsor will overcome this problem (as in the Nixon "Wrong Road" piece). Instead, it merely raises the negative and leaves the audience to ponder that predicament.

The Negative Frames: The Satire

To Burke (1959), the satire is a complicated story form in that "the satirist attacks *in others* the weaknesses and temptations that are really *within himself* (p. 49). Burke illustrated his point through this example: "A and B have a private vice in common. . . . At the same time, on some platform of the public arena they are opponents. . . . A is a satirist. In excoriating B for his political views, A draws upon the imagery of the secret vice within himself" (p. 49). It is this facet of satire—the projection of traits by the source—that makes it a distinctive rhetorical strategy.

Holman (1980) described the two major forms of satire as the "formal or direct" and "indirect" (p. 399). In the former, "the satiric voice speaks . . . either directly to the [audience] or to a character" in the story, whereas the latter is "expressed through a narrative" in which "the characters or groups who are the satiric butt are ridiculed not by what is said about them but by what they themselves say and do" (p. 399).

The satire presents an interesting mixture of identification strategies, as it casts the negative regarding a trait potentially shared by the attacker. Subsequently, the plot may feature an imposing scene and cast of characters or it may downplay the scene and characters in favor of an emphasis on some flaw in one or both. In all cases, this tale addresses some negative quality through a direct expression (Holman's formal satire) or through an enactment of the traits attributed to the butt of the story (the indirect approach).

Our sample of presidential ads contained a spot that employed Holman's direct approach through an attack on McGovern's 1972 candidacy. This "Democrats for Nixon" piece featured a photograph of McGovern connected to a pole. A male announcer intoned, "In 1967, Senator George McGovern said he was not an advocate of unilateral withdrawal of our troops from Viet Nam." The photo suddenly flipped toward the opposite direction while the voice-over declared, "Now, of course, he is." The story continued with similar claims, such as, "Last January, Senator McGovern suggested a welfare plan that would give a thousand dollar bill to every man, woman, and child in the country [photo flip] and now he says maybe the thousand dollar figure isn't right." After several more such flips, the spot ended with the photo spinning wildly as the announcer remarked, "Last year, this year, the question is what about next year," as the "Democrats for Nixon" graphic appeared. This example demonstrated the essential ingredients of Burkean satire as the "Democrats for Nixon" attacked McGovern regarding a vice shared by the attacker. That is, politicians change their minds on issues. Therefore, to attack the opposition on such a matter was to cast the negative in satiric terms. After all, the Democrats had changed *their* positions in order to vote for Nixon, a Republican.

The satire is risky business, as narrators may inadvertently promote identifications *against* their causes as often as they facilitate positive associations. Although satires may employ humor to gain attention, their resolutions remain distinctive endings that do not stress the positive, but merely leave the viewer to contemplate the traits portrayed within the stories.

The Negative Frames: The Burlesque

Burke (1959) defined the burlesque as "the depiction of very despicable, forlorn, and dissipated people" (p. 53). He claimed that these attacks are basically "external," as authors make "no attempt to get inside the psyche of [the] victim"; they are "content to select the externals of behavior, driving them to a 'logical conclusion' that becomes their 'reduction to absurdity' " (p. 54).

Holman (1980) observed how burlesque is "characterized by ridiculous exaggeration . . . secured in a variety of ways," such as making the sublime appear absurd or honest emotions being turned into sentimentality or "a serious subject may be treated frivolously or a frivolous subject seriously" (p. 63). The essential quality of burlesque is "the discrepancy between subject matter and style" (p. 63).

The burlesque's plot provides for audience identification through its exaggeration of some negative quality associated with the attacked. This story line may either exaggerate the scene, certain characteristics of the attacked, an activity attributed to the attacked, or a combination of these. As a result, this strategy often resorts to caricature to construct its realities.

The burlesque enjoys widespread popularity with political storytellers. Consider the 1964 Johnson ad that cast the negative through a rather humorous scene. The spot opened with a map of the United States, with a saw slowly severing the east coast from the continent. As the saw reached the tip of North Carolina, a male announcer said, "In a recent *Saturday Evening Post* article dated August 31, 1963, Barry Goldwater said, 'Sometimes I think this country would be better off if we could just saw off the eastern seaboard and let it float out to sea.' " The voice-over continued, "Can a man who makes statements like this be expected to serve all the people justly and fairly?" Suddenly, the east coast fell off and floated away. The story concluded with a graphic and this voice-over: "Vote for President Johnson on November 3rd. The stakes are too high for you to stay home."

This ad certainly exaggerated the "externals of behavior." For Democrats to attack Goldwater as either a regional candidate who fails to represent the entire country or to lament his lack of experience with the executive branch would have taken us into the realm of satire (no candidate can be a "national" candidate) or elegy. Instead, the ad resorted to caricature through scenes that portrayed a serious subject frivolously. To suggest that anyone would sever the thirteen original states from the union is ludicrous.

The burlesque attacks with recklessness. Although it concentrates on the negative, the "woe is me" or "beware of the other person" dimensions observed in the elegic and satiric story lines are omitted in favor of caricature. But, as Burke (1959) suggested, the burlesque narrator should exercise care not to imagine these characters with "too great [an] intimacy. . . . For to picture them intimately, he must be one of them" (p. 53).

The Burkean Frames: A Summary

Each of these frames employs distinct styles of organization as it depicts scenes of heroism, foolishness, or sorrow. It comes as little surprise that some rhythms are better suited for some jobs than others. With regard to this effort, the narrators in our sample felt portrayals of heroism and sorrow served them best. Table 8.1 indicates the frequency of usage for each frame in our sample of presidential commercials.

Although two frames dominate our sample, this is not a reflection on the utility of the other story lines. Instead, this finding is the product of two factors: (a) epic and elegies are simplistic story lines that lend themselves to simple forms of expression (almost all early spots are one or the other) and, (b) they appear to satisfy the often unimaginative needs of political narrators. Perhaps a review of each strategy would provide an instructive summary.

The epic is distinctive, due to its emphasis on the activities of the central character, the hero (a person, place, or cause). In this strategy, the heroism always overcomes the story's setting. This tale's objective involves the audience's identification with the attributes of the heroic force. The key to this strategy relates to the projection of heroism for specific audiences, as one person's hero may be another's fool.

In direct contrast to the epic, comedy stresses the scene more than character activity. In the comedy, characters act foolishly in situations of consequence. However, this strategy emphasizes a *correction* of the central character's foolishness, which, in turn, produces a positive ending. The comedy presents a mistake, corrects it, and leaves the audience to identify not only with the humorous actions of the central character, but the correction as well. Although this story line appears often in nonpolitical spots, not one example emerged from our sample.

Positive endings are also produced through the tragedy, but in the tragic story line a character with heroic-like qualities experiences a fall.

The central character has some flaw that prompts a violation of an acknowledged principle, hence the character is punished. In this anecdote, the audience identifies with the principle violated, the punishment rendered, and the moral of the story. Again, this frame enjoys more prominence in nonpolitical advertising. The tragedy and the comedy are the two most complicated story lines in our taxonomy.

The elegy, satire, and burlesque organize realities through strategies that elevate the negative aspects of some situation and leave the audience to ponder the condition. In the elegy, the central character laments an unhappy circumstance. Emphasis may be placed on a character trait, a setting, or society as a whole; in all cases, the story's strategy involves the introduction of the negative and identification with the sad state. As evidenced in Table 8.1, this frame appears often in political advertising since narrators project the "sorry state" of the situation and/or the opposition with some regularity.

In the satire, the narrator raises concerns regarding some attribute potentially shared by the source. Unlike the elegy, which advances a "woe is me" plot, this anecdote suggests "woe is the *other* person." Here, audience identification is pursued through a rather risky strategy, as the narrator may inadvertently discredit the source rather than the attacked. Although few examples emerged in our sample, this frame enjoys some popularity among political narrators, due to the satire's ability to cast the negative in graphic terms.

Finally, the burlesque attacks with severity, often resorting to caricature to promote audience identification as it assails some cause, institution, person, trait, or a variety of topics. Indeed, these distortions make the burlesque a most distinctive—and potentially dangerous—strategy. Although examples of this frame were not plentiful in our sample, these exaggerated attacks appear frequently in American elections.

The potential advantages and disadvantages of each frame suggests the strategic nature of the process. For political narrators, blatant attacks on the opposition's character may be acceptable; however, for their nonpolitical counterparts, graphic expressions of the negative are more controversial. In both cases, it is the selection of the story's structure that establishes the parameters of interpretation and, in turn, the mental equipment projected through the narrative.

CONCLUSIONS

Regarding our methodology, Scodari (1987) characterized Burke's sociological criticism as a "treasure chest of tools for rhetorical and media criticism" (p. 111). In this instance, that treasure chest yielded Burke's literary frames, which we used to devise a taxonomy of narrative styles.

Although these frames display distinctive features, there are always limitations to this type of venture: (a) stories may appear that fail to reflect any internal consistency (there were three "others" in our sample) and (b) critics may disagree in evaluations of story content. Moreover, our concerns were in the internal workings of the anecdotes' *content*, not in the technical facets of the production (their manifestations). Although our efforts reflect these limitations, Burke's treasure chest produced meaningful insights into the world of political advertising.

In terms of subject matter, we implicitly observed the growth of television technology through the evolution of these productions. During the early days of television, narrators relied on simplistic story structures to complement their technically constrained productions. Consequently, the epic and elegy dominated the early portions of our sample. As technical sophistication advanced, the story lines expanded as narrators had the capacity to graphically portray tragedy, satire, and burlesque. Still, television's inclination toward imitation appeared to limit the imaginations of political narrators, as their productions displayed little innovation.

Specifically, we wonder why more examples of comedy are not present. This story form, perhaps more than any other, maintains a capacity to portray foolishness in a positive way. In contrast, storytellers turn to negative humor as they cast shadows over the opposition's campaign.

Nevertheless, the prolific use of this form of mass communication requires critics to pursue this enterprise through all available means. Whether a bear is used to express the dangers associated with foreign affairs or big business is used as a villain, these scenarios feature knowledge of life's situations that viewers use in the construction of their personal realities.

In no way, however, can we infer that what is encoded in an ad determines what will be decoded by audiences. By examining an ad's internal workings in terms of narrative, we can explore the ways in which a commercial attempts to assist audiences in the reading of the ad—at least the reading that the sponsor desires. As Allen (1987) argued, television does not reflect the world; "rather it constructs representations of the world on the basis of complex sets of conventions—conventions whose operations are hidden by their transparency" (p. 2). Thus, sponsors construct a range of possible audience interpretations through the use of certain strategic devices (i.e., Allen's conventions), which were discussed in terms of Burke's story frames. These rhythms of expression are fascinating topics for the sociological critic and operate in the context of political advertising.

REFERENCES

Allen, R. C. (1987). *Channels of discourse*. Chapel Hill, NC: University of North Carolina.

Andrew, D. (1984). *Concepts in film theory*. New York: Oxford University Press.

Barker, D. (1988). "It's been real": Forms of television representation. *Critical Studies in Mass Communication, 5,* 42–56.

Brummett, B. (1984a). Burke's representative anecdote as a method in media criticism. *Critical Studies in Mass Communication, 1,* 161–176.

Brummett, B. (1984b). The representative anecdote as a Burkean method, applied to evangelical rhetoric. *The Southern Speech Communication Journal, 50,* 1–23.

Brummett, B. (1984c). Burkean comedy and tragedy, illustrated in reactions to the arrest of John DeLorean. *Central States Speech Journal, 35,* 217–227.

Brummett, B. (1985). Electric literature as equipment for living: Haunted house films. *Critical Studies in Mass Communication, 2,* 247–261.

Burke, K. (1959). *Attitudes toward history*. Los Altos, CA: Hermes Publications.

Burke, K. (1965). *Permanence and change*. Indianapolis, IN: Bobbs-Merrill Educational Publishing.

Burke, K. (1966). *Language as symbolic action*. Berkeley, CA: University of California Press.

Burke, K. (1967). Dramatism. In L. Thayer (Ed.), *Communication: Concepts and perspectives* (pp. 327–360). Washington, DC: Spartan Books.

Burke, K. (1969a). *A grammar of motives*. Berkeley, CA: University of California Press.

Burke, K. (1969b). *A rhetoric of motives*. Berkeley, CA: University of California Press.

Burke, K. (1973). *The philosophy of literary form*. Berkeley, CA: University of California Press.

Chatman, S. (1978). *Story and discourse: Narrative structure in fiction and film*. Ithaca, NY: Cornell University Press.

Corcoran, F. (1984). Television as ideological apparatus: The power and the pleasure. *Critical Studies in Mass Communication, 2,* 1–22.

Devlin, L. P. (1986). An analysis of presidential television commercials, 1952–1984. In L. L. Kaid, D. Nimmo, & K. R. Sanders (Eds.), *New perspectives on political advertising* (pp. 21–54). Carbondale, IL: Southern Illinois University.

Diamond, E., & Bates, S. (1984). *The spot*. Cambridge, MA: MIT Press.

Fiske, J., & Hartley, J. (1978). *Reading television*. London: Methuen.

Hall, L. (1965). *A grammar of literary criticism*. New York: The Macmillan Company.

Hall, S. (1980). Encoding/decoding. In S. Hall, D. Hobson, A. Lowe, & P. Willis (Eds.), *Culture, media, language* (pp. 128–138). London: Hutchinson.

Hartley, J. (1982). *Understanding news*. London: Methuen.

Hofstetter, C. R., & Zukin, C. (1979). TV network news and advertising in the Nixon and McGovern campaigns. *Journalism Quarterly, 56,* 106–115.

Holman, C. H. (1980). *A handbook to literature*. Indianapolis, IN: Bobbs-Merrill Educational Publishing.

Jamieson, K. H. (1984). *Packaging the presidency: A history and criticism of presidential advertising*. New York: Oxford University Press.

Joslyn, R. A. (1980). The content of political spot ads. *Journalism Quarterly, 57,* 92–98.

Kaid, L. (1981). Political advertising. In D. Nimmo & K. Sanders (Eds.), *Handbook of political communication* (pp. 249–272). Beverly Hills, CA: Sage.

Kaid, L. L., & Davidson, D. K. (1986). Elements of videostyle: Candidate presentation through television advertising. In L. L. Kaid, D. Nimmo, & K. R. Sanders (Eds.), *New perspectives on political advertising* (pp. 184–209). Carbondale, IL: Southern Illinois University Press.

Kaid, L. L., Nimmo, D., & Sanders, K. (1986). *New perspectives on political advertising.* Carbondale, IL: Southern Illinois University Press.

Latimer, M. K. (1984). Policy issues and personal images in political advertising in a state election. *Journalism Quarterly, 61,* 776–784, 852.

Nimmo, D., & Combs, J. (1983). *Mediated political realities.* New York: Longman.

Patterson, T. E. (1980). *The mass media election: How Americans choose their president.* New York: Praeger.

Patterson, T. E., & McClure, R. D. (1976). *The unseeing eye.* New York: Putnam.

Payne, J. G., & Baukus, R. A. (1985, April). *Trend analysis of the 1984 GOP senatorial spot.* Paper presented at the McElroy Symposia: Current Trends in Broadcast Advertising, University of Northern Iowa, Cedar Falls, IA.

Sabato, L. J. (1981). *The rise of political consultants.* New York: Basic Books.

Shyles, L. (1983). Defining the issues of a presidential election from televised political spot advertisements. *Journal of Broadcasting, 27,* 333–343.

Shyles, L. (1984). The relationship of images, issues and presentational methods in televised spot advertisements for 1980's American presidential primaries. *Journal of Broadcasting, 28,* 405–421.

Shyles, L. (1986). The televised political spot advertisement: Its structure, content, and role in the political system. In L. L. Kaid, D. Nimmo, & K. R. Sanders (Eds.), *New perspectives on political advertising* (pp. 107–138). Carbondale, IL: Southern Illinois University Press.

Scodari, C. (1987). Contemporary film and the representative anecdote of "Unmasking": Coping strategies for a narcissistic society. *Central States Speech Journal, 38,* 111–121.

Smith, L. D., & Golden, J. L. (1988). Electronic story telling in electoral politics: An anecdotal analysis of television advertising in the Helms-Hunt senate race. *The Southern Speech Communication Journal, 53,* 244–250.

9

Issue Content and Legitimacy in 1988 Televised Political Advertising: Hubris and Synecdoche in Promoting Presidential Candidates

Leonard Shyles
Villanova University

INTRODUCTION AND RATIONALE

For several decades, political observers and analysts have lamented the negative impact that television has purportedly had on the American presidential election process. Among the foremost complaints have been those leveled at televised political spot advertisements. Critics have maintained since the inception of political spots in the 1952 campaign that the use of such messages has weakened rational debate of important issues by focusing instead on slick and often misleading candidate images and frivolous emotional appeals more suitable for peddling perfume than leaders. In addition, such messages have repeatedly been condemned for being too short to permit adequate coverage of complex issues, even when such topics are the chief focus of their content. Nowadays, most political announcements are 30 seconds long, some 60 seconds; critics argue that such time frames offer little opportunity for anything but the most abbreviated presentations of issue information, argument, and debate.

As early as 1969, the Twentieth Century Fund Commission framed debate over the value of televised political spot advertisement for the political system as follows:

> Specifically, does a series of short "spot" announcements contribute as much to the voter's knowledge of the issues and of the candidates as longer programs where issues are discussed and candidates are exposed to view?

The answer is almost certainly no.

> (Minow, Burch, Corcoran, Heard, & Price, 1969, p. 2)

Debate over the possibility that political spot advertisements do not contain significant issue information has stemmed from the ideological view that the democratic process depends on an informed electorate:

> . . . the democratic process requires open forums for political ideas and the widest possible dissemination of information. . . . [F]ostering the development of commercial-like campaign spots rather than rational political discussions may in time subvert the democratic process . . . (Minow et al., 1969, p. 17)

Patterson and McClure (1973) further described the controversy over the alleged value of political spots:

> . . . conflicting claims are made about the impact of televised political spots. Critics contend that televised ads fail to provide the voters meaningful information, that they degrade the electoral process by selling candidates as if they were soap, that they emphasize image-making while ignoring political issues. . . . (p. 7)

Writers who have agreed that televised political spots have been preoccupied with images at the expense of issues include scholars, journalists, political observers, and campaign workers. Devlin (1973) and O'Keefe and Sheinkopf (1974) recount the emergence of the television candidate as the product of "image-merchants and media specialists" (Devlin, 1973, p. 18; O'Keefe and Sheinkopf, 1974, p. 403). In 1958, *New York Times* columnist James Reston expressed the image-issue controversy this way:

> Instead of the old-fashioned emphasis on what a candidate thinks, or what he says, the emphasis now seems to be on how he looks, especially on television, and on what kind of personality he has. (Rubin, 1967, p. 32)

RobertMacNeil (1968) criticized political commercials as featuring image at the expense of issue:

> . . . [Political commercials] are intended to influence us vividly and emotionally in as short a time as possible. They imply that the ingredients of a political decision can be encapsulated like the ingredients of any trivial commercial decision. They reduce the complexities of public life [and] . . . are so indefensible by any criterion of public service that politicians do not even pretend otherwise. (p. 194).

Although such criticism is common, there are substantial reasons for the continued lavish use of such messages by campaign organizations. First, such spots offer a practical application from the lessons of repetition research in brand-name advertising. Furthermore, political spots represent a low cost-per-thousand purchase, and, as reported elsewhere, they succeed better than longer political programs in reaching undecideds and nonsupporters, thereby permitting a sensible approach to regional and statewide campaigns in critical areas (Patterson & McClure, 1973; Minow et al., 1969; Ogden & Peterson, 1968; Shyles, 1986). For these pragmatic reasons, there is little likelihood that the use of such messages will cease in the near future.

Critical debate and analysis of televised political advertisements followed the proliferation of such spots into the 1980s during the Reagan presidential campaigns, which featured in 1984 the now famous "It's Morning Again in America" commercials, a nostalgic and patriotic advertising promotion that presented the quintessential image candidate in a pastiche of Norman Rockwell-like portrayals reminiscent of 19th-century idealized innocence. In these spots, the incumbent Reagan was shown presiding over a problem-free America re-awakening to a renaissance of national well-being resulting from the policies of Reagan's first term (see a review and analysis of these commercials in Shyles, 1984, 1988). Although such an appeal appears to have resonated with enough voters for Reagan to win reelection in 1984, the aftermath of the Reagan era raises significant questions about the legitimacy of using such appeals for inducing the body politic to select and empower its leaders to guide and direct the ship of state.

In the year since Reagan left office and his vice president, George Bush, took over, it appears now that the Reagan years were not so much a reason to celebrate a renaissance of national well-being as it was a period marked by a slide into a slothful slumber of neglect and avoidance of a plethora of painful problems which, in the nineties, looms as perhaps the most difficult and complex set of issues ever to plague our peacetime republic. In no special order, we can identify some of these worsening predicaments as (a) fiscal (unprecedented growth in our national debt and trade imbalance); (b) educational (i.e., education experts recognize the poor performance of America's students compared to that of other industrialized nations); (c) drug-health-crime related (i.e., the crack-cocaine and AIDS epidemic); and (d) environmental (i.e., growth in toxic and nuclear waste disposal problems). The problems left over by the Reagan stewardship are by no means exhausted by this short list. Add to the ledger the unprecedented growth in homelessness over the last decade, as well as the recent Savings & Loan crisis destined to cost taxpayers several hundred billion dollars, and we begin to realize that the Reagan era, once touted in its campaign commercials as a grand return to an era of prosperity, may actually have been a period that papered over a ledger of liabilities. Certainly the prior description of our current state, if accurate, suggests the possibility that the Reagan era may have bequeathed not prosperity but a domestic legacy of economic debt and social uncertainty well into the future. It is from this perspective that we examine the advertising content of the 1988 presidential campaign, and that of the general election campaign in particular, and offer a means by which we can come to understand how, among other things, through political hubris and an advertising appeal that made trenchant use of the stylistic device of synecdoche, George Bush's presidential campaign managed to deflect criticism from his major opponent.

It is essential for America's political health not only to try to explain the outcome of the 1988 campaign, but perhaps, more importantly, to reflect on what the legitimate (rather than merely pragmatic) role of a political campaign in a properly functioning representative democracy should be. When we witness through television the recent blatant attempts by tyrants to mock the democratic process by stealing elections by thievery and vote fraud, physical brutality and intimidation (i.e., Marcos, Noriega), we feel fortunate and even blessed to live in a nation that routinely conducts peaceful elections, where citizens are offered the opportunity to freely cast ballots, in order to voice their political will. Americans pride themselves on conducting their voting ritual with regularity, legitimacy, and decorum. Voters here feel confident that "their vote will count," that anything less than an honest count would constitute a sad parody of the election process. In theory, it is through the mechanism of fair elections that we invest our contemporary leadership with the legitimate right to deliberate our futures, to represent us, to carry out our will, and to conduct the people's business.

But the voting process requires more than just a fair count in order to secure genuine representation; it is a logical prerequisite that before a vote is correctly counted, it is essential that the hand casting the ballot be directed by a citizen exercising informed choice. Media scholars and others have long recognized and bemoaned that segment of the citizenry that either fails to vote or, perhaps even worse, votes without knowing the candidates and issues—this latter group merely apes the voting process and mimics more than it participates. Political scholars lamentably characterize them as the "narcotized" electorate. Conversely, we exult and rejoice that rare subgroup of active participants who bring informed choice to the ballot box, for it is said of them that they bring "good and right reason" to their actions, thereby helping to legitimize the voting process.

Finally, if all goes according to classic democratic theory, after the rational vote is cast and fairly counted, the elected candidate takes an oath of public office and then carries out his campaign pledges *in good faith,* a condition that presupposes that pledges are made in good faith to begin with—anything less would be an infelicitous outcome.

In the language of J. L. Austin's (1977) speech act theory, as it has come to be called, unless all of these conditions are present, "voting in an election" has perhaps not really occurred; that is, if the process in the main falls short of meeting all three conditions (namely, informed choice, a fair count, and an honest candidate), we can say, in the words of Austin, that the "election" that results is an inauthentic imposter, the flawed product of "hitches," "misfires," "misexecutions," "insinceri- ties," "miscarriages," "nonfulfillments," "breaches," or, generally, "infelicities" (pp. 18, 14–45, 136–161).

So, in America, at the same time that we are hopeful that our votes are intelligently deliberated and counted fairly, and that our process of casting ballots is allowed to proceed with regularity and decorum, we must also be concerned with the need to protect ourselves from campaigns that may knowingly promise fantasy while intentionally diverting attention away from salient issues. In short, it is important for citizens who vote in a representative democracy to feel able to judge when they are being hoodwinked by political advertising. With regard to this concern, the present analysis of televised political advertising in the '88 campaign can help optimize the function of the active electorate in future campaigns.

A WORD ABOUT RATIONAL CHOICE

Of course, there are those who say that the rational classic democratic model articulated earlier has never existed and has always been a myth; however, it is a fitting response to answer that even though irrational and nonrational impulses may be at work in the election process (particularly in voters' private deliberations over complex emotional and controversial issues), the model of the voter may be incomplete, which views the citizen in the voting booth as playing pin-the-tail-on-the-donkey (or elephant). Casting a vote is more than that.

The preponderance of research on voting behavior over the last few decades seems to indicate that the model of the voter as either purely rational or irrational is incorrect. For example, Key (1966), in his masterful analysis of voting behavior and motivation, concluded that the electorate is responsible, that voters are not fools, and that the voter is neither " 'straightjacketed by social determinants,' nor 'moved by subconscious urges triggered by devilishly skillful propagandists.' The portrait that emerges is rather that of 'an electorate moved by concern about central and relevant questions of public policy, of governmental performance, and of executive personality" (p. vii). Key uses voting results from the 1964 presidential election to advance his central thesis that "voters . . . base their . . . decisions on the issue positions of the candidates and on their expectations concerning how . . . candidates would perform as president" (p. xiv).

Himmelweit, Humphreys, Jaeger, and Katz (1981) claim that the "decision models of voting . . . are . . . 'rational' models in that they assume that the voter wishes to maximize his or her expected utilities . . . that might accrue from . . . competing choices. Voting masochists, out to select a party which would make matters worse, have no place in these models nor do voters who choose at random" (p. 112). They concede, however, that voters may differ with respect to their "decision horizons," that is, the point "in the future beyond which the voter does not go when considering the consequences" of his vote (p. 112).

Similarly, Pomper's (1973) research on voting behavior suggests that the voter is neither the ideal citizen who "individually seek[s] the common good by attention to policy issues [and] upon fair consideration . . . supports the candidate most likely to advance the general welfare; [nor is he] a subject susceptible to manipulation by . . . propaganda and glamorous candidates" (p. 68). Rather, for Pomper, both these models "can be shown to be empirically invalid" (p. 69). For Pomper, the truth is somewhere in between.

Finally, in an in-depth treatment and review of political theory and empirical research of voting behavior, Dalton (1988) calls for a reassessment of the model of the rational voter, concluding that voters are neither ideal citizens who are fully informed, nor are they fully unsophisticated and uninvolved. Rather, Dalton suggests that the relevant criterion of participation that would satisfy the perspective of classic democratic theory should be "whether the public possesses a sufficient basis for rational political action" (p. 32) when a particular election takes place. In line with these findings, the model of the voter that is adopted for the present study is one that includes rational dimensions.

Hence, in the case of the contemporary controversy over abortion, for example, although this issue is highly emotional, it is not on purely irrational grounds that people who are pro-life or pro-choice base their arguments. Even though points of view about abortion are widely divergent, strongly felt, and intensely debated, the content of such passionate debate can be, nevertheless, high in logos and rational argument. Voters who are highly polarized by the abortion issue, who base their voting decisions on how their views will be represented by their chosen representative, do not see themselves as playing dice (and are not blindfolded) when they enter the voting booth. Much to the contrary, the voter may actually be registering his or her commitment to a point of view, and could feel betrayed in the extreme by that candidate who promised to pursue policy X while knowing he lacked either the inclination and/or the resources to follow through on his pledges. Voters who discovered that they had entrusted their endorsement to such a candidate might feel the same sense of loss as that felt by victims of stolen elections whose views are summarily discounted, and who are powerless and at the mercy of a dictator or tyrant who stages a mock election, steals the ballot boxes, stuffs them with fraudulent ballots, and counts only those "votes" that guarantee the outcome the dictator wants.

In part it is for these reasons that the present study views political advertising as consequential among voters who rely on television as their main source of political information during presidential campaigns. According to Dalton (1988), "Television is uniformly cited [by 62% of respondents] as the most frequently used information source" (p. 21) for political information in America. Since television is such a pervasive factor, it is therefore important to assess the content of political advertising; part of that assessment lies in judging its information value and its accuracy.

STATEMENT OF RESEARCH OBJECTIVES

From the foregoing rationale, the purpose of this research is to analyze the issue content presented on behalf of candidates in televised political spots for the 1988 presidential campaign and to focus most closely on the campaigns of the major party nominees. In addition, emphasis is placed on examining advertising content and styles of the Bush and Dukakis campaigns for the general election periods, as well as the meaning and value of the Bush campaign in particular (especially in terms of the match between its promise and its performance) in the context of some salient contemporary issues since his victory.

Methods

In order to isolate the issue content of the 1988 presidential campaign as it was presented in televised advertisements, a justifiable definition of issue content was required. It was first necessary to acquire copies of all political spots available for both the primary and general election periods from all major party campaign hopefuls. To do this, videotapes of all 30- and 60-second political commercials were solicited from thirteen campaign organizations from the Democratic and Republican parties; then, issue information was coded for all spots. The candidates whose spots were included for analysis are listed in Table 9.1. In all analyses, the data in this study were treated not as a sample but as a census.

The Issue Concept in Political Research

For this study, "issue content" has been taken to refer to information dealing with specific policy stands and to topics tied to the civic concerns of the citizenry (Hofstetter & Judge, 1974). We defined *issues* as "current topics and civic concerns linked to the national interest" (Kaid & Sanders, 1978; Patterson & McClure, 1974).

Operational Definition of Issue

An issue was defined for each commercial as: the total number of *positive evaluations* made by coders of terms found in each advertise-

Table 9.1 Distribution and Frequency of Advertisements by Candidate, Party

	Last Elected Office	Total Number of ADS	Number of 30-sec. Spots	Number of 60-sec. Spots
Candidate				
Bruce Babbitt* (D)	Governor, Arizona	8	6	2
George Bush (R)	Vice President, United States	34(19,15)**	32	2(1,1)
Robert Dole (R)	Senatory, Kansas	5	5	0
Michael Dukakis (D)	Governor, Massachusetts	37(12,25)	32	5(1,4)
Pierre DuPont (R)	Governor, Delaware	4	4	0
Richard Gephardt (D)	Congressman, Missouri	8	6	2
Albert Gore (D)	Senator, Tennessee	9	8	1
Alexander Haig (R)	None	3	3	0
Gary Hart (D)	Senator, Colorado	3	0	3
Jesse Jackson (D)	None	4	4	0
Jack Kemp (R)	Congressmen, New York	9	7	2
Pat Robertson (R)	None	8	8	0
Paul Simon (D)	Senator, Illinois	10	8	2
Party				
Democrat		79	64	15
Republican		63	59	4
Total		142	123	19

*D, Democrat; R, Republican.
**Primary and general election spots, respectively.

ment that matched terms featured in a list (supplied by the analyst) of current topics linked to the national interest. This method of coding issue scores for each commercial was a partial reduction of semantical content analysis (Lasswell & Leites, 1949, pp. 57–65) to what has been called *sign vehicle analysis,* and uses a set of sign vehicles as a representative of a semantic class (in this case, campaign issues).

A positive evaluation occurred when coders determined that a sign vehicle from a commercial referred to a "current topic linked to the national interest" rather than to some entity that was not a current topic. (Example: if a coder watched a commercial wherein the word *war* was used, and if the word also appeared in the sign vehicle list, then it was considered for inclusion in that commercial's issue score; if, however, the reference of the term was judged by a coder to be a historical reference about World War II, for example, rather than to a current military involvement [i.e., the Contra effort], the term was not included in the commercial's issue score.)

Development of the Operational Definition of the Issue Construct

Delphi Panel

An expert panel of five political scientists familiar with political propaganda discourse generated a list of issue terms contained in a subsample of advertisements analyzed in this study. This Delphi Panel (Cegala & Bassett, 1976) watched a 25% subsample of commercials (35 spots) and wrote key words and phrases, used in the advertisements, that referred to current topics linked to the national interest. In addition, the panel was asked to keep track of the frequencies with which issue terms were used.

After viewing, panel members discussed all terms used and their frequency of usage; this additional information allowed a rationale to form for using frequently used terms as category divisions under which to subsume all others representing issues.

Follow-up to Delphi Panel Efforts

A follow-up effort was made to expand the list made by the Delphi panel; the researcher selected terms, from the remaining 75% of advertisements, that were semantically similar to those selected by the panel but were absent from the subsample viewed by the panel. This was done to certify that issue terms contained in the final sign vehicle list would represent issues contained in all 142 spots.

Classification Scheme of Issue Categories

The category divisions for all issue terms consisted of the following seven headings, adopted from frequency information and prior issue research (Shyles, 1983) on political advertising content: (a) domestic issues; (b) economy; (c) environment; (d) foreign policy/foreign relations; (e) government management; (f) national security/military strength; and (g) national well-being.[1]

Plan for Coding Issue Terms

The final sign vehicle list and category divisions were submitted to coders (students enrolled in advanced political communication courses) who viewed each advertisement. In each case where a term on the list matched a term in a commercial, an evaluation was made to determine whether the term actually referred to a "current topic linked to the national interest." Each time a positive evaluation was made, a score of one point was assigned to the category selected for the term under examination. In this way, semantic issue material for each commercial was scored. Finally, a grand composite issue score was computed for each commercial.

The Reliability of Coder Judgements

Category reliability for issue scores was computed as a percent of agreement for two coders for a 10% random subsample of commercials. The percent of agreement was 85%. This value was deemed acceptable,

---

[1]"Domestic" issues specifically concerned national and social welfare problems, for example, education, crime, civil rights, industry, and nongovernmental institutions. "Economy" focused on economic growth and the effect of the recession on the standard of living, the status of business and finance, costs, prices, the work force, earning and buying potential, and so on. "Environment" included mentions focusing on nuclear dumping, nuclear waste, pollution, and ecological policies (i.e., the impact of the EPA on the nation and the world). "Foreign Policy/Foreign Relations" included international relationships, agreements, expectations, resolutions, occurrences and negotiations between nations, foreign trade, foreign trouble spots, and institutions negotiating foreign affairs. "Government Management" focused on financial government programs, policies of taxation, and budgetary and financial policies of government. "National Security/ Military Strength" focused on safety of the nation from military aggression of potential international enemies, the maintenance of a safe margin of weapons protection against threats to the physical survival of the nation's people, and references to peace and avoidance of war. "National Well-Being" focused on the vision of the American Dream, the hope of all Americans for the continued growth of the nation, subsequent status of the nation in the long run, and values and commitment of citizens to strive for the continued success of America.

and coding for all commercials was completed. Disagreements were resolved by discussion and debate among the coders and the principal investigator.

RESULTS

The Primary Campaigns

Table 9.2 reveals the proportions of issue mentions comparing Democratic and Republican parties, and the population for all issue categories. As coded, the total number of issue mentions for all 142 commercials was 647, nearly 36% of which belonged to the domestic issue category. Next highest was the economy, with 20.7% of all mentions, followed by the categories of foreign policy (15%) and government management (11.6%). Just under 10% of all issue mentions were devoted to the national well-being category; only 6% dealt with national security/ military strength. Surprisingly, only 1.4 percent dealt with environmental issues. This is initially surprising, since a good deal of campaign rhetoric outside of that featured in spot advertising dealt with environmental issues. It remains to be seen upon examination of the rest of the data broken down by candidate whether emphasis on the environment will emerge for a particular candidate during the primaries or the general election.

It is immediately obvious that over half of the issue emphasis in televised advertising for the 1988 campaign was on domestic and

Table 9.2 Proportions of Issue Mention Comparing Democratic, Republican Parties and Population (Percentages)

	Population	*Democratic*	*Republican*
N*	647	369	278
*M***	80.5	47.0	33.5
Domestic	35.9	41.5	28.4
Economy	20.7	17.6	24.8
Environment	1.4	1.6	1.1
Foreign Policy	15.0	17.9	11.1
Genverment Management	11.6	6.0	19.1
National Security	6.0	3.3	9.7
National Well-being	9.7	12.5	6.1
Total	100.0	100.0	100.0

*N, Total Number of Issue Mentions.
**M, Total Commercial Time in Minutes.

economic issues, including social programs dealing with education, crime, drugs, health care, and jobs on the domestic side, and concerns with deficits, taxes, and interest rates on the economic side. Table 9.2 also enables comparisons with respect to parties. In spots made on behalf of democrats, over 40% of all mentions were devoted to domestic issues, with emphasis on the economy and foreign policy following as distant seconds, with under 18% of issue mentions for each. Of the remaining issue categories coded, only the national well-being category scored more than 10% of issue mentions for Democrats (12.5%). Issue emphases for the categories of government management (6%), national security (only about 3%), and the environment (less than 2%) were quite low.

By contrast, Republican candidates' spots overall were coded such that emphasis on domestic issues was low compared to Democrats (only 28% for Republicans). However, among Republicans' spots, domestic issues still had the greatest proportion of issue mentions. After domestic issues, it appears that Republicans were most concerned with the economy (24.8% of all mentions), followed by government management (19.1%). Next in emphasis were issues dealing with foreign policy (11.1%) and national security (9.7%).

Republican emphasis on government management was over three times that scored for Democrats, whereas emphasis on domestic concerns on behalf of Democrats was nearly 1½ times greater than that scored for Republicans. These outcomes reflect traditional differences that have distinguished the two parties since at least the Great Depression, when major social programs were forged by the Roosevelt administration and continued to receive support and/or expansion during the Kennedy, Johnson, and Carter administrations and the Mondale and Dukakis campaigns. Emphasis on government management, on the other hand, has traditionally been associated with Republican party positions, especially as applied to policies of taxation and budget (especially during the Reagan era). Therefore, to the extent that these results are consonant with the traditional character of the two major political parties, it appears that the procedures used to score commercials for issue content were adequate. These results lend credibility to the methods used here to measure issue information as presented in televised political advertising.

Table 9.3 shows the proportions of issue mentions, comparing candidates and the population across all issues. As Table 9.3 illustrates, over two-thirds of mentions made in commercials representing candidates Gore and DuPont concerned domestic issues. Domestic issues also dominated commercials made on behalf of candidates Gephardt (47.5%), Jackson (63.2%), Robertson (44.4%), Simon (35%), Dukakis

Table 9.3 Proportions of Issue Mentions Comparing Candidates and Population (Percentages)

	Population	Babbitt	Bush	Dole	Dukakis	Dupont	Gephardt
N*	647	26	139	18	194	16	40
M**	80.5	5.0	18.0	2.5	21.0	2.0	5.0
Domestic	35.9	26.9	25.9	33.3	36.6	68.8	47.5
Economic	20.7	23.1	23.8	38.9	21.6	25.0	15.0
Environmental	1.4	0.0	2.2	0.0	1.1	0.0	0.0
Foreign Policy	15.0	3.8	10.1	16.6	21.6	6.2	30.0
Government Management	11.6	3.8	13.7	5.6	7.7	0.0	0.0
National Security	6.0	0.0	14.4	5.6	1.0	0.0	0.0
National Well-being	9.7	42.3	10.1	0.0	11.3	0.0	7.5
Total	100.0	100.0	100.0	100.0	100.0	100.0	100.0
	Gore	Haig	Hart	Jackson	Kemp	Robertson	Simon
N*	37	11	13	19	58	36	40
M**	5.0	1.5	3.0	2.0	5.5	4.0	6.0
Domestic	67.6	0.0	38.5	63.2	17.2	44.4	35.0
Economic	5.4	27.2	0.0	10.5	24.1	22.2	20.0
Environmental	2.7	0.0	0.0	0.0	0.0	0.0	7.5
Foreign Policy	2.7	18.2	0.0	26.3	12.1	8.3	12.5
Government Management	2.7	0.0	0.0	0.0	44.8	19.4	12.5
National Security	5.4	45.5	46.2	0.0	1.7	0.0	5.0
National Well-being	13.5	9.1	15.4	0.0	0.0	5.6	7.5
Total	100.0	100.0	100.0	100.0	100.0	100.0	100.0

Note: *N, Total Number of Issue Mentions.
**M, Total Commercial Time in Minutes.

(36%), and Bush (25.9%), thus underscoring the pervasive importance of such concerns for 8 of the 13 featured candidates. By contrast, not one candidate's spots emphasized environmental issues. The highest rate of such mentions was 7.5% for the environment, featured in spots made on behalf of Senator Paul Simon. The reader is cautioned that the total amount of commercial time for some candidates is quite low; for this reason, some candidates are considered to be minor players. For example, the spot campaigns on behalf of candidates Haig, Hart, DuPont, Dole, and Jackson did not exceed 19 total issue mentions for any one candidate. It is important to view the proportion scores for these candidates with this limitation in mind.

Of the remaining candidates, it is interesting to note the emphasis placed on government management in spots made on behalf of Jack Kemp (R), who is now Secretary of Housing and Urban Development (HUD). In Kemp's spots, over 44% of issue mentions dealt with government management, an area in which his expertise seems to be finding current application. In addition, nearly a quarter of all issue mentions in Kemp spots were devoted to economic concerns. These outcomes are consonant with Kemp's present cabinet post and presage that candidate's efforts in these areas.

As for spots made on behalf of candidate Gephardt, after the 47.5% score for the domestic category, the next highest issue concentration was in the area of foreign policy (30%). These outcomes are reflective of Gephardt's theme during the primary campaigns, which advocated more equitable competition from foreign business interests. For example, in *Trade,* candidate Gephardt was shown face-to-face addressing citizens about competition from Korea. Gephardt (1987) said:

> [Chrysler employees] work their hearts out every day trying to turn out a good product at a decent price. Then the Korean government slaps on nine separate taxes and tariffs. And when that government's done, a $10,000 Chrysler K-car costs $48,000 in Korea. We can't sell our cars in a market like that and I'm tired of hearing American workers blamed for it. It's time to open up markets, . . . push down those trade barriers. . . .

Gephardt's focus on foreign trade policy reform was the centerpiece of his primary campaign.

Of all the commercials analyzed, those of candidates George Bush and Michael Dukakis are of greatest interest since these were the candidates chosen to represent their parties in the general election. As Table 9.3 shows, nearly half of all commercials analyzed were made on behalf of either George Bush or Michael Dukakis. Issue emphasis for Bush and Dukakis follows traditional party lines, with spots made on behalf of George Bush putting less emphasis on domestic issues than did Dukakis spots (25.9% and 36.6%, respectively).

Conversely, the Dukakis campaign put only about half the emphasis on government management issues (7.7%) as did the Bush campaign (nearly 14%). As for foreign policy, surprisingly, Dukakis spots devoted over 21% of mentions to such issues as compared to Bush's 10%. One reason for this might be that during the primary period, the Dukakis organization felt it needed to offset the perception that Dukakis lacked foreign policy acumen. This sensitivity may be felt by governors who run for president, since they don't acquire much foreign policy experience in their statehouses. In the 1988 election in particular, this possible weakness might have been even more sorely felt because George Bush had a demonstrably impressive background in foreign policy. Hence, during the primary period, Dukakis's organization compensated by airing foreign policy statements. In *Central America,* for example, the candidate's own voice is featured over a montage of grim war images:

End the fiasco, stop the killing war, and stop the conflict, and begin the process of peace and human rights and economic opportunity in Central America. Stop the shooting war and start the war against poverty, injustice, and exploitation . . . with the U.S. as full partners.

In having Dukakis speak these lines, it lends credence to the view that the candidate is conversant with issues beyond our borders. In summary, the Dukakis campaign during the primary period established issue emphases in domestic, economic, and foreign policy arenas. The only other issue category receiving more than 10% of issue mentions in Dukakis spots was that of national well-being (11.3%), a category traditionally free from controversy, since all Americans are theoretically in favor of America's future growth and success.

As for spots representing George Bush during the primaries, Table 9.3 indicates greatest emphases in the areas of domestic issues (25.9% of all mentions), economic concerns (23.8%), national security (14.4%), and government management (13.7%). Foreign policy and national well-being categories received only 10.1% each of all issue mentions, with the environment a distant last, with only 2.2% of all mentions. Upon closer inspection, we see that during the primary period, most references to domestic issues in Bush spots dealt with education, the need for jobs, and the need to fight drugs. For example, in *Education,* candidate Bush speaks about a centerpiece of his campaign:

Every dollar that we invest in our schools comes back ten-fold, twenty-fold. It's the most certain investment there is. It's an investment in our children and therefore an investment in the future, in the future of our farmland, our technology, our factories, our entire economy. When I said I'd like to be the education president, I said it because education just doesn't mean education, it means everything. . . .

As for economic issues, a separate Bush primary spot stressed the need to get the deficit under control by the use of a flexible spending freeze while pledging protection for the social security fund and promising to allow more money for education. Bush's homage to education in this different spot on economic issues was consistent with Bush's statement that education was "the most certain investment there is." With respect to these two spots, there was great unity, such that the subject of education was juxtaposed with "investment," thereby dovetailing nicely with pronouncements on the economy. Calling education an investment and bringing up the topic of education in a commercial focused primarily on the economy offered consistency with Bush's other commercials and avoided dissonance and disparity in Bush's overall campaign. However, the audience was not told which segments of the economy would undergo a freeze to "get the deficit under control" while protecting the social security fund and increasing education funding; at best, what we gained from the spots was an outline of intention. Furthermore, there was no mention of the current cross-pressure against forging a major education program in an economy laden with Reagan's left-over deficit and trade problems. Instead, investment and education issues were made chummy bedfellows.

As for national security issues, Bush primary spots dealt directly with the Reagan defense build-up, the negotiation of the intermediate nuclear force treaty, and the theme that Reagan's strong defense posture would not change if George Bush were to become president. Here candidate Bush offered continuity in defense policy, a promise to stay on course with his predecessor, a position likely to comfort constituents. In summary, the Bush organization during the primaries cast itself in a campaign of consistency and continuity with the Reagan philosophy, especially as far as defense and economic issues were concerned.

The General Election Period

The general election spots for the two nominees continued to stress domestic, economic, foreign policy, and national security concerns, but the rhetorical and presentational formats of the Democratic contender's spots used several different stylistic approaches, whereas those used by the Bush campaign were more conventional, stable, and unified throughout the fall campaign. Specifically, inspection of the Dukakis advertisements reveals that in addition to spots that continued to present the nominee's experience and accomplishments as governor of Massachusetts, several attack spots were produced that broke with the conventional style used in the primaries; the attack spots aimed at different themes. One incorporated a popular refrain derisive of what Democrats saw as George Bush's abdication of responsibility during the Reagan years. This commercial, entitled *Telephone,* excerpted Ted Kennedy's convention speech by lifting the rhetorical question "Where was George?" in order to denounce Bush's own statement that he was "out of the loop" on some key Reagan policies. The "Where was George?" chant was used in an attempt to win the state of Texas in the general election:

> For eight years, Texans called George Bush for help. But when the oil business collapsed for lack of a national energy policy, where was George? When a quarter of a million Texans' jobs were lost, where was George? When 192 Texan banks closed and 23,000 Texan businesses failed, where

was George? Now George Bush is calling on Texas for help. Where was George when we needed him?

A different set of attack spots directed at the Bush candidacy recounts what was perceived by Democrats as Bush's leadership failures during the Reagan years: in all of these commercials, an announcer delivers the tag line: ". . . that's not leadership. That's Bush." Among the most definitive of these commercials is a 60-second spot entitled *That's Bush-leadership,* featuring an announcer reviewing Bush's record on assignments for which he was supposedly placed in a leadership role by the Reagan administration:

> George Bush says he's got experienced leadership. So far it's been quite an experience. While George Bush was head of the task force on drugs, drug smuggling increased 400%, and Panama's General Noriega was allowed to run the biggest drug dealing operation in Central America. He was put in charge of a presidential task force on banking. Bank failures rose from 10 in 1981 to over 200 in 1987—the most since the Great Depression. He was asked to improve our trade relations with Japan. America's trade deficit with Japan rose from 18 to 60 billion dollars. He called this relationship "superb." He was put in charge of reducing red tape in government. The red tape he cut, cut regulations intended to warn Americans about harmful chemicals. While George Bush was in charge of a task force on terrorism, he took part in four meetings he won't discuss and approved the sale of weapons and missiles to the Ayatollah. That's not experience. That's not leadership—that's Bush.

In addition to the "Where was George?" and the "That's not leadership-that's Bush" attacks (two relatively standard formats for direct attack spots), the Dukakis campaign also released a separate set of more complicated indirect attack spots against Bush's choice of Dan Quayle as a running mate, as well as against Bush's criticism of the Massachusetts furlough program, and what was perceived by Democrats as Bush's propensity to divert debate on substantive issues by wrapping himself in the flag.

Beyond content, what is most important about these commercials is their oblique presentational format: they were presented by actors pretending to be the Bush campaign staff at work; hence the audience was given the initial impression that they were eavesdropping on real campaign workers' candid views. But the format made it difficult to discern the actual source of the message until the end. It was also hard to identify the supposed political affiliation of the "campaign workers" featured in the advertisements. For example, in a spot entitled *Crazy,* the fictional "campaign workers," observed via cinema verite (in black and white, grainy and shaky), were overheard dealing with what they perceive as a disaster:

> First campaign worker (CW1): "We got a disaster on our hands."
> CW2: "After all that rehearsal, I thought we had Quayle totally programmed."
> CW3: "Not totally."
> CW4: "Suddenly the words 'President Quayle' even make me nervous."
> CW3: "Bentsen looked great."
> CW5: "You know, what if . . . no, it's too crazy."
> CW4: "What is it?"
> CW5: "Is it too late to drop him, bring in Bob Dole?"
> CW3: "Yeah. Dole."
> CW2: "You're right. It's too crazy."
> CW1: "Not that crazy. . . . Rosemary" (reaching for an intercom)
> ANNOUNCER: 'They'd like to sell you a package. Wouldn't you rather choose a president?"

In this spot it was not until the closing speech by the off-camera announcer that the audience was made aware that it had *not* been privy to a behind-the-scenes look at a Bush campaign strategy session but rather a fictional account of some put-on by the Dukakis camp. This realization in itself, apart from the commercial content, ultimately damaged the credibility of the source, an outcome that can be viewed as an ironic backfire of intent. The intent, as revealed by the announcer, was to get the audience to believe that the Bush campaign was more interested in packaging than substance. But in trying to deliver this message, the Democrats were forced by the announcer's tagline to admit that it was they themselves who relied on actors and pretense. One unintended effect of this spot was to reveal how inept the Democrats were at accomplishing their objectives. Both the announcer's tagline and the inevitable legal requirement to identify the sponsor of the message doomed the announcement to failure. By using such an approach, the Democrats were politically gunning for their foot, first by confusing their constituents, and second by ironically revealing that they too were preoccupied with packaging over substance.

In another Dukakis spot featuring the same audio/visual format, entitled *How Many More?,* the fictional Bush "campaign workers" were overheard discussing strategy options:

> Campaign Worker 1 (CW1): "Well, I think we need another TV commercial on this furlough thing."
> CW2: "No way. They're beginning to write about Dukakis's real crime record."

CW3: "Nobody reads anymore."

CW2: "Let's hope not. First of all, Dukakis changed that furlough program. Now look at this: more cops on the streets; more drug offenders behind bars; crime down 13% in Massachusetts."

CW3: "That's what I mean. How long do they expect to get away with this furlough thing?"

CW1: "How many more weeks to the election, Bernie?"

ANNOUNCER: "They'd like to sell you a package. Wouldn't you rather choose a President?"

These spots failed to achieve their objectives because they were too reflexive and convoluted (therefore confusing) to accomplish their goals in the abbreviated time frame of a general election period. In addition, as mentioned, the announcer's tag and the legal requirement to identify the party responsible for the message ultimately negated the force of the implication that only the Bush campaign is preoccupied with images over issues, since inevitably the content must be revealed to be fabricated fare made by Democrats! In short, such conditions featured a logical misstep that betrayed the intent of the spots to the detriment of the Democrats. Furthermore, this format raises questions regarding the propriety of using fabricated dramatizations to criticize opponents in political campaigns. Finally, this format is arguably too subtle and abstract to be successful in a campaign where simple slogans and direct appeals are the order of the day. Perhaps national campaigns, especially in the latter stages, cannot benefit from such subtlety and complexity; campaigns may be better served by appeals presented simply, expediently, and directly.

By contrast, the Bush campaign painted concrete and vivid general election images with a broader brush. For example, inspection of Bush's general election spots shows that one major area of domestic concern dealt with crime. In several attack spots, the Bush campaign used the case of Massachusetts convicted felon Willie Horton in order to attack opponent Dukakis as too soft on crime. In an infamous spot entitled *Horton PAC Ad,* an announcer's voice intones:

Bush and Dukakis on Crime: Bush suggests the death penalty for first degree murderers. Dukakis not only opposes the death penalty; he allowed first degree murderers to have weekend passes from prison. One was Willie Horton, who murdered a boy in a robbery, stabbing him nineteen times. Despite a life sentence, Horton received ten weekend passes from prison. Horton fled, kidnapped a young couple, stabbing the man and repeatedly raping his girlfriend. Weekend prison passes—Dukakis on crime.

What is noteworthy about this spot is that its subject matter was essentially limited to one anecdote concerning a Massachusetts prison furlough case, but by virtue of the announcer's tag-line, its content was projected as a synecdoche (using the part for the whole, i.e., calling the kingdom the "crown") of all of Michael Dukakis's criminal justice policy and philosophy. The phrase at the end, "Dukakis on Crime," *could* follow a statement of the Massachusetts governor's complete crime policy. But this spot made no effort to describe the qualities of the Massachusetts furlough program, thereby criticizing it to political advantage, nor did it report how the Massachusetts criminal justice system dealt with the Horton tragedy, nor what the failure rate of the Massachusetts furlough program was, nor how it compared to other such programs. Rather, from one anecdote, accompanied by vivid description but little or no argument, the transfer of culpability was made from felon Horton's criminal escapade to candidate Dukakis's political judgment; the transfer is as exquisite as it is expedient. The commercial never expounded a rational argument for why the Horton incident was enough of a case for doubting the soundness of Dukakis's judgment or his crime policy. Furthermore, the commercial omitted to inform the viewer (an omission reflective of hubris) that while Massachusetts had a furlough program, such programs were quite common, and that even the Reagan-Bush administration had one on the federal level! Nevertheless, pragmatically the commercial succeeded powerfully for the Bush campaign as an indictment without argument of Dukakis's overall crime policy. Willie Horton was successfully cast as a symbol of Dukakis's supposed weakness regarding criminal justice, law, and order, not through argument but through the shorthand of synecdoche, that is, of letting Willie Horton stand for the failure of the entire furlough program and, by association, the failure of the governor.

Similarly, in another attack spot, the Bush campaign used a single case, namely, the pollution problem of Boston Harbor, in order to imply that candidate Dukakis was negligent and insensitive on environmental issues. In *Harbor* an announcer states:

> As a candidate, Michael Dukakis called Boston Harbor "an open sewer." As governor, he had the opportunity to do something about it but chose not to. The environmental protection agency called his lack of action the most expensive public policy mistake in the history of New England. Now, Boston Harbor, the dirtiest harbor in America, will cost residents 6 billion dollars to clean. And Michael Dukakis promises to do for America what he's done for Massachusetts.

In this spot, subject matter was essentially limited to the case of the polluted Boston Harbor, but the announcement implied that if elected,

President Dukakis would neglect the nation's environmental problems the way he purportedly neglected those of Boston Harbor. Thus, the commercial presented Boston Harbor as a synecdoche to imply that all of the nation's pollution problems would be exacerbated under a Dukakis administration. The tag-line "And Michael Dukakis promises to do for America what he's done for Massachusetts" bears this out.

Of course, what was omitted from this spot was that cutbacks in Environmental Protection Aid (EPA) funding by the Reagan-Bush administration beginning as early as 1982 (see Epstein, Brown, & Pope, 1982) hampered state governments' abilities to administer environmental rectification projects. In this respect, political hubris was involved again, since the group responsible for *Harbor* may be reasonably viewed as partly responsible for the problems described in the spot in the first place. This is analogous to the perverse situation of the defendant in a criminal trial who has ordered the murder of his parents but begs for mercy from the court because he is an orphan.

The Willie Horton and the Boston Harbor commercials succeeded in establishing links (although unsupported ones) between Dukakis's general policies on crime and the environment, and specific concrete anecdotal cases of offensive and vivid criminal and environmental violations, and they did so without the use of conventional evidence or rational argument. Although such a practice may not stand up to critical scrutiny from a forensic standpoint, the spots nevertheless succeeded in damaging Dukakis with compelling power, especially when aimed at voters who might not have availed themselves of the additional information necessary to blunt their impact.

In terms of strategy, these spots exemplified Aristotle's advice that orators should use those devices that "set [ideas] more distinctly before our eyes" (Cooper, 1960, p. 189). The Bush campaign used these spots in the same way as Aristotle advised orators to use metaphors and lively sayings: "[Audiences] like words that set an event before their eyes; for they must see the thing occurring now, not hear of it as in the future. The speaker must aim at . . . metaphor [and] . . . actuality" (Cooper, 1960, pp. 207–208).

In this passage, Aristotle advocates using vivid, concrete examples rather than abstract descriptions to move an audience. And whereas the Dukakis campaign chose to show complicated dramatizations of ersatz Bush campaign operatives conducting strategy sessions on abstract topics, the Bush campaign, by contrast, featured striking images of water pollution and actual criminal mugshots from prison files to make its points.

From this perspective, the Dukakis campaign squandered its opportunity to articulate its case clearly against the Republican record or to defend itself against attack by Bush's advertising; it failed in part by failing to identify clearly and directly the political hubris involved in the content of Bush's attacks, especially as presented in the Willie Horton and Boston Harbor spots. Instead, the Dukakis campaign responded with a set of oblique, confusing, abstract spots incapable of carrying a forceful and convincing indictment of the Bush record and vulnerable campaign tactics to the public.

PROMISE VERSUS PERFORMANCE IN THE BUSH PRESIDENCY

Among the themes advanced in this chapter is the view that George Bush exhibited hubris in promoting himself as a champion of education and the environment while serving in an administration that cut funding for such programs. Further hubris was demonstrated when Bush attacked Michael Dukakis for supposedly being insensitive on environmental issues, even though it was the Republican administration's cuts in EPA funding and personnel that weakened states' abilities to administer environmental rectification projects.

In order for Bush the candidate to assume such a position and maintain credibility, it was necessary either to court votes from citizens ignorant of Reagan-Bush White House policies or, with respect to voters cognizant of such policies, to disassociate Bush from his predecessor in some way. This latter task George Bush accomplished in two ways. First, while Vice President, Bush admitted on several occasions that he was "out of the loop" (i.e., uninformed) on some Reagan policy initiatives and, therefore, could not be reasonably held accountable for shaping policies forged without his counsel. Second, during the campaign, Bush the candidate was heard pledging *in conditional terms* to support environmental and educational programs. Thus we remember Bush saying that *if elected,* he *would be* "the education president" and "the environmental president." Strictly speaking, during the campaign, such pronouncements could not be falsified, since, at that time, Vice President Bush had not yet become president and, therefore, his performance as president could not be judged.

However, in the years since George Bush took office, it has become possible to begin to assess the sincerity of President Bush's campaign promises regarding several salient issues. With respect to pledges to protect the environment, it is to the President's credit that Congressional debate on amending The Clean Air Act was given a boost by the Bush administration, which, according to French, "submitted a plan . . . that will halve emissions that cause acid rain, tighten emissions standards for automobiles significantly, and require much stricter control of toxic air pollutants'' (Brown, 1990, pp. 114–115). However, French points out that the "administration's proposal misses the opportunity to address the problem at a fundamental level through energy efficiency, transportation reform, and waste reduction'' (Brown, 1990, pp. 114–115). As of this writing, the plan submitted by the Bush White House has not yet become law.

On other environmental fronts, the record is less convincing. For example, although President Bush at his first State of the Union address announced that he was elevating the EPA Administration post to cabinet status (a symbolic gesture that strictly speaking does not remove an iota of pollution from anyone's environment), White House Chief of Staff John Sununu has been playing an active role in a blunting progress on proposed environmental programs. According to a report in *The Phila-delphia Inquirer* (Weisskopf, 1990, Feb. 14), Sununu decided to "weaken an agreement to preserve the nation's dwindling wet lands . . . [while toning down] a Bush speech on the danger of global warming'' (p. 12-D). The report notes that while candidate Bush "made promises during the presidential campaign,'' including a policy of "no net loss of wetlands'' and "the use of the 'White House effect' to combat the 'greenhouse effect' [in practice], the administration has often pulled back from its rhetoric, eschewing tough decisions in favor of relatively inexpensive symbolic gestures'' (p. 12-D). With respect to global warm-ing, Christopher Flavin, Vice President of Worldwatch Institute, as-sessed Bush in these words: "[Bush's refusal to endorse action to stem the emission of gases] was strong on rhetoric but light on substance'' (Thomma, 1990, Feb. 6, p. 2-A). And Senator Albert Gore (D, Tennessee) in the same article pointed out that Bush's 1991 budget would "cut energy conservation funds by nearly 50 percent, from $437 million . . . to $213 million'' (Thomma, 1990, Feb. 6, p. 2-A).

As for the infamous and filthy Boston Harbor, since Bush became president, "the first budget Bush has presented . . . would cut $20 million that Congress had authorized to clean it up'' (Epstein, 1990, Feb. 1, p. 12-A). According to the *Philadelphia Inquirer:*

In September 1988 Bush hired a ferry, filled it with reporters . . . and cruised the . . . harbor saying: "Two hundred years ago tea was spilled in the Boston Harbor in the name of liberty. If tea were spilled in the Boston Harbor today, it would dissolve in the residue of my opponent's neglect and delay.''

Political consultants praised the event as brilliant campaign strategy. Bush at the time brushed aside the fact that it was the EPA that took three years to act on the state's request for money for the harbor. He said he was more interested in directing attention to what he would do if president. . . . The

$20 million Bush left out of his budget would pay for a five-mile tunnel that would carry sewage to a new treatment plant. It is a key component of the harbor cleanup. (Epstein, 1990, Feb. 1, p. 12-A).

As for Bush's response to the worst environmental disaster on record since he has taken office, namely the Exxon Valdez accident, the latest development in the legal imbroglio to follow in the wake of our nation's worst oil spill serves as an indication of where The White House seems to be headed. According to *U.S. News and World Report* ("Is Exxon Slipping the Hook in Alaska," 1990, Mar. 5):

The Exxon Corporation . . . moved toward a plea bargain with the Justice Department that had both the state of Alaska and the environmentalists in an uproar. Exxon faces some 150 civil lawsuits filed by the state, environmental organizations, fishermen, native Americans and others seeking payment for damages. It is threatened, too, with future state and federal criminal indictments that could cost it billions more in compensatory damages. Top Exxon officials also fear pollution statute felony charges that carry stiff fines and long jail terms.

Little wonder that Exxon is drawn toward a deal with the Justice Department that would require it to pay just $500 million more for environmental restoration [and] block plans for federal criminal prosecution. . . . Environmentalists fear it could . . . hamper Alaska's ability to file criminal charges. . . . Jay Hair, president of the National Wildlife Federation . . . grumbled that the Bush administration was letting Exxon off the hook with a "nod and a wink." (p. 10).

Such recent reports, if accurate, are hardly the hallmark of a president destined to be known as a champion of the causes of environmentalists. However, Bush's stay in office has not elapsed; perhaps we should not rush to judgment. On the other hand, from the perspective of history, most modern administrations successful at forging centerpiece legislation manage to act sooner. According to Hedrick Smith (1988), in his comprehensive book analyzing political power in Washington, speed is an essential element in introducing the nation's agenda; as examples, Smith cites FDR's famous First Hundred Days, as well as Reagan's first term.

If environmental rights and remedies are not the strong suit of the Bush presidency, what of his performance since taking office in the area of fiscal management (traditionally a major theme of Republicans) and support for education? As for Bush's moves to "get the deficit under control" (as his campaign promised), a recent review (Feb. 4, 1990) quotes high-ranking budget committee Democrats and Republicans as admitting that the budget process is "pretty close to a sham." The deficit

. . . has become a metaphor for ineffectual government. "An enormous amount of talent and energy goes into creating a budget which many . . . think is pretty close to a sham" says Rep. Lee Hamilton (D-Ind) Chairman of The Joint Economic Committee . . .

Could 1990 be the year for decisive action on the deficit?

"No", Senate Republican leader Bob Dole says. "We'll just continue to paper over it . . .". Stanley Collender, director of federal budget policy for the accounting firm of Price Waterhouse [says] . . . "Everybody wants the deficit eliminated, but nobody wants to cut spending . . . so you look for quick, magic solutions" . . . like using the Social Security surplus to mask the true deficit, moving military paydays from one fiscal year to the next . . . (p. 1-D)

David Broder (1990, Feb. 1) criticized Bush's first budget along similar lines:

The gap between Bush's own rhetoric and his resolve is awesome.

That is . . . the case when it comes to the basic obligation of any executive: financing the programs he proposes. The first budget . . . continues the pattern of systematic prevarication. . . .

If you accept that budget's golden economic-growth assumptions and if you ignore the $200 billion—plus cost of the savings and loan bailout, and if you count the Social Security Trust Fund surplus against the unfunded annual operating budget, then you can get down to a "mere" $63 billion.

But the reality is different. . . . (p. 18-A)

In addition to the description of the budget by high-ranking budget officials, including Republican Senator Bob Dole, we find the following criticism of Bush's first budget by Mortimer Zuckerman, editor-in-chief of *U.S. News and World Report.* In an editorial entitled "Deja Voo-doo All Over Again" (Zuckerman, 1990, Oct. 9) we read:

You can fool all of the people all of the time . . . they got away with fiscal deceit in the last administration and now they are cynically casual about it. . . . Government paydates that fall at the end of the fiscal year are shunted back and forth so that they fall in whatever fiscal year suits . . . suspension of Gramm Rudman reality. Expenses such as the Savings and Loan bailout are put "off budget," even though their funding comes from the federal treasury. More than $100 bilion a year is being expropriated from surplus trust funds intended for other purposes . . . when you read the president's lips, what he has been saying is that the U.S. budget will remain a fraud, but a kinder, gentler fraud. . . .

Bush administration officials put forth new ideas for schools, for drugs, for
space exploration, for the environment. Then, in small print, you find they
do not have the money . . . the question . . . is . . . has [George Bush] the
. . . vision to build a better nation? Or is he just a talker?'' (p. 84)

What is most interesting about these views regarding President Bush's
first budget is the extent to which officials and observers from both sides
of the aisle characterize the budget as essentially deceptive. This outcome is most regrettable when one remembers the Bush campaign
promise to ''get the deficit under control'' without threatening the
Social Security fund. What we seem to be discovering, however, is that
the budget is still out of control and continues to threaten the Social
Security trust fund.

Finally, in the area of education, although candidate George Bush
presented himself as wanting to be ''the education president,'' his
current appropriation for such funding ($500 million) increases the
education budget by only 2%, most or all of which is at this time
earmarked for Project Headstart, a program benefitting preschoolers
only. At this rate, the overall education budget would barely outpace
inflation. The president blunted this criticism at his first State of the
Union Address by countering that America's approach for improving
education would be ''not to spend more, but to *expect* more from
schools, teachers and students . . . [so that] by the year 2000, U.S.
students must be first in math and science in the world.'' Although it is
admirable to try to keep expenses down and to expect better performance from our educational institutions, such a view is seemingly
inconsistent and advocates economic austerity and better performance
from educational institutions while earmarking hundreds of billions of
dollars from the federal treasury for bailing out bankrupt savings and
loan institutions. Perhaps it would be more consistent to appropriate
fewer tax dollars for bankrupt savings and loan institutions and advocate
more financially sound performance from banking institutions.

It is unfortunate that terms such as *sham, deceit, prevarication,
voodoo,* and *fraud* are used to describe the current administration's
fiscal policies. However, it would be a mistake to think that such charges
of deception are limited only to budgetary matters in the Bush presidency. On the contrary, such characterizations extend to a broad array
of policy matters (Ullman, 1990, Feb. 16):

When President Bush's national security adviser turned up in Beijing
toasting China's leaders in December, people were stunned. After all, Bush
had banned high level exchanges with the Chinese government.

When he announced that he would meet with Soviet President Mikhail S.
Gorbachev, the news also came as a surprise. Until then, Bush had said he

was not interested in an early summit—even after secretly arranging the Malta meeting . . .

Increasingly, Bush is being accused by the White House press corps of misstating facts and deceiving the public, and yesterday the accusation prompted an angry denial from the president. (p. 8-A)

In the same article (Ullman, 1990, Feb. 16), it is conceded that deception is a common pattern for modern-day presidents, but the practice is not without risks:

"At one time or another, all presidents manipulate the truth, but they pay a price," said Nelson W. Polsby, Director of the Institute of Governmental Studies. . . . Lyndon Johnson . . . wound up with . . . a credibility gap. People did not trust him or believe him. . . . The next time Bush says 'Trust Me', people may say 'Why?' (p. 8-A)

In a functioning democracy, it is ultimately the responsibility of individual citizens to make political judgments. Implicit in this responsibility is the assumption that citizens exercise their right to judge for themselves whether politicians' performances match their promises. In that spirit, the goal of this chapter has been to invite citizens to judge for themselves the veracity of the 1988 presidential campaign as it was presented in televised political spot advertisements, and to judge the quality of the fit between promises made and the performance that has transpired since the 1988 election.

This goal is important for the following reasons: it is commonplace among political scholars that most members of the electorate do not gain information useful for making voting decisions from direct encounters with candidates for public office; rather, most voters must rely instead on the mass media in order to get political information upon which to base their action. In today's world, for better or worse, it is television that has become the preeminent medium in America for the transmission of political information.

In this way, television stands in as a proxy for candidates; television "re-presents" candidates to the electorate. Therefore, it is a preselected array of fabricated televised images and edited words of candidates that voters come to rely on as their main source of information (and in many cases, their only source) in making voting decisions.

To the extent that television so mediates between candidates and voters, it is of paramount importance to the classic democratic theory of generating informed choice in the citizenry to try to determine the degree to which televised fabricated portrayals of candidates through their paid political advertising are, insofar as possible, accurate representations of these candidates. Of course, determining the accuracy of a candidate's televised presentation is difficult for a voter to do, especially when it is the only source of information a voter avails himself of during an election campaign. Without access to the original candidate through direct encounter or some other alternative, independent, and reliable source of information, determining the accuracy of a candidate's projected televised image is analogous to trying to determine whether a bill is genuine or counterfeit without access to the original article. It has been the general concern of this research to provide a precise description of candidates' projected televised portrayals that voters can then compare with independent sources in order to better judge the accuracy of candidates' televised presentations.

Finally, a major conclusion of this research is that although political spots do have the potential to clarify issue information for the electorate, in spite of the time constraints inherent to the format, mere potential to inform is no guarantee. After all, inconsistencies between politicians' advertised promises and their subsequent policy actions most certainly predate television. Therefore, in order to improve reliability in the video age, voters need a means by which to check, to their satisfaction, the adequacy of the information presented to them in political commercials. It is only through a mechanism of independent scrutiny that voters will be able to judge for themselves the veracity of televised political advertising content and thereby invest the modern political system with greater legitimacy when they vote. In the absence of such a mechanism, voters remain prey to mendacious advertising campaigns that can grossly mislead the public—an outcome that constitutes a general threat to the legitimacy of the electoral process.

REFERENCES

Austin, J. L. (1977). *How to do things with words*. Cambridge, MA: Harvard University Press.

Broder, D. (1990, Feb. 1). Bush wastes his popularity by proposing a wimpy budget that just nibbles. *Philadephia Inquirer,* p. 18-A, col. 1.

Brown, L. R., Flavin, C., Postel, S., Starke, L., Durning, A., Jacobson, J., Renner, M., French, H., Lowe, M., and Young, J. (1990). *State of the World*. New York: Norton.

Cegala, D., & Bassett, R. (1976). The goals of speech communication instruction: The teacher's perspective. In R. R. Allen and K. C. Brown (Eds.), *Developing communication competence in children* (pp. 225–242). Skokie, IL: National Textbook Co.

"Central America" (1987). Michael Dukakis campaign commercial from a video reel made available to the author by The Dukakis for President Campaign.

Cooper, L. (1960). *The rhetoric of Aristotle*. London: Prentice Hall.

"Crazy" (1988). Michael Dukakis campaign commercial made available to the author by The Dukakis for President Campaign.

Dalton, R. J. (1988). *Citizen politics in western democracies*. NJ: Chatham House.

Devlin, L. P. (1973, Winter) Contrasts in presidential campaign commercials of 1972. *Journal of Broadcasting, 18,* 18.

"Education" (1988). George Bush campaign commercial made available to the author by The Bush for President Campaign.

Epstein, E. (1990, Feb. 1). Campaign issue falls from Bush's favor. *Philadelphia Inquirer,* p. 12-A, col. 1.

Epstein, S., Brown, L., & Pope, C. (1982). *Hazardous waste in America.* San Francisco, CA: Sierra Club Books.

"Harbor" (1988). George Bush campaign commercial made available to the author by The Bush for President Campaign.

Himmelweit, H. T., Humphreys, P., Jaeger, M., & Katz, M. (1981). *How voters decide: A longitudinal study of political attitudes and voting extending over fifteen years.* New York: Academic Press.

Hofstetter, C. R., & Judge, M. (1974). Content analysis of typed television stories: Coding manual. The Ohio State University Polimetrics Laboratory, Working Paper #2.

"Horton, PAC AD" (1988). George Bush campaign commercial made available to the author by The Bush for President Campaign.

"How Many More" (1988). Michael Dukakis campaign commercial made available to the author by the Dukakis for President Campaign.

Is Exxon slipping the hook in Alaska? (1990, Mar. 5). *U.S. News and World Report,* p. 10, col. 1.

Kaid, L., & Sanders, J. (1978). Political television and commercials: An experimental study of type and length. *Communication Research, 5,* 57–70.

Key, V. O., Jr. (1966). *The responsible electorate: Rationality in presidential voting: 1936–1960.* Cambridge, MA: Harvard University Press.

Lasswell, H., & Leites, N. (1949). *The language of politics: Studies in quantitative semantics.* New York: George W. Stewart.

Lutz, W. (1989). *Doublespeak.* New York: Harper & Row.

MacNeil, R. (1968). *The people machine: The influence of television on American politics.* New York: Harper & Row.

Minow, N. N., Burch, D., Corcoran, T. G., Heard, A., & Price, R. (1969). *Voter's time: Report of the twentieth century fund commission on campaign cost in the electronic era.* New York: Twentieth Century Fund.

Ogden, D. M., Jr., & Peterson, A. L. (1968). *Electing the president.* San Francisco, CA: Chandler Publishing.

O'Keefe, T., & Sheinkopf, K. G. (1974). The voter decides: Candidate image or campaign issue. *Journal of Broadcasting, 18*(4), 403.

Patterson, T., & McClure, R. (1973). *Political advertising: Voter reaction to televised political commercials.* Princeton, NJ: Citizen's Research Foundation.

Patterson, T., & McClure, R. (1974). Television news and political advertising. *Communication Research, 1,* 3–31.

Pomper, G. (1973). *Elections in America: Control and influence in Democratic politics.* New York: Dodd, Mead & Co.

Rubin, B. (1967). *Political Television.* Belmont, CA: Wadsworth Publishing Co.

Shyles, L. (1983). Defining the issues of a presidential election from televised political spot advertisements. *Journal of Broadcasting, 27*(4), 333–343.

Shyles, L. (1984, September). Special report: Political spots images and issues. *Videos System,* pp. 20–25.

Shyles, L. (1986). The televised political spot advertisement: Its structure, content, and role in the political system. In L. Kaid, D. Nimmo, & K. Sanders (Eds.), *New Perspectives on Political Advertising* (pp. 107–137). Carbondale, IL: Southern Illinois University Press.

Shyles, L. (1988). Profiling candidate images in televised political spot advertisements for 1984: Roles and realities of presidential jousters at the height of the Reagan era. *Political Communication and Persuasion, 5,* 15–31.

Smith, Hedrick (1988). *The Power Game: How Washington Really Works.* Random House: New York.

"Telephone" (1988). Michael Dukakis campaign commercial made available to the author by The Dukakis for President Campaign.

"That's Bush—Leadership" (1988). Michael Dukakis campaign commercial made available to the author by The Dukakis for President Campaign.

Thomma, S. (1990, Feb. 6). Bush backs more study of global warming. *Philadelphia Inquirer,* p. 2-A, col. 1.

"Trade" (1987). Richard Gephardt campaign commercial from a video reel made available to the author by The Gephardt for President Committee.

Ullman, O. (1990, Feb. 16). Bush denies charge that he's deceptive. *Philadelphia Inquirer,* p. 8-A, col. 1.

Weisskopf, M. (1990, Feb. 14). On environment, officials turn to White House, not EPA chief. *Philadelphia Inquirer,* p. 12-D, col. 1.

Zaldivar, R. A. (1990, Feb. 4). "Who Will Exorcise the Demon Deficit?" *Philadelphia Inquirer,* p. 1-D, col. 5.Zuckerman, M. B. (1989, Oct. 9). Deja voodoo all over again. *U.S. News and World Report,* p. 84.

10

Toward an Integration of Textual and Response Analysis Applied to the 1988 Presidential Campaign

Gary Cronkhite
Jo Liska
David Schrader
Indiana University

The semiotic analysis of texts seems to have proceeded relatively independently of the analyses of receiver perceptions of those texts. It is the purpose of this chapter to illustrate one way in which textual analysis and perceptual analyses might be used to complement one another. Our thesis is that the combination of two such approaches can be useful in describing a media campaign, such as the television commercials of the 1988 presidential campaign.

The term *text,* as used in semiotic analyses, is far broader than mere discourse, and certainly broader than written discourse. Berger (1982) described such analysis as applied to media events and campaigns. He wrote of two types of semiotic analysis of texts, the synchronic and the diachronic. We are concerned with synchronic analysis.

Synchronic, or paradigmatic, analysis is based on Saussure's (1966) statement that "in language there are only differences." Jonathan Culler (1976) wrote in this regard:

> Structuralists have generally followed Jacobsen and taken the binary opposition as a fundamental operation of the human mind basic to the production of meaning. (p. 15)

Berger (1982) wrote quite explicitly, "The paradigmatic analysis of a text involves searching for a hidden pattern of meanings that are buried in it and that generate meaning" (p. 30).

The connection that so tantalized us was that between this sort of textual analysis and the semantic differential technique of Charles Osgood, described in detail in *The Measurement of Meaning* (1957) and widely used since as a measure of receiver perceptions. A semantic differential scale is a bipolar scale bounded by adjectives opposite in meaning. Respondents are asked to register their perceptions of concepts, including people, objects, ideas, words, and oral or written passages on a number of seven-point scales connecting such adjective pairs. Ratings can then be factor-analyzed to identify the underlying dimensions of the *semantic space* within which the meaning of a concept lies for a given group of respondents. Osgood originally believed that there were three general dimensions of semantic space: evaluation, activity, and potency. However, it has since been demonstrated that the dimensionality of semantic space changes from concept to concept, from one type of rater to another, and from situation to situation. Two of the present authors have analyzed that literature and have proposed that semantic space be determined for any given concept, especially for potential communicators, and that the structure of semantic space for that concept be used to define its meaning (Cronkhite, 1977; Cronkhite & Liska, 1976; Liska, 1978). It was this approach we used in this chapter.

Our expectation was that there would be some correspondence, but not necessarily identity, between the sets of oppositions derived from the presidential campaign commercial "text" by paradigmatic analysis and those identified by factor analysis of semantic differential ratings.

In addition to factor analysis, we proposed to use discriminate analysis to identify the dimensions, or oppositions, on which different groups of respondents could be distinguished.

Our hope was that the semiotic analysis and the response analyses would shed light on the "meanings" of the 1988 presidential campaign commercials.

The papers by Liska and Cronkhite to which we referred earlier were critical analyses of a deluge of studies using factor analyses of semantic differential scales to identify the dimensions of source credibility. This deluge followed the original study by Berlo, Lemert, and Mertz (19), which was actually conducted in 1959 and presented at a convention that year, but did not appear in print until 1969. The studies that occupied the succeeding 15 years were designed to find generalizable dimensions on which the credibility of any source could be assessed. The search had been unsuccessful, had already occupied too much research time and energy, and should be abandoned in favor of other approaches. Nimmo and Savage (1976) summarized research designed to discern images of political candidates through the mid-1970s, but such research has languished since then in favor of other approaches, especially Q-sort methodology. The approaches used in the analysis of political images are surveyed by Swanson and Nimmo (1990).

TEXTUAL OPPOSITIONS

A political campaign between two candidates makes oppositions at one level obvious. Each issue that develops is an opposition in the overall text of the campaign. Issues, of course, are important in their own right, but a presidential election is not a direct referendum on the issues. Rather, the candidates are evaluated on the basis of their positions on the issues and the ways in which they deal with those issues in interviews and commercials. Thus, issues and images are not separable aspects of a presidential campaign. It is the function of the issues to contribute to the candidates' images, since it is the images on which the vote is taken.

Our first step in identifying oppositions in the campaign was to develop a list of the overt issues. Our initial list included abortion, education, defense, crime, drugs, the budget deficit, the environment, taxes, jobs, ethics in government, patriotism, health care, farm policies, and the qualifications of the vice-presidential candidates to be president. It was not difficult to develop such a list, because each of these issues was mentioned several times during the course of the campaign, in paid political spots, interviews, and/or the debates.

But these were at best surface-level oppositions. It is our belief that each contributed to candidate comparisons at a deeper level.

We observed, for example, that a major opposition between the two candidates seemed to be the extent to which they were open or closed, accessible or inaccessible, emotional or controlled. Thus Dukakis was seldom pictured with his family, whereas Bush's family appeared with him frequently and he talked about them frequently. Bush's gestures were open and expansive, whereas those of Dukakis were tight and close to the body. And near the end of the campaign, although Bush had fought what some thought to be a decidedly aggressive campaign, he told us he would create a "kinder, gentler" America. One of the obvious signs of this opposition was the interminably repeated scene of Bush's granddaughter rushing into his open arms, obviously representing the hope and trust he wished the American electorate to place in him. On the other hand, the best Dukakis could muster was to remove his sport coat in the opening scene of the election eve commercial. He squandered his best opportunity to demonstrate the depth of his emotionality when he was asked in the debate what his position would be on the death penalty if Kitty were raped and murdered. Instead of condemning the inanity of the question and then answering, as he did in the election eve commercial, that he would want to kill the murderer with his bare hands, he coolly analyzed the question with no show of emotion and gave the viewer no access into his private world.

A second opposition seemed to be what the media early in the campaign referred to as Bush's "wimp factor." Recall that this problem existed at least as early as his campaign as Reagan's vice-presidential nominee in the 1984 campaign. Two of our graduate students at Cleveland State University videotaped the debate between Bush and Ferraro, showed the tape to groups of respondents, and had those subjects rate the two candidates on semantic differential scales. One of those scales was "masculine–feminine." It turned out that Bush was rated significantly more feminine than was Ferraro. He claimed afterward that he had "kicked a little butt"—femininely speaking, of course.

In the 1988 campaign, however, it was clear that Bush was determined to erase that image. He was tough on crime, drugs, and national defense issues; he pictured Dukakis as soft on crime, coddling drug users and pushers, and determined to reduce the country's defense capabilities. Of course, Dukakis was not well equipped physically to confront Bush on such an issue; he was simply too short to be imposing. So the shot of the prison tower that began the Willie Horton commercial became a sign of Bush's strength and Dukakis's weakness. In fact, those "attack commercials" became examples—signs—of Bush's masculine, Texan inclination to "kick a little butt," something a wimp would never do.

Closely related to the wimp factor was the emphasis on patriotism. Bush persistently questioned Dukakis's patriotism and proclaimed his own, frequently equating patriotism with national security and military strength. He almost literally wrapped himself in the flag when he visited the flag factory in the waning days of the campaign. Dukakis tried to respond by donning a helmet and riding in a tank, but some combination of his stature and his smile made him appear merely silly rather than strong or patriotic. Throughout the campaign Bush emphasized his war record, and in the opening scene of the election eve commercial we saw him being plucked from the ocean after crashing the plane he had piloted, predestined for greatness, a virile savior for America.

There appeared a clear opposition between the future and the past. Dukakis's campaign slogan was "The best America is yet to come." Bush emphasized the Reagan record and his participation in it.

Another opposition involved leadership/experience versus inexperience. Bush emphasized his varied resume, and especially his foreign policy experience. Dukakis attacked the Bush record with the series of spots that ended with "That's not leadership, that's Bush," and tried to make the question "Where was George?" part of everyone's repertoire of cliches. He questioned Bush's ability to lead when his first decision after being nominated was to choose Quayle as his running mate. He presented himself as the Governor of Massachusetts and spoke of the "Massacahusetts Miracle." But Bush used the image of a polluted Boston Harbor to question not only his devotion to a clean environment, but also his administrative ability.

The opposition between forthrightness and hedging pervaded the campaign. Both men were pressed to be specific as to their programs, especially with the sorts of budgets they would advocate. Bush, in particular, was pressed to explain how he could pledge "no new taxes" and still advocate health care, job programs, improved educational systems, stimulating the economy, reducing the deficit, and maintaining a sound social security system. The difference was especially reflected in the election eve commercials, in which Dukakis was simply a "talking torso" throughout most of his 30 minutes, responding to audience questions regarding his positions on the issues, whereas Bush used his 30 minutes to deal with almost everything except his positions on those issues.

Finally, there was an evident opposition between thrift and spend-thrift, with Bush depicting Dukakis as a liberal spender and himself as following the Reagan promise just mentioned, "No new taxes."

These, then, were the oppositions we identified from a prior examination of the campaign commercials, which were also expressed by the candidates in personal appearances and interviews: open versus closed, tough versus soft, patriotic versus nonpatriotic, future versus past, experience versus naivete, forthrightness versus hedging, and thrifty versus extravagant.

Next we designed a study to determine what dimensions respondents perceived in the campaign, and what relation those perceptual dimensions bore to the oppositions we had identified by textual analysis.

Our specific research questions were:

1. What were the *personal* dimensions on which viewers perceived the two candidates?

2. On what dimensions did viewers perceive the *issues* as to their importance and the comparative stands of the candidates?

3. On what *personal* perceptions and on what *issue* perceptions can viewers of differing political views be distinguished?

    (a) On the basis of what perceptions can *extreme* conservatives be distinguished from *extreme* liberals?

    (b) On the basis of what perceptions can conservatives in general be distinguished from liberals in general?

Another question, not relating to our semiotic analysis, was asked, concerning the question of whether extreme partisans or moderates are more knowledgeable about political issues and candidates. On the one hand, extreme partisans are likely to be more motivated to attend to political information, but they may also engage in biased scanning of that information. Two of the most recent papers dealing with the question and reviewing the relevant literature are those by Sidanius (1988) and Ottati, Fishbein, and Middlestadt (1988). Our question did not have to do with residual political knowledge, however. Rather, we were interested in whether extreme partisans or moderates retained more information from these commercials as measured by an immediate post-test. Thus our fourth research question:

4. To what extent do viewers of different political views differ in their retention of information from the commercials?
(a) To what extent do extreme conservatives, moderate conservatives, moderate liberals, and extreme liberals differ in their retention of information from the commercials?
(b) To what extent do extreme conservatives, moderates, and extreme liberals differ in their retention of information from the commercials?

Our fifth question was not directly related to our original analysis either, nor was it especially imaginative. Since the beginning of the recorded history of social psychology and communication research, scholars have been interested in the extent to which prior opinions affect receivers' evaluations of new information. We had an excellent opportunity to investigate that issue by attempting to determine the extent to which viewers of different political persuasions assessed the effectiveness of the commercials differently. Thus, our fifth and final question:

5. In what ways do viewers' political views relate to their judgments of the comparative effectiveness of the two commercials?

METHOD

Basically, we (a) exposed viewers to videotapes of the two election eve commercials, (b) aksed them to rate the two candidates on a set of semantic differential scales, (c) asked them to rate the candidates' positions on the issues on a set of bipolar scales of our own devising, which used the basic semantic differential format, (d) asked them to respond to multiple-choice items designed to test their recollections of selected information from the commercials, and (e) performed statistical analyses on those responses designed to answer our research questions.

Subjects

Respondents consisted of 232 undergraduates enrolled in communication courses at Indiana University in the spring semester of 1989. Actually, more respondents viewed the commercials and responded to them, but only 232 response sheets were useable; others were not completed or respondents did not follow directions. Most of the students came from introductory service courses, but because students have a proclivity to delay fulfilling their communication requirement, the preponderance of those students were juniors and seniors. Respondents were all volunteers whose participation was solicited during classes, but most, in fact, volunteered in part to fulfill a required listening assignment.

Materials

We recorded the two election eve commercials on videotape as broadcast by all three major networks (recorded from cable television to assure high-quality recording). From the three videotapes, we chose the one that appeared to have the best quality. The two commercials appeared on the tape in the order in which they were broadcast, with the Dukakis commercial appearing before the Bush commercial. Each commercial occupied approximately one-half hour and was viewed in a moderately darkened classroom on a television monitor having a 21 inch screen.

A response booklet was used to measure viewers' responses. The first six items to which subjects responded asked them to identify themselves only by the last four digits of their social security/student identification numbers, to indicate their biological sex and their class standing, to identify which presidential ticket they voted for or would have voted for if they had voted, to indicate the political party with which they considered themselves to be affiliated, and to indicate whether they considered themselves to be politically conservative or liberal.

Two sets of 14 semantic differential scales followed, one set eliciting responses to Bush and the other set eliciting responses to Dukakis. The semantic differential scales used were chosen from those identified by Liska (1978), Cronkhite and Liska (1976), and Cronkhite (1977), since they were especially useful and robust for use by respondents rating communication sources.

Following the semantic differential scales was a list of the 14 issues as having been important in the campaign. These issues were "qualifications of the vice-presidential candidates to be president," "abortion," "education," "defense," "crime," "drugs," "budget deficit," "environment," "taxes," "jobs," "ethics in government," "patriotism," "health care," and "farm policies." These issues were chosen from a somewhat longer list on the basis of the importance they seemed to have assumed in the campaign. For the most part, however, issues were not eliminated; rather, they were consolidated into more encompassing terms. Following each issue were two scales, each having seven response positions, the first ranging from "important" on the left to "unimportant" on the right, and the second from "Bush/Quayle" on the left to "Dukakis/Bentsen" on the right. Respondents were instructed to use the scales to indicate what they considered to be the importance of each issue and the extent to which one pair of candidates or the other had the better position on that issue. They were asked to try to respond as they would have if the commercials they had just seen had provided their only information about the candidates and the issues. (We fully realize it is not possible for viewers to follow such instructions, but we hoped the focus on these commercials would help them recall the issues dealt with in the campaign.)

Next, respondents were asked to respond to 14 multiple-choice items designed to test their recollection of information presented in one or the other of the commercials. Six of those items were drawn from the Dukakis commercial and eight from the Bush commercial.

Finally, respondents were asked to indicate which ticket they would vote for if they were voting on the basis of the commercials alone.

Procedure

The viewing/response sessions were conducted during February 1989, at least 3 months after the election. Respondents signed a schedule to indicate which showing of the commercials they would attend. At the appointed time the researcher distributed the first page of the questionnaire and a mark-sense data sheet, and briefly explained the purpose of the study. No attempt was made to conceal the general purpose of the study, but none of the research questions was revealed. Respondents completed the first six items as instructed on the first page of the questionnaire and then viewed the two commercials in succession, the Dukakis commercial appearing first. At the conclusion of the second commercial, the researcher distributed the remaining pages of the booklet and asked respondents to follow the instructions on those pages. The booklets were collected from respondents after they had finished. No time pressure was imposed; respondents were allowed as much time as necessary. Those respondents who were using the study to satisfy a listening assignment signed a roll sheet before they left.

RESULTS

Statistical Analysis

Principal-axis factor analyses with the eigenvalues set at one, followed by oblique (Oblimin) rotation were performed on the Bush semantic differential scales and on the Dukakis semantic differential scales. We had planned to perform the same analysis on the responses to the issues, but when Oblimin failed to converge after 25 iterations, we abandoned it and reported the principal-axis loadings instead.

Groups of respondents were then formed according to their responses regarding their voting, party affiliation, and political philosophy. The Conservative Extreme (CE) group consisted of those respondents who indicated they voted for or would have voted for Bush *and* were Republican *and* considered themselves conservatives. The Liberal Extreme (LE) group consisted of those respondents who indicated they voted for or would have voted for Dukakis *and* were Democrats *and* considered themselves liberals. The Conservative Moderate (CM) group consisted of those respondents who met two of the three criteria for the CE group but failed the third, and the Liberal Moderate (LM) group consisted of respondents who met two of the three criteria for the LE group but failed the third. Respondents who did not meet at least two of the three criteria for either the CE or the LE group were not placed in any group. (Respondents would achieve such distinction by using the "undecided," "other," or "independent" categories more than once, for example.)

A stepwise discriminate analysis was conducted between the CE and LE groups over the semantic differential items applied to both candidates and the responses on the issues.

A "conservative" group was formed by combining the CE and CM groups, a "liberal" group was formed by combining the LE and LM groups, and a stepwise discriminate analysis was performed between these two combined groups over the semantic differential items and the responses to the issues.

A simple randomized analysis of variance (ANOVA) was performed among the CE, CM, LM, and LE groups using the retention scores as the dependent variable.

A "moderate" group was formed by combining the CM and LM

groups, and a simple randomized ANOVA was performed among this moderate group, the CE group, and the LE group.

A chi-square was performed using the subjects present voting preferences as the criterion, but omitting respondents who were undecided, to determine which commercial was preferred by viewers, regardless of their political views. The more important analysis was a contingency chi-square performed across subgroups (CE, CM, LM, LE) using the same postelection voting preference question.

Question 1

What were the *personal* dimensions on which viewers perceived the two candidates as represented in the commercials, and did those dimensions differ between the candidates?

Bush Dimensions. The first factor analysis, using 232 cases conducted over the semantic differential scales on which subjects rated George Bush as he appeared in the commercial, yielded three factors that produced eigenvalues greater than one, and thus met the criterion for rotation. After oblique rotation (Oblimin procedure), the first factor accounted for 45.5% of the total variance, the second factor accounted for 9.3%, and the third factor accounted for 7.8%.

Scales that loaded at least 0.50 on the factors, along with their pattern matrix loadings, are displayed in Table 10.1 in order of the sizes of those loadings.

We termed the first factor the "deferential/assertive" dimension,

Table 10.1 Bush Dimensions

	Loading
Factor 1 (45.5% of the variance)	
67. takes a stand—doesn't take a stand	0.82
18. assertive—not assertive	0.79
20. informed—uninformed	0.60
23. reliable—unreliable	0.53
Factor 2 (9.3% of the variance)	
16. annoying—pleasing	0.80
15. bad—good	0.73
10. foolish—wise	0.71
14. right—wrong	− 0.68
22. similar to me—different from me	− 0.68
Factor 3 (7.8% of the variance)	
13. friendly—unfriendly	− 0.92
12. responsible—irrespondible	− 0.82

given the scales of which it consisted. It is important to remember that respondents did not necessarily perceive Bush as either deferential or assertive, since their ratings of him varied across these scales. Rather, this was the dimension they viewed as most important in judging him, at least as reflected in their ratings.

We termed the second factor the "likeability" dimension. The positive and negative signs are only indicative of the direction this factor was rotated relative to each individual scale, not of Bush's ratings on those scales.

In order to name the third factor, we looked at the next two scales; although they did not reach our criterion loading, they seemed to shed some light on the nature of the factor. Those were:

11. honest	—	dishonest	−0.46
21. sincere	—	insincere	−0.28

We termed this third factor the "demeanor" dimension, especially in view of the fact that respondents had been instructed to judge such characteristics as honesty and responsibility on the basis of the commercials, not the candidates' prior reputations. Although we do not have enough faith in those instructions to make general causal attributions, it does seem likely that their judgments of Bush's personal demeanor were based on his behavior in the commercial that was so salient to them at that time, at least likely enough to justify this factor naming.

"Deference/assertiveness" showed a negative correlation of −0.41 with "likeability" and −0.36 with "demeanor," whereas "likeability" correlated 0.43 with "demeanor."

Respondents in this study, then, perceived George Bush on the basis of his "deference/assertiveness" first, and then likeability and demeanor.

Dukakis Dimensions.   The principle-axis factor analysis using the ratings of Michael Dukakis produced two factors with eigenvalues above 1.0, which, when rotated obliquely, accounted for 46.3% and 9.2% of the variance. The factor loadings for the component scales are shown in Table 10.2.

The first factor clearly appears to be an undifferentiated "general personal evaluation" factor. That is, some of the scales that loaded on different factors for the Bush ratings were subsumed under "general personal evaluation" for Dukakis. More importantly, most of the scales loading on this first dimension have strongly evaluative connotations. Many were identified as such in Osgood, Suci, and Tannenbaum's (1957)

Table 10.2 Dukakis Dimensions

	Loading
Factor 1 (46.3% of the variance)	
35. sincere—insincere	0.85
36. similar to me—different from me	0.80
29. bad—good	−0.76
30. annoying—pleasing	−0.72
28. right—wrong	0.69
37. reliable—unreliable	0.69
24. foolish—wise	−0.67
25. honest—dishonest	0.67
27. friendly—unfriendly	0.60
26. responsible—irresponsible	0.58
Factor 2 (9.2% of the variance)	
31. takes a stand—doesn't take a stand	0.86
32. assertive—not assertive	0.83
33. masculine—feminine	0.69
34. informed—uninformed	0.56

original description of the semantic differential technique and, more recently, were identified as robustly evaluative by Cronkhite (1977).

This second dimension appears to be nearly identical to the first Bush dimension, lacking only the "reliability" scale, which, for Dukakis, loaded instead on "general personal evaluation." The "masculine-feminine" scale that loaded here for Dukakis actually loaded 0.42 on the same factor for Bush, barely missing the 0.50 criterion. Thus we decided to term this the "deference/assertiveness" dimension. "General personal evaluation" and "deference/assertiveness" correlated 0.55 with one another.

Dukakis, then, was perceived primarily on a "general personal evaluation" dimension and secondarily on a "deference/assertiveness" dimension, whereas Bush was judged primarily on "deference/assertiveness" and to a lesser extent on likeability and demeanor, but never on "general personal evaluation." It appears that Dukakis's "general personal evaluation" dimension, which was primary for him, was split into two much lesser dimensions in respondent perceptions of Bush.

Question 2

On what dimensions did viewers perceive the *issues* treated in the commercials as to their importance and the comparative stands of the candidates? When the scales asking for judgments regarding the issues were submitted to a principle-axis factor analysis, six dimensions were identified with eigenvalues greater than one. But when these dimensions were rotated obliquely, Oblimin failed to converge after 25 iterations and so was abandoned. Principle-axis loadings are reported in Table 10.3, but since principle-axis analysis produces orthogonal factors, a scale is reported as achieving criteria on a factor only if it loads at least 0.50 on that factor (strength) and does not load 0.30 on any other factor (purity). The purity criterion is irrelevant to oblique loadings, since the factors themselves are intercorrelated.

Ten additional items met the strength criterion but not the purity criterion for this factor, and all were items judging the importance of issues—specifically, the issues of defense, patriotism, the environment, ethics, health care, drugs, the budget deficit, farm policies, the qualifications of the vice-presidential candidates, and abortion. That includes all 14 issues covered in the questionnaire, so this is simply an undifferentiated "importance" dimension.

Since all of the "importance" scales loaded above 0.30 on the importance factor, none could meet the purity criterion on the remaining factors. Thus, the remaining factors all consisted of scales asking viewers to judge which candidate took the better position on each issue in the commercials.

But the "importance" dimension so contaminated even the scales that did not ask for "importance" judgments that no other scales could meet the purity criterion. If we abandon the purity criterion, other scales that load at least 0.50 on this second factor are health care (0.65), education (0.63), crime (0.56), and drugs (0.53). This factor seems to be a "social issues (problems)" dimension.

Only two scales met the strength criterion on the third factor, and

Table 10.3 Issue Dimensions

	Loading
Factor 1 (22.2% of the variance)	
46. Importance of crime	0.70
56. Importance of jobs	0.68
42. Importance of education	0.66
54. Importance of taxes	0.65
Factor 2 (16.7% of the variance)	
53. Environment	0.69
65. Farm policies	0.56
Factor 3 (5.6% of the variance)	
45. Defense	−0.58
61. Patriotism	−0.50

neither of those met the purity criterion. The two scales that load high on the dimension seem to identify it quite adequately, however, as "defense/patriotism."

The remaining three factors that achieved eigenvalues above 1.0 nevertheless were so drained by the first three factors that there was not enough residual variance to allow any scale to achieve the strength criterion on any one of them.

The issues that emerged in the campaign and the commercials seem to have been judged by viewers of the commercials primarily according to their "importance" and secondarily on the basis of the extent to which they were social issues or had to do with defense/patriotism.

Question 3

On what *personal* perceptions and on what *issue* perceptions can viewers of differing political views be distinguished?

(a) On the basis of what perceptions can *extreme* conservatives be distinguished from *extreme* liberals?

(b) On the basis of what perceptions can conservatives in general be distinguished from liberals in general?

Unfortunately, by the criteria used to define extreme conservatives and extreme liberals, 85 viewers qualified as extreme conservatives but only 13 as extreme liberals for this analysis. We recognize and deplore the hazards of proceeding with discriminate analysis under these circumstances, but we did so anyway, hoping that these findings would be confirmed later when we compared all conservatives and all liberals. As it turned out, that was a forlorn hope.

Twenty-five of the 56 person–perception and issue–perception items were entered into a function capable of correctly classifying 98.1% of the cases before the F-to-remove fell below 1.0.

All items that either were entered into the function or produced a significant univariate F-value are listed in Table 10.4, followed by their correlations with the canonical discriminate function (i.e., their loadings on the function), followed in turn by their univariate F-values at step zero, before any variables were entered into the function. Those F-values indicate how strongly the item *by itself* discriminated between the two groups. An item that discriminates strongly when taken alone may not be entered into the function because it may be so strongly related to another variable already entered that it does little to improve the discriminative strength of the function.

The difference between this next analysis and that immediately preceding was that responses of all conservatives were compared to

Table 10.4 Discriminate Analysis Between Extreme Political Groups

Item Number and Description	Function Loading	F-value
14. Bush: right—wrong	0.44*	55.33*
36. Dukakis: similar—different	−0.43*	52.72*
23. Bush: reliable—unreliable	0.38*	42.70*
57. Whose position is better on jobs?	0.32	37.52*
47. Whose position is better on crime?	0.31*	28.36*
59. Whose position is better on ethics in government?	0.28*	22.94*
43. Whose position is better on education?	0.28*	22.07*
22. Bush: similar—different	0.27*	21.17*
24. Dukakis: foolish—wise	0.26*	19.16*
39. Which VP better qualified?	0.25	7.12*
11. Bush: honest—dishonest	0.25	12.41*
61. Whose better on patriotism?	0.25*	18.19*
28. Dukakis: right—wrong	−0.24	8.62*
49. Whose position is better on drugs?	0.23	12.86*
21. Bush: sincere—insincere	0.23	16.35*
17. Bush: takes a stand—doesn't	0.22*	14.36*
29. Dukakis: bad—good	0.20	13.62*
30. Dukakis: annoying—pleasing	0.20	18.47*
32. Dukakis: assertive—not assertive	−0.20*	12.04*
55. Whose position better on taxes?	0.19	7.,34*
35. Dukakis: sincere—insincere	−0.18	11.64*
10. Bush: foolish—wise	−0.18	7.97*
45. Whose position better on defense?	0.18	7.79*
15. Bush: bad—good	−0.18	9.40*
41. Whose position better on abortion	0.18	13.09*
63. Whose position is better on health care?	0.17*	8.27*
51. Whose position is better on the budget deficit?	0.16*	7.24*
20. Bush: informed—uninformed	0.16	15.53*
34. Dukakis: informed—uninformed	−0.15*	6.72
37. Dukakis:reliable—unreliable	−0.15	14.02*
56. Importance of jobs	0.14*	5.95
44. Importance of defense	0.11*	3.34
18. Bush: assertive—not assertive	0.10	7.99*
31. Dukakis:takes a stand—doesn't	−0.09*	2.56
54. Importance of taxes	0.09*	2.19
12. Bush: responsible—irresponsible	0.08*	2.00
65. Whose position is better on farm policies?	0.08*	1.64
58. Importance of ethics in government	−0.06*	1.31
64. Importance of farm policies	0.04*	0.49
13. Bush:friendly—unfriendly	0.04*	0.45
48. Importance of drugs	−0.01*	0.06
52. Importance of the environment	0.01	0.01

An * in the Function Loading column designates an item that was entered into the function; in the F-value column, an * designates an F-value significant at the 0.01 level.

those of all liberals, moderate or extreme. Again, unfortunately, the group sizes were widely disparate, there being 136 respondents defined as conservative and only 31 liberals.

In this case, 19 of the person–perception and issue–perception items were entered into a discriminant function capable of correctly classifying 93.9% of the cases before the F to remove fell below 1.0. With 1 and 166 degrees of freedom, the F required for significance at the 0.01 level is 6.8. All the items that either were entered into the function or produced significant univariate Fs are listed in Table 10.5, with the same information as in Table 10.4.

One finding that seems to achieve interocular significance is that the items that discriminate strongly between *all* conservatives and *all* liberals are almost exclusively *person–perception* items rather than *issue–perception* items. However, the items that discriminate between *extreme* liberals and conservatives are a mixture of person–perception and issue–perception items.

Question 4

To what extent do viewers of different political views differ in their retention of information from the commercials?

(a) To what extent do extreme conservatives, moderate conservatives, moderate liberals, and extreme liberals differ in their retention of information from the commercials?

(b) To what extent do extreme conservatives, moderates, and extreme liberals differ in their retention of information from the commercials?

Retention was operationally defined by a test included as part of the questionnaire as described in the procedure section. The four groups used in the first ANOVA were defined as CE, CM, LM, and LE by criteria also described on page 171. The three groups used in the second ANOVA consisted of the CE and LE groups, and a third group formed by combining the two groups previously defined as "moderate."

Simple randomized ANOVAs comparing first the mean retention scores of the four groups and then the mean retention scores of the three groups produced no significant differences in retention among groups. The summary F-table for the four-group ANOVA constitutes Table 10.6. The summary F-table for the three-group ANOVA constitutes Table 10.7.

Once again, these analyses are flawed by the fact that there are quite disparate cell sizes, with 93 CEs, 16 LEs, 57 CMs, and 19 LMs, with 47 fitting none of the four group definitions.

Table 10.5 Discriminate Analysis Between Liberals and Conservatives

Item Number and Description	Function Loading	F-value
14. Bush: right—wrong	−0.65*	93.08*
22. Bush: similar—different	−0.53*	62.03*
23. Bush: reliable—unreliable	−0.48*	49.78*
36. Dukakis: similar—different	0.47*	47.64*
15. Bush: bad—good	0.40	33.65*
57. Whose position is better on jobs?	−0.40	40.24*
10. Bush: foolish—wise	0.38*	32.13*
17. Bush: takes a stand—doesn't	−0.33	16.79*
11. Bush: honest—dishonest	−0.31*	21.41*
37. Dukakis:reliable—unreliable	0.31*	20.52*
30. Dukakis: annoying—pleasing	−0.31	11.09*
43. Whose position is better on education?	−0.30*	19.50*
51. Whose position is better on the budget deficit?	−0.30	12.82*
34. Dukakis: informed—uninformed	0.29	11.80*
16. Bush: annoying—pleasing	0.29	11.56*
47. Whose position is better on crime?	−0.29	22.99*
21. Bush: sincere—insincere	−0.26*	14.92*
20. Bush: informed—uninformed	−0.26	18.82*
19. Bush: masculine—feminine	−0.26	10.61*
18. Bush: assertive—not assertive	−0.26	11.31*
35. Dukakis: sincere—insincere	0.24*	12.34*
24. Dukakis: foolish—wise	−0.23	8.05*
41. Whose position better on abortion	−0.23	14.34*
25. Dukakis: honest—dishonest	0.22	9.38*
39. Which VP better qualified?	−0.22	6.81*
63. Whose position is better on health care?	−0.21	16.84*
49. Whose position is better on drugs?	−0.21	14.09*
45. Whose position better on defense?	−0.21	18.18*
29. Dukakis: bad—good	−0.21	6.91*
65. Whose position is better on farm policies?	−0.20	6.98*
12. Bush: responsible—irresponsible	−0.20*	8.44*
32. Dukakis: assertive—not assertive	0.19	8.71*
59. Whose position is better on ethics in government?	−0.19	11.50*
61. Whose better on patriotism?	−0.18	14.77*
28. Dukakis: right—wrong	0.17	11.29*
26. Dukakis: responsible—irresponsible	0.17	8.66*
13. Bush: friendly—unfriendly	−0.16*	5.60
60. Importance of patriotism	−0.15*	4.62
27. Dukakis: friendly—unfriendly	0.12*	3.06
64. Importance of farm policies	0.05*	0.66
40. Importance of abortion	−0.05*	0.53
58. Importance of ethics in government	0.04*	0.38
62. Importance of health care	0.03*	0.25
48. Importance of drugs	−0.03*	0.17

An * in the Function Loading column designates an item that was entered into the function; in the F-value column, an * designates an F-value significant at the 0.01 level.

Table 10.6 Summary Table for the Four-Group Anova

Source	D.F.	Sum of Squares	Mean Square	F	F-prob
Between	3	17.2278	5.7426	1.7072	0.1671
Within	181	608.8263	3.3637		
Total	184	626.0541			

Table 10.7 Summary Table for the Three-Group Anova

Source	D.F.	Sum of Squares	Mean Square	F	F-prob
Between	2	16.6068	8.3034	2.0849	0.1267
Within	229	912.0441	3.9827		
Total	231	928.6509			

Question 5

In what ways do viewers' political views relate to their judgments of the comparative effectiveness of the two commercials?

First, it is clear that viewers preferred the Bush commercial. When they registered their views on the question, "If you were voting on the basis of the commercials alone, which ticket would you vote for now?" 158 viewers chose Bush/Quayle and 39 chose Dukakis/Bentsen. There were 35 viewers who expressed no preference. They could not be included in the chi-square analysis because there was no basis for any a priori expectation regarding their number. The imbalance of preferences produced a chi-square of 71.88, which, with one degree of freedom, is significant well beyond the 0.01 level.

Of greater importance, however, was the contingency chi-square to determine whether the distribution of preferences depended on the viewers' political views. The distribution of preferences by political view is shown in Table 10.8.

This distribution produced a chi-square of 29.84, which with three degrees of freedom is significant far beyond the 0.01 level.

It is interesting that there is such an imbalance in Bush's direction among both the conservative groups, but no imbalance at all in Dukakis's direction among the two liberal groups. Looking at the table between rows, there is relatively little difference among groups for Dukakis, but a great deal of discrepancy among groups for Bush.

DISCUSSION

Because most of us were educated in either a "humanistic" or "social science" tradition, we bring sets of biases to this sort of enterprise that

Table 10.8 Contingency Table of Viewer Preferences for the Two Commercials

	CE	CM	LM	LE	Row
Bush	74	38	9	7	128(81.5%)
Dukakis	3	11	8	7	29(18.5%)
Column	77	49	17	14	157
	(49%)	(31.2%)	(10.8%)	(8.9%)	

CE, conserative extreme; CM, conservative moderate; LM, liberal moderate; LE, liberal extreme.

The reason that the total is 157 rather than the 197 who indicated preferences is that 40 viewers who expressed preferences could not be classified into any political group.

may not be productive. In considering an attempt to integrate a humanistic and social science approach, we must abandon an excessive fascination with either. There are those who suffer from the debilitating academic disease of quantiphobia, causing them to go weak at the sight of numbers, as Superman does with exposure to Krypton. Others suffer equally from quantifilia, a condition in which they treasure—nay, worship—numbers as the harbingers of truth.

We are not engaged in a search for truth, and we must abandon the fond delusion that truth is identifiable by either approach. The question is: to what extent do various research approaches lead us to useful conclusions, especially to new questions and hypotheses that are heuristic in that they inspire further research?

Neither the textual analysis nor the response analysis described here is "right" or even more right. In a few cases they provide mutual confirmation, convergent validation. In other cases they provide alternative interpretations that may be mutually complementary. In any case, we hope, taken together they provide enjoyable cognitive fodder.

Textual and Response Relationships

The first of the oppositions we identified by a priori textual examination was the "open-closed," "accessible-inaccessible," "emotional-controlled." Factor II, "likeability," seems to reflect this opposition to some extent, although one would expect the "friendly-unfriendly" scale to be a part of such a factor, and it was not. In fact, the third factor for Bush, which we have termed "demeanor," included friendliness, honesty, and responsibility. This "likeability" factor, in fact, lacks content. It consists almost entirely of purely evaluative scales. The only hint we have of the reasons for the liking comes from the scale "similar to me—different from me." Neither was any "openness" dimension observed in the ratings of Dukakis. Thus, we have to say that our respondents do not appear to have used the "open-closed" opposition in the way we expected.

The second opposition we identified was what was termed the *wimp factor* for Bush. We noted that Bush made a determined effort to rid himself of that label. It is clear from the response analysis that our respondents, at least, perceived that opposition to be a major consideration in their judgments of Bush; what we have termed the "dominance/assertiveness" factor accounted for almost half the variance in their ratings of Bush. The emergence of such a factor does not tell us whether he came to be perceived as dominant. In fact, it tells us that this was the part of Bush's image on which respondents most disagreed, which is why it accounted for so much of the variance. Essentially the same factor emerged for Dukakis, but it was much weaker, accounting for only 9.2% of the variance.

Our third opposition, "patriotism," did not emerge from the factor analysis of the ratings of the candidates, but it did emerge from the ratings of the issues. The first factor in that analysis related to the importance of all the issues, so there were two major dimensions on which respondents judged the candidates' stands on the issues. One of these, accounting for 5.6% of the variance, was "defense/patriotism."

We perceived an opposition between the future and the past in the literature of the campaign, but no such dimension emerged from the factor analyses of either the candidates' ratings or the ratings of the issues, unless "social issues" can be interpreted in those terms, and that is tenuous. Apparently neither Dukakis's slogan, "The best America is yet to come," nor Bush's espousal of the glorious past of the Reagan Administration had much impact on the respondents, at least not in terms of chronology.

The opposition between leadership/experience and naivete did not emerge as a separate response factor, either. Looking back at the scales we made available to our respondents, however, we realize that those scales probably militated against such a separate factor. It may well have been submerged somewhere in the "dominant/assertive" factor.

The "forthrightness/hedging" opposition appears to have been a part of the "dominance/assertiveness" dimension, since the highest loading on that factor for both Bush and Dukakis went to the scale "takes a stand—doesn't take a stand."

Finally, the "thrift/spendthrift" opposition was not reflected in the response factors, although there is no question that it was hidden somewhere between the "social issues (problems)" and "defense/patriotism" factors. Bush wanted to spend money on defense, whereas Dukakis wanted to spend the same money on social problems.

None of our a priori oppositions are reflected in the discriminate analyses identifying the differences between those of different political allegiances.

The Specific Research Questions

The foregoing discussion answered in some detail the first two of our research questions: On what personal and issue dimensions did our respondents perceive the two candidates?

Our third question asked: What personal and issue perceptions can viewers of differing political views distinguish? This can best be answered by an examination of Tables 10.4 and 10.5. The one finding that may be generalizable, although the dearth of liberals in the sample makes it suspect, is that although conservatives in general seem to be distinguishable from liberals in general, primarily on the basis of their ratings of the candidates, extreme conservatives can be distinguished from extreme liberals on a mix of personal and issue perceptions.

Our fourth question was: To what extent do viewers of different political views differ in their retention of information from the commercials? We found no evidence for retention differences among extremists and moderates of both stripes.

The fifth question was: In what ways do viewers' political views relate to their judgments of the comparative effectiveness of the two commercials? Of tangential interest is the fact that viewers overwhelmingly preferred the Bush commercial, but more importantly, although political conservatism was overwhelmingly related to preference for the Bush commercial, Dukakis enjoyed no such bias in his favor on the part of liberals.

CONCLUSION

Not surprisingly, we concluded that the use of both textual and response analysis provided a much richer view of the election than either method could have produced alone. Frequently the two types of analysis complemented one another or, as someone less charitable or biased might put it, contradicted one another. In some cases they confirmed one another. But in all cases, we believe, they provided a wealth of information that helps us to better understand what transpired in the presidential election of 1988.

REFERENCES

Berger, A. A. (1982). *Media analysis techniques*. Beverly Hills, CA: Sage.
Berlo, D. K., J. B. Lemert, and R. J. Mertz (1969). Dimensions for evaluating the acceptability of message sources. *Public Opinion Quarterly 33;*563–576.

Cronkhite, G. (1976). Effects of rater-concept-scale interactions and use of different factoring procedures upon evaluative factor structure. *Human Communication Research 2;*316–329.

Cronkhite, G. (1977). Scales measuring general evaluation with minimal distortion. *Public Opinion Quarterly 41;*65–73.

Cronkhite, G. & Liska, J. (1976). A critique of factor-analytic approaches to the study of credibility. *Communication Monographs 43;*91–107.

Culler, J. (1976). *Structuralist Poetics: Structuralism, linguistics, and the study of literature.* Ithaca, NY: Cornell University.

Liska, J. (1978). Situational and topical variations in credibility criteria. *Communication Monographs, 45;*85–92.

Nimmo, D. and R. L. Savage (1976). *Candidates and Their Images: Concepts, Methods, and Findings.* Pacific Palisades, CA: Goodyear.

Osgood, C., Suci, G. J. & Tannenbaum, P. (1957). *The measurement of meaning.* Urbana, IL: University of Illinois.

Ottati, V., Fishbein, M., & Middlestadt, S. E. (1988). Determinants of voters' beliefs about the candidates' stands on the issues: The role of evaluative bias heuristics and the candidates' expressed message. *Journal of Personality and Social Psychology 55;*517–529.

Saussure, F. de (1966). *Course in general linguistics.* New York: McGraw-Hill.

Sidanius, J. (1988). Political sophistication and political deviance: A structural equation examination of context theory. *Journal of Personality and Social Psychology, 55;*37–51.

Swanson, D. and D. Nimmo (1990). *New Directions in Political Communication.* Beverly Hills, CA: Sage.

III

The Campaign Documentary as an Ad

11

The Political Campaign Film: Epideictic Rhetoric in a Documentary Frame

Joanne Morreale
Northeastern University

Students of rhetoric have contributed much to our understanding of the interplay of visual communication forms, politics, and contemporary American culture. Most studies have focused on televised political advertising, speechmaking, and news coverage of political candidates. However, the political campaign film is one genre that combines characteristics of all three modes of political communication. As a hybrid documentary and advertisement, film and mode of public address, this genre marks a rich site where politics, culture, and communication intersect.

In the guise of entertaining television, the political campaign film can define a candidate and the broad themes that shape a campaign; thus, in modern media-dominated political campaigns, it has gained in importance as a tool that can reach millions of voters at one showing. In fact, in recent years the film has substituted for the introductory speech for the presidential candidate at the national conventions. In 1984, the Reagan campaign incited much controversy when it aired the lushly produced film, *A New Beginning,* in place of the nominating speech at the Republican National Convention. By 1988, both Republican and Democratic candidates were introduced to the American people by way of videotaped presentations.

The style and structure of the Reagan film, widely regarded to be a landmark in the art of political filmmaking (Raines, 1984), was emulated by the producers of the Bush film, and both offer great insight into political discourse in a media age. The increased visibility of the political campaign film echoes the emphasis upon sight and sound which characterizes modern-day, advertising-based political campaigns. Candidates and their media advisors are acutely aware of television's dominance in American life and how its requirements and capabilities differ from those of oratory. An orator may require 15 minutes to argue a point; in 15 minutes of film, the candidate's ethos and message can be put forth and illustrated through the strategic interplay of words, music, and pictures. As opposed to the nominating speech, in the political campaign film words can be supported with visual "proofs," just as visual images can overpower and render words unnecessary. Moreover, musical backdrops establish an emotional tone that directs feelings about the words and images on screen. Not only are more channels of communication open in a film than in a speech, but sound and pictures can be used to communicate by implication and innuendo. Pictures do not assert so much as suggest and their meaning remains ambiguous on some level. In the film there is more freedom to mislead than there is in the speech.

Thus, the political campaign film, as a genre that replaces oratory, marks a cultural shift whereby political discourse serves more to subvert than to extend democratic processes that are based on informed and reasoned dialogue. In order to demonstrate the above and to assess its implications, I begin by describing the modern political campaign film as an epideictic rather than deliberative genre of political rhetoric. As such, it serves to celebrate values rather than to persuade by virtue of rational argument. It can best be understood through recourse to the oral logic of television. Visual cliches that evoke myths and values, rather than the devices of formal logic and reasoning, enable the viewer to make sense of the film. As an illustration, I examine the opening scene from *A New Beginning* (1984), the first campaign film to fully exploit the capabilities of television as a visual communication form. I then explore the way that the placement of cliched images within a documentary frame enables candidates to communicate to the viewing public in a manner that far exceeds the persuasive power of televised speechmaking alone. Here I analyze one scene from George Bush's 1988 campaign film (Bush Political Campaign Documentary, 1988), which continues the strategies employed by Ronald Reagan in 1984.

THE POLITICAL CAMPAIGN FILM AS EPIDEICTIC RHETORICAL GENRE

The political campaign film as a genre of discourse has been in existence at least since 1952 (Jamieson, 1984). Both the Eisenhower and Stevenson campaigns aired films at their respective conventions, although these did not attain the prominent positions accorded the films of 1984 and 1988. In 1960, Kennedy had a 30-min "biography," *The New Frontier,* which is the structural and thematic prototype of the genre. Structurally, the early campaign films simulate newsreel footage, using stark black-and-white images, the anonymous voice of a narrator, and a static camera. The bulk of the film consists of prerecorded campaign speeches along with still photographs that depict the candidate's personal life. *The New Frontier,* for example, includes a chronological record of the candidate's life, featuring Kennedy's school career, military duty, and public service. As in every other political campaign film to date, the candidate is shown to be a family man.

All political campaign films, like the introductory speech that they have come to replace, celebrate the candidate's personal and public qualifications for the job. In addition, their themes offer a sneak preview of the campaign to come: candidates promise to improve the economy, to keep America strong militarily, and to achieve or maintain peace. All are shown to be leaders and men of the people, although one of these qualities may be emphasized more than another. Candidates are shown meeting with military and foreign leaders, and, at the film's conclusion, their commitment to peace is stressed.

As politicians increasingly have made use of media techniques based upon advertising, political campaign films have become correspondingly more sophisticated. This is particularly the case with the films produced for Republican candidates; since 1968, when Richard Nixon placed his future in the hands of Madison Avenue, the Republican party has been committed to the use of advertising experts to "sell" their candidates on television (Fineman, 1988). As more campaign funds have been used to produce these films, they have been put to broader use in the ensuing campaigns. In 1984, the Republicans spent nearly a half million dollars on their film, *A New Beginning* (Mermigas, 1984). In addition to the 1984 convention, it was used as a half-hour paid political advertisement, and at the 1988 convention a reedited version was used as a homage to the Reagan years. Likewise, George Bush later reedited his 1988 convention film and combined it with shots of the convention itself, some of his spot commercials, and images from *A New Beginning* (among other footage), and aired the montage as an election eve paid political special.

The primary distinction between contemporary and past campaign films, as between the film and the nominating speech, is the extent to which the structure and function of current films have shifted away from deliberative rhetoric. Deliberative rhetoric, concerned with exhorting or dissuading, moves from point to point in an effort to gain the reasoned agreement of its audience. The political campaign films, however, are structured as a nonsequential series of short vignettes that make use of visual and verbal modes of presentation characteristic of news and documentary genres (Hartley, 1982). For example, interviews with "talking heads" are filmed in medium-to-close shot as they address the camera. In the 1988 Dukakis film, the film actress Olympia Dukakis acts as on-camera host to walk the viewer through the film. More characteristic of these films is the use of the "eyewitness" who attests to the character of the candidate, as George Bush did for Ronald Reagan in 1984, and that Ronald Reagan reciprocated for Bush in 1988. Photographs of the Bush family trekking West to Texas also give the film a documentary feel, as do still images of Bush meeting with ordinary Americans, Lech Walesa, a contra, Gorbachev, and Ronald Reagan. The perceived "reality effect" of documentary has been well established in the literature of both speech and film theory (e.g., Gronbeck, 1976; Nichols, 1976/77; Nimmo and Combs, 1983; Worth and Gross, 1980). Thus, images that emulate news and documentary genres give the film an aura of authenticity and create the impression that deliberative matters of substance are being presented on screen.

Although the political campaign film borrows many of the devices of a documentary or news vehicle, its function is persuasive. Unlike deliberative rhetoric, where propositions are overtly stated, the film uses subtle persuasive devices that are characteristic of an advertisement. In the words of the editor of *A New Beginning,* "You have to say this is a product [referring to Ronald Reagan] and the market is the USA. . . . You're selling an ideal, a way of life" (Maniaci, 1984). In order to achieve this aim, the filmmakers make use of actors, props, and staged settings; lighting, color, and camerawork are manipulated to give the film a soothing feel; the film has a musical score that includes a popular country music song; it is ordered thematically rather than chronologically, and its message is entirely upbeat. The Bush film is much the same; it begins with a slow-motion image of a small child running through the grass, which dissolves into documentary footage of World War II.

Previous campaign films also used this admixture of documentary and advertising techniques. Both the Ford and Carter films in 1976 included news footage and a theme song; Carter's film, an anomaly for the Democratic party, even made use of animation. Overall, the Democrats' films are less highly produced than the Republicans' and reflect their lack of media savvy. The Dukakis film ran like a home movie, using only one location, Dukakis's Brookline home, throughout. Although Walter Mondale had a campaign film in 1984, it did not compare with its competition, Reagan's *A New Beginning.* For example, both films made use of mythic images and cliches such as the American flag and the Statue of Liberty. In the Mondale film, however, the statue was shown before its massive reconstruction project had begun. The footage was old and outdated, and there was no camera movement in the shot. In *A New Beginning,* a dynamic camera zoomed in on the statue that was being repaired, thus reinforcing the entire message of the film. It, like America, was being "rebuilt."

What is most outstanding about the Reagan and Bush political campaign films is the degree to which they are designed as specifically televisual communication forms. Images and events from different times and places are decontextualized, fragmented, and placed in juxtaposition to one another in order to leave the viewer with a positive impression of the candidate. In so doing, each film creates a rhetorical event that could not have occurred in actuality. Editing techniques, music, and sound overlays all intensify the impact of the whole. The themes, which reflect American values such as work, family, patriotism, and defense, are linked through montage rather than the linear logic of formal argument. It is not the case that a speaker puts forth propositions and claims, supported by evidence, in order to promote some future action. Instead, the political campaign film is primarily an epideictic form of rhetorical "argument." Implications, associations, and juxtapositions are used in order to identify the candidate with images, ideas, and values representative of the dominant American culture. Perelman (1969) explained the epideictic genre:

> Unlike the demonstration of a geometrical theorem, which establishes once and for all a logical connection between speculative truths, the argumentation in epidictic [sic] discourse sets out to increase the intensity of adherence to certain values, which might not be contested on their own but may nevertheless not prevail against other values that might come into conflict with them. The speaker tries to establish a sense of communion centered around particular values recognized by the audience, and to this end he uses the whole range of means available to the rhetorician for purposes of amplification and enhancement. (p. 51)

In other words, these films are epideictic discourses in that they aim to move their audiences by unifying them around a common set of values that all Americans are presumed to share; the emotional responses evoked are not based upon informed and reasoned analysis. This is accomplished by the artful use of rhetorical depictions—simple but mythic pictures that embody common values and goals (Osborn, 1986). As is the norm for political campaigns in the media age, campaign managers make extensive use of population polls, surveys, demographic data, and market pretesting strategies in order to get a sense of their audience and its preeminent values and goals (Diamond and Bates, 1984; Jamieson, 1984). The resultant films consist largely of visual cliches, or "culturetypes"—repetitive, familiar images, all of which resonate the American mythos (Osborn, 1986). These cliched images become identified with the candidate. According to political advertising expert Hal Riney, this identification process is the aim of a "soft-sell" advertising approach, where "the product is associated with wholesome, yet otherwise unrelated images" (Buck, Friend, & Wipple, 1984, p. 82). The resultant montage of images builds to an overall positive impression that the viewer takes away from the advertisement.

The strategic use of visual cliche, employed by Ronald Reagan in 1984 and George Bush in 1988, enabled the Republicans to "sell" their candidate's version of America to the viewing audience. The Republicans wished to consolidate the political majority in 1984 and to retain their base in 1988. The middle and working classes, who had defected to their camp in 1980, had historically been Democrats; thus, Reagan's and Bush's populist appeals to the "people" served as an attempt to secure more firmly a shift in party allegiances that had already begun (see Wilson, 1980). In addition, the Republicans wanted to take advantage of a basic political fact—most American voters have a superficial relationship to politics. Fewer than 50% of the eligible voters went to the polls in 1988 (*New York Times,* Nov. 10, 1988, p. B6) and this was not significantly different from 1984. Thus, television—entertaining television—was the best way to reach a lethargic populace.

THE ORAL LOGIC OF EPIDEICTIC RHETORIC

The cliched images and segments that structure the Reagan and Bush films and unify Americans around a common set of values that are identified with the candidate, suggest that the films are best conceived as epideictic rhetoric. Individual depictions, like many advertising images, may be condensed narratives that tell a story, but none of the segments is arranged in a linear, sequential order. The films more readily conform to what Nichols (1981) has defined as an "image mosaic." He wrote:

> The whole is organized not as a narrative but poetically, as a mosaic. Only the parts have a diegetic unity. Between sequences editing seldom establishes a chronological relationship; sequences follow each other consecutively but without a clearly marked temporal relationship. The whole thus tends towards poetry (metaphor, synchronicity, paradigmatic relations)—an all at once slice through an institutional matrix re-presented in time—rather than narrative. (p. 211)

Meaning is arrived at through metaphors, associations, juxtapositions, and paradigmatic relations. This is not to say that no "formal" logic or argument occurs within the films. On the contrary, the narrators perform this overtly instrumental function.

Yet, as an epideictic form, the political campaign film implicitly "argues" that it represents a social reality, and, in this way, it implies a course for future action. It does so by creating a favorable psychological image, by fostering an impression or attitude and not by persuading with logical arguments, information, or "facts." Strategically positioned pictures construct the arguments made in the film, thus avoiding the need for the more logical processes of reflection and analysis required to evaluate more linear, deliberative arguments.

Stated another way, the political campaign film is organized more by the oral logic of epideictic televisual communication than by the linear, formal logic of deliberation more characteristic of print media. Fiske and Hartley (1978) explained in *Reading Television:*

> . . . television discourse is not "immutable and impersonal" in nature, and its mode is the reverse of literate or formal logic: its mode is that of rhetoric. For instance, the television message if validated by its context, by the opposition of elements (often visual/verbal), and not by the deductive requirements of the syllogism. The kind of consistency which requires an alphabetic means of recording and retrieval in order to be known, and which imposes its own kind of constraints on, for instance, the style of the novel, is alien to the television discourse. (p. 117)

Scene I of *A New Beginning* provides an excellent example of the oral logic of television. The internal structure of this opening scene indicates the way that meaning is arrived at in *A New Beginning* through metaphor, association, and juxtaposition, rather than through formal argument. It demonstrates how rhetorical devices such as visual cliches create meaning in the political campaign film through their evocation of familiar myths; in addition, this scene makes apparent the way that the mosaic structure of the film, which enables the filmmakers to juxtapose visual cliches with the voice and image of Ronald Reagan, intensifies the impact of the entirety.

The film begins conventionally with the date of Reagan's 1980 inauguration shown on a black screen as he begins his oath of office. Although the Inauguration itself is linear and sequential, the images that are interspersed are atemporal and have no overtly logical relationship to the words that are being spoken. The aim of this scene is to create a mood, tone, or feeling that, as part of the image mosaic comprising the film, will contribute to the overall positive impression, or image, the viewer takes away from it.

The voice and figure of Ronald Reagan contain the other images in this scene. His image—a re-presentation of past actuality—surrounds those of ordinary America and Americans; his voice conjures these images, and, ultimately, he explains their significance: "Yes, it was quite a day, a new beginning." This refers to both the inauguration and the images of Americans beginning a new day, which are cross-cut within it. Furthermore, it is the qualities and values that these images of a new day connote that are transferred to Ronald Reagan. The initial image of a plow furrowing the earth in the early morning sun suggests growth, fertility, fecundity. It is a simple image, yet one that is evocative of America's agrarian roots; this is especially the case when this image is joined to that of a farmhouse. This, too, evokes a simple American untarnished by industry and technology. The cock crows, the flowers bloom, and there is work to be done, as indicated by the dump truck with an empty bed that is moving out of frame. A cowboy and his horse dissolve into a city laborer at work. Both country and city are unified, both are peopled by men at work. The laborer's upward pointing gesture is, like the sun-lit images that have come before, an indication of optimism. Through the juxtaposition of these images and their connotations (and their unification through the implication of a beginning, a new day), Reagan is imbued with the positive qualities of traditional America—its fecundity, beauty, optimism, hope.

Reagan's America also encompasses the grassy suburbs, where, still cross-cut with the inauguration, a young boy delivers papers on his bicycle. A man with a briefcase greets him by name as their paths cross. Both are part of a community where people know one another. Through these images, the values of work, neighborhood, and community are conveyed. It is these values that are associated with Ronald Reagan.

Protection and defense, which are important themes throughout *A New Beginning,* are also implied in this initial scene of the film. A traffic policeman, prominently wearing his badge, guides a group of construction workers across the street. This invites associations with law and order, particularly because the word *defend,* spoken by the Chief Justice as Reagan takes his oath of office, accompanies this image. Then Reagan's voice promises to "preserve and protect," and the image that appears is that of a wooded camp area where a group of children watch as a flag is being hoisted. This shot could create associations with Reagan as an environmentalist, implicitly mitigating criticism of him in this area. Another association is that of the flag being raised amidst a group of children. The flag is rising—as is the sun in the previous images. The flag connotes freedom and patriotism, and, in conjunction with the sun, productivity, hope, and a new day. The children gaze upward, children implying innocence and the future. A close-up of one child's face is coupled with Reagan's voice saying "defend" as he completes his oath of office. The implication is that he speaks of defending the nation's children, rather than "the Constitution of the United States," which is the continuation of this dialogue in the next shot. These words are then paired with an image of the White House, the unifying center of political stability and authority. Besides serving this metonymic function, the White House links the opening images of America and Americans to Ronald Reagan and his presidency. The depiction of the White House dissolves into another image that positions Ronald Reagan securely within its confines, seated at his desk in the Oval Office. He is "at home" in the White House, surrounded by family photographs, a navigator's compass, and a plaque that reads, "It can be done."

Thus, this initial two-and-one-half–minute scene, composed of simple, commonplace images, constructs a highly complex "image" of Ronald Reagan and what he represents: tradition, hope, productivity, defense, patriotism, innocence, the future, authority. These connections are not made through logical argument, but rather through the "oral logic" of televisual communication. Nor could these messages have been conveyed in two-and-one-half minutes of a speech. Overall, the film aimed to create an impression of spritual rebirth, of optimism, patriotism, and productivity across the land; most importantly, this renewal was inextricably related to Ronald Reagan by juxtaposing images with conventional, generally positive associations and the voice/image of Ronald Reagan.

These images are, moreover, reassuring, which is one important function of epideictic rhetoric (Osborn, 1986). The images are pleasurable because they are so effortlessly recognizable. They reinforce conventional images of social reality and one's place in it. These cliched depictions serve as points of orientation; their connotations, implications, and associations appear to be self-evident.

THE FRAMING OF THE POLITICAL CAMPAIGN FILM

By re-presenting familiar myths and cliches through a variety of modes and genres of televisual discourse, and by tying these to a particular candidate, the Republicans in 1984 and 1988 were able to present a coherent ideological stance, one that was perceived to be a truth rather than a version of it. Although their conservative positions make up a political ideology (using the term in a narrow sense), this was presented to the American people through appeals that were ideological in Althusser's (1969) definition of the term as "a system (possessing its own logic and rigour) of representation (images, myths, ideas or concepts, as the

case may be) existing and having a historical role within a given society"
(p. 231). Ideology, then, is materialized as a body of ideas and pictures
of reality that appear to be self-evidently true.

This suggests that it is not the case that the cliched depictions that
make up the films can be opposed to everyday reality. On the contrary,
these are presentational strategies that mediate and make experience
meaningful. They reinforce a particular way of interpreting experience,
and because they are ideological, this interpretation is perceived to be
nonproblematic, transparent, and "natural."[1] Nor is it the case that
symbolic or "fictional" mediations of experience are necessarily less
true than those that are interpreted to be less mediated representations,
such as news or technical accounts. The frames, or boundaries, that
differentiate these discursive forms and genres are themselves socially
constructed means whereby meaning and sense are made communica-
ble. Thus, attending to the framing of the political campaign film can
provide insight into the way in which a noncontradictory ideological
position is both represented by the film and created in the process of
viewing it, in other words, the way in which a version of reality is
constituted in the film by "framing" frames.

It is important to recognize that, as with all processes of communication, meaning can only be made with the participation of the receiver, or
audience, or, in this case, the viewer. Chaney (1979) wrote:

> . . . each social process of communication invites agreement on the order
> to be followed. Of course this order is only rarely explicitly addressed,
> rather it is inferred from cues such as context and memories of other
> similar expressions and performances. We cannot get inside an author's
> head, but we can infer the grounds through which his use of imagery is
> potentially meaningful by situating his work within features of a tradition
> or genre. The performance is the occasion of our inference of meaning, but
> we accumulate sense through reference to shared grounds so that perfor-
> mances make sense through each other. (p. 23)

It is in a similar fashion that Osborn (1986) suggested that rhetorical
depictions have a "cumulative impact" in the construction of reality. It
is these "shared grounds," or interpretive frameworks, that are evoked
by "simple mythic images." These "shared grounds," in the forms of
myths, cliches, and commonplaces, are perceived to represent truths

---

[1]Goffman (1974) distinguishes primary frameworks as either natural or social, whereas
Worth and Gross (1980) make parallel distinctions between natural and symbolic sign
events. Natural signs are believed to be unmediated, transparent, and "caused" by reality,
rather than produced by vested interests. Although television is obviously a mediation, it
is believed to have the capacity to reflect reality transparently.

rather than to be propositional constructs. It is for this reason, too, that Zijderveld (1979) wrote that at the core of frames are cliches, which he referred to as "the social knots of communication" (pp. 57–58). They unify and provide a common interpretive frame for large numbers of social groups, and through their repetition in a variety of cultural forms, they become imprinted in the collective consciousness.

Neither Osborn nor Zijderveld, however, discussed framing as a means to explain how these shared grounds are created and maintained. In the political campaign film, different levels of mediation become reframed as one, their common cliches reinforcing one another and creating a shared interpretive ground. Consequently, by blurring the boundaries that differentiate interpretive frames, the film is rendered all the more persuasive.

LENDING CREDIBILITY TO CLICHE THROUGH FRAMING

One of the most apparent ways in which the campaign film obscures boundaries that differentiate interpretive frames is through its internal structure. The opening scene from George Bush's convention film demonstrates the way that seamlessly intercut images signify many familiar televisual genres, although these genres may typically be perceived to be incompatible means of communicating a single message: news, documentary, fiction, advertisement, and biography. The admixture of visual forms and genres in the Bush film range from those that are considered to be highly mediated, and obviously rhetorical, to those that are regarded to be unmediated reflections of reality. By blurring the distinctions between forms and genres of televisual discourse, messages of different levels of mediation that are conventionally interpreted to be real or true (such as news or documentary), along with more explicitly mediated representations, together become interpreted to be authentic representations of reality.

The Bush film begins with a headline, "August 1988," on a blank screen, ostensibly to locate the viewer in present time. This initial gambit is followed by a "timeless" slow-motion image of a young girl running through a grassy field. She is in soft focus, and the image is accompanied by sentimental music. This gentle image, which mimics an advertisement, quickly dissolves to white and is replaced by another headline that locates the viewer in the distant past, December 1941. Stark black-and-white footage is accompanied by harsh, throbbing music. As this dissolves to white, an anonymous narrator explains that America has faced many challenges throughout the twentieth century and has found many people to meet those challenges. The unstated implication is that one of these people is George Bush. The narrator's voice is accompanied by black-and-white images of soldiers leaving for war, which dissolve into shots of them kissing women goodbye. Rather than addressing current challenges, such as the deficit, the viewers are nostalgically returned to the site of one of America's last great victories. The use of graphics and black-and-white footage serve as illustrative "proof" of the events to which the narrator alludes; along with his anonymous "voice of God" (Nichols, 1981), they cue the viewer to the authenticity of the film.[2]

Authenticity is also signaled by the use of still photographs in lieu of moving images. Bush's own voice follows that of the narrator, as Bush explains that he joined the army at age 18 because he wanted to become a pilot. Two still photographs accompany his words: one of the young George with his wife Barbara, and the second of Bush wearing a pilot's cap and army uniform. These pictures, like the black-and-white footage, serve as corroborative testimony to his words. The off-screen narrator then returns to extol Bush's virtues as a war hero. He describes the young army pilot's exploits when he earned a distinguished flying cross on a bombing run. His words, again, are illustrated by black-and-white images of planes and smoke.

Then, for the first time, there is a disjunctive cut in the film and Bush's voice and image are united in one shot. The use of color also indicates a shift to the present, as Bush, seated comfortably in the White House, retells the experience that made him a hero. As he speaks, his words are verified by documentary footage of World War II. Further documentation of the somewhat blurry images is provided by a graphic that proclaims itself to be "U.S. File Footage" and another that labels a shadowy figure on the deck of the rescue boat "Lt.(JG) Bush."

Pragmaticaily, this scene serves to dispel charges of "wimpiness," which plagued the candidate early in his campaign. In addition, along with these labored attempts to be framed as "authentic," Bush's mission is metaphorical as well as literal. His heroism fulfills the mythic pattern of the leader who is tested, overcomes challenge, and is the wiser for it (Campbell, 1988). Once the myth is established, there is another dissolve to the headlines on a movie marquee. The marquee advertises a newsreel that is titled "War Ends." This use of headlines is a way to narrate, or fictionalize, the film in a way that retains the audience's perception of its authenticity. Headlines are transitional devices that appear in fiction

---

[2]Nichols (1981) discusses the function of the narrator as voice of authority in documentary films. The narrator who directly addresses the audience from a position off-camera is referred to as the "voice of God" who, from a position of knowledge outside of the film, conveys the "truth" of the film to the viewing audience.

films of the thirties as well as in nonfiction newsreels and documentaries. In all cases, they are used both to show the passage of significant, eventful moments of time, and as illustrative "proof" of an event (Neale, 1981). The movie image serves as an unintended reminder of the mediated nature of news then and now, and of the mediated nature of the Bush film itself, that the viewer is, at that moment, watching a movie about "reality." The marquee is followed by still photographs of sailors returning and people hugging. The bombastic music that accompanies the World War II battle footage becomes soft and sentimental. George Bush becomes part of the saga of American history, an important contributor to one of its most significant moments. The film then cuts back to the "present," with Bush again seated in the White House, and he articulates his desire to unify Americans, to make all a part of the same kind of team effort that resulted in victory in World War II. This scene finally ends with Barbara Bush, who appears on camera to remind the viewers that her husband is, indeed, a caring man.

Not only does this opening scene implicitly set up Bush's alternating campaign strategy, advocating a nation that is kind and gentle, yet strong and prepared; it also articulates this message by a blurring of televisual genres. Overall, the preponderance of documentary images, intercut with more obviously mediated events constructed for the camera, disguise the fact that the film is, above all, an advertisement for George Bush. The advertisement is signaled by the young child in soft focus who appears at the very beginning (and later closes the film); yet this initial impression is overridden by the insistence of the documentary images to be perceived as reflections of reality. The boundaries between different levels of mediation remain unclear, and different televisual genres are seamlessly linked through use of dissolves that blur distinctions. In this way, the film bolsters the candidate's credibility, and, on an ideological level, creates a version of reality that appears to be "natural" and self-evident.

CONCLUSION

The Republicans recognize the political mileage to be gained by presenting themselves through television images that can be rendered comprehensible and credible in a seemingly effortless manner. They are keenly aware of television's dominance in American life, and they seem to embrace the assumption that epideictic rhetoric, the domain of television, is more effective than the deliberative rhetoric associated with stump oratory and the print media. More so than previous contenders, and certainly more so than Democratic challengers, the Republican strategists understand that the aims and requirements of televisual communication differ from those of oratory or print. To an unprecedented extent, deliberative oratory has receded in importance during presidential campaigns; this is signified by the form, content, and framing of the political campaign film.

It is thus that the ascendance of the political campaign film may mark a turning point in American political discourse, one that is representative of a society that is more receptive to the visual than to the verbal. All signs point to the continuing entrenchment of the political campaign film in American politics. It is a truly postmodern phenomenon, one that promulgates an ideology not by informing, but by entertaining, by providing mythic images and cliches that evoke common beliefs and values, and by manipulating the interpretive frames by which meaning and sense are accrued.

In consequence, the political campaign film as a genre that replaces oratory subtracts from rather than augments the democratic process based upon informed and reasoned dialogue. Its techniques reproduce and mimic the idiom of "the people," but there is no common ground of discourse on which the electorate can discuss and debate. Overall, there are few propositions presented to be analyzed and assessed; there are few claims to be critiqued on the grounds of formal logic and reason. Instead, what is offered is a reassuring form of entertainment that can be consumed effortlessly.

REFERENCES

Althusser, L. (1969). *For Marx.* Harmondsworth: Penguin Books.
A New Beginning (1984). Produced by the Committee to Re-elect President Reagan.
Buck, R., Friend, D., & Wipple, C. (1984, June). The Soft Sell. *Life,* 75–82.
Bush Political Campaign Documentary (1988). Produced by the Committee to Elect George Bush.
Campbell, J. (1988) *The Power of Myth* with Bill Moyers, New York: Doubleday.
Chaney, D. (1979). *Fictions and ceremonies: Representations of popular experience.* New York: St. Martin's Press.
Change without Chaos (1972). Produced by the Committee to Re-Elect President Nixon.
The Democratic faith: The Johnson years (1968). Official Democratic party film.
Diamond, E., & Bates, S. (1984). *The spot: The rise of political advertising on television.* Cambridge, MA: MIT Press.
Fineman, H. (1988, October). Why Bush is Winning. *Newsweek,* 18–20.
Fiske, J., & Hartley, J. (1978). *Reading Television.* London: Methuen.
Goffman, E. (1974). *Frame Analysis.* New York: Harper and Row.
Gronbeck, B. (1976). Celluloid rhetoric: On genres of documentary. In K. Campbell & K. Jamieson (Eds.), *From and genre: Shaping rhetorical action.* Falls Church, VA: Speech Communication Association.
Hartley, J. (1982). *Understanding news.* London: Methuen.

Jamieson, K. (1984). *Packaging the presidency: A history and criticism of presidential campaign advertising.* New York: Oxford University Press.

Maniaci, T. (1984, November 14). Personal interview.

Mermigas, D. (1984, August 23). Nets pressured on Reagan film. *Advertising Age,* pp. 1,53.

Neale, S. (1981). Genre and Cinema. In T. Bennett, S. Boyd-Bowman, C. Mercer and J. Woollacott (Eds.), *Popular Television and Film* (pp. 6–25). London: British Film Institute.

The New Frontier (1960). Produced by the Committee to Elect Kennedy.

New York Times (1988, November 10). B6. Chart.

Nichols, B. (1976–77). Documentary Theory and Practice. *Screen* 17.4, pp. 34–48.

Nichols, B. (1981). *Ideology and the Image.* Bloomington, IN: Indiana University Press.

Nimmo, D., & Combs, J. E. (1983). *Mediated political realities.* New York: Longman Inc.

Osborn, M. (1986). Rhetorical depiction. In H. Simons & A. Agharazarian (Eds.), *Form, genre, and the study of political discourse.* (pp. 79–107) Columbia, SC: University of South Carolina Press.

Perelman, C. (1969). *The new rhetoric: A treatise on argumentation.* South Bend, IN: University of Notre Dame.

Raines, H. (1984, August 24). Reagan sees clear choice. *New York Times,* p. A1.

Wilson, J. Q. (1980). Reagan and the Republican revival. *Commentary, 70,*(4), 25–32.

Worth, S., & Gross, L. (1980). *Studying visual communication.* New York: Mouton.

Zijderveld, A. (1979). *On cliches: The supersedure of meaning by function in modernity.* London: Routledge and Kegan Paul.

12

Network Coverage of Video Politics: "A New Beginning" in the Limits of Criticism

Herbert W. Simons
Temple University

Don J. Stewart
University of South Carolina at Aiken

> Television watching has become America's true national pastime, and Ronald Reagan has shown the nation's political strategists how it is possible to reduce the pronouncements of the medium's news stars to mere network chatter.
>
> *Washington Post* reporter Martin Schram on manipulation of the networks by image-makers during the 1984 presidential contest
>
> —Schram (1987)

> We have to do something. If you see how we were all being led around by the nose, and how our access was restricted, and how the commercials took the place of thoughtful interviews, it's a very serious problem. The political process isn't working, and our part in it is not working at all.
>
> ABC News President Roone Arledge on manipulation of the networks by image-makers during the 1988 Presidential election
>
> —Polman (1989)

From the 1988 presidential election at least one thing seems perfectly clear: that the major commercial networks have little better idea how to cover and cope with today's video politics than they did during the Reagan years. Complicating the task of presidential campaign coverage was the vast superiority of the Republicans at the game of video politics. For the networks this too proved to be something of an embarrassment, for the Republicans succeeded once again by exploiting television's own vulnerabilities. The photo opportunities granted to the news media by the Bush people were engineered with the same meticulous care as the Reagan handlers gave to his appearance at a D-day ceremony or to a Fourth of July visit to a stock car race. They showed a refurbished candidate, smiling and confident—no longer a wimp or a patrician. As during the Reagan campaigns, they served as an effective substitute for press conferences and interviews, during which the candidate might have been forced to elaborate on campaign promises and to explain away seeming inconsistencies between them.[1]

The Reagan presidency marks the beginning of a new era in political mass persuasion, one in which, as Roone Arledge lamented, the networks are no longer in control of their political coverage. To be sure, the age of video politics begins much earlier, in the 1952 contest between Stevenson and Eisenhower. Since that time, television has assumed increasing importance both in the management of the presidency and for presidential candidates seeking office. But it was not until the Reagan presidency that a politician was able to exploit so completely television's distinctive rhetorical potential.

The primary concern of this chapter is with the possibilities for effective network response to televised presidential campaign hype. While the focus of this essay is on network coverage of presidential campaigns, it has obvious bearing on other political campaigns as well and on coverage of video politics generally. Our interest in network coverage stems in part from the conviction that the networks have a special responsibility to educate their viewers about the nature of video politics. Surely no other medium than television reaches such a wide audience or has so much impact.[2] Indeed, suggested Jamieson (1988), the effects of even the most trenchant critiques appearing in the print media tend to be relatively insubstantial due to the lag time between the critiques and the televised messages that they criticize.

But if television is where the action is, and if it is via television that Americans must also be expected to get the bulk of their education in how to resist today's video politics, then we fear for the American electorate. In the Fall of 1984 we conducted a quasi-experimental

---

[1]As we argue later in this chapter, there is a recurrent tension in assessments of campaign hype. Journalists (as well as viewers) are frequently poised between condemning on grounds of inaccuracy and deceptiveness messages that they admire for their power and effectiveness. This tension was repeatedly manifested in NBC's treatment of the film. How, then, could viewers resolve the tension for themselves in evaluating the overall worth or value of the film? Considerations of this kind dictated the choice of dimensions and scales used in the study.

[2]In the study that will be reported on later in this chapter, Simons, Stewart, and Harvey (1989) found that network critiques of a campaign film may have enhanced Ss ratings of the film's accuracy, power, and value, rather than blunting its effects.

comparison of the effects of three network treatments of a Reagan campaign film known as *A New Beginning* (ANB) (Simons, Stewart, & Harvey, 1989). The study added research support for what until then had been largely anecdotal evidence of the difficulties that television commentators on political campaign hype are apt to confront in countering politicians' video depictions with conventional journalistic commentary (Jamieson, 1988; Osborn, 1986; Schram, 1987). That study's findings were underscored in the 1988 presidential contest. Thus, in addition to summarizing in some detail the findings from our earlier study, we place the findings in context and show how they are part of an ongoing pattern.

THE NEW VIDEO POLITICS

The new video politics is a combination of paid political spots and "free TV," the latter consisting for the most part of manufactured "video moments" on network, cable, and local news. In some respects it is a continuation of the old: a politics of image over substance; of repetition with variation; of learning from the voters what it is they want to see and hear, then tailoring one's message accordingly. In other respects, however, it truly is distinctive. For example, the 1980 Reagan campaign marked the first concerted effort to integrate day-to-day national polling with test marketing of presidential campaign spots on focus groups and trial displays of ads in bellwether cities. In that campaign there were strong pressures from within Republican ranks to use professional actors in entertaining attack commercials depicting President Carter as a bumbling incompetent. But the test-marketing revealed that ads of this kind would only reinforce the negative image of Reagan as actor. Selected instead were ads that were known to be far duller, but elicited favorable ratings toward Reagan from Democrats (Simons, 1986).

Particularly as practiced by the Republicans, the new video politics also provides evidence of increased sophistication at what Osborn (1986) calls rhetorical depiction. ANB is a spectacular example. Whether presented verbally or nonverbally, rhetorical depiction offers visual images and dramatizations in place of documented arguments. It plays fancifully, analogically on associative linkages rather than on deductive or inductive connections. It is a nonpropositional logic of mythic evocations and sensory connotations—if it is a logic at all (Jamieson, 1988). Close cousin to ANB in 1984 were the "Morning in America" ads, awash in bright sunshine and middle-class prosperity, scenes of happy Americans brought to us in slow motion and soft focus by the same people who brought us the Pepsico commercials. Some of these same actors and scenes appear in the 1988 Bush videos; few people noticed. What they did notice was that the video gave them an upbeat feeling about themselves, about America, about George Bush. This was what counted.

So too were they warmed by the "grandaughter" ads, showing Bush relaxed, a family man, playing with grandaughter, being doted on by an adoring wife. Here, as in the "Morning in America" ads, the television camera does most of the communicating. What it presents to us, again in soft focus, is a Hallmark-like world of idyllic people, who are removed from the real one, which we voyeurs are free to enter and vicariously enjoy. The ad contains messages of middle-class identification and reassurance but they are implicit, nonpropositional, largely visual messages that call upon us to feel, not to think. In a swing through California during the course of the campaign, David Broder (1988) noted that the ads of Bush with his grandchild played extremely well in sports bars, where viewers watched with the sound off, shifting their attention from table talk of the moment to television sets in much the same way that they might have been distracted by the instant replay of a touchdown pass. So too did the Bush attack commercials have this effect.

Of special importance both to presidents and presidential hopefuls in the decade of the eighties has been the exploitation of free TV. Here, once again, the Republicans have been far more astute than the Democrats. For example, on the Fourth of July, 1984, Reagan is prominently shown on all three networks kicking off a Daytona Firecracker 400 stock car race by use of a telephone aboard Air Force One, subsequently joining in the viewing of the race from a position in the stands. Viewers then see Reagan alongside country star Tammy Wynette who sings "Stand by Your Man" in full throttle, then presses against him to deliver a kiss. Reagan later basks in the reflected glory of winner Richard Petty, who is heard to express great admiration for the president. On the same day, Walter Mondale is shown hard at work, meeting first with a group of women pushing to have one of their gender nominated for vice-president, then meeting with San Antonio mayor Henry Cisneros as the television screen scrolls down a list of the special interests Mondale could curry with that nomination. Wittingly or unwittingly Mondale has conveyed the image of a man too busy currying favors with special interests to celebrate America's Independence Day (Schram, 1987).

The foregoing contrast provides some indication of the respective styles and competencies of the two parties in their use of video politics in presidential campaigns. They provide, in turn, some measure of the problems that the networks confronted in covering campaign events. The Republicans, it appears, are far more astute at the game of video politics. They have understood that it is far more important to field a likeable candidate than one in command of a great deal of technical knowledge. In pitching their campaign to the eighty-plus percent of the American people who get their news exclusively from television, they have recognized that most such viewers care little at all about complex affairs of state.

So, too, have they understood that television is essentially an entertainment medium that thrives on the new, the exciting, the dramatic; moreover, that television is also a predominantly visual medium. Whereas the print media will organize its coverage around what a candidate says, television organizes its coverage around what viewers see (Schram, 1987). Consistent with these precepts is yet another: much as network correspondents might complain about packaged video politics, television producers and cameramen like nothing more than pretty pictures.

Finally, a rule that the Dukakis campaign adhered to reluctantly and belatedly is that it is possible and strategically desirable to control what gets put over the air. This entails, first, that the candidate and his handlers have a clear plan as to what they want shown on the networks on any given day; second, that they avoid interviews and press conferences that the candidate cannot control; third, that they arrange events and engage in activities that have at least the semblance of being newsworthy so as to give the media the excuse that they need to cover them; finally, that in their selection and staging of video moments, they provide clear signals to reporters and cameramen of when important things are likely to be said or done—in effect helping the networks to edit the news in their own behalf.

These precepts of free video politics are hardly our own invention. Indeed, from time to time, the networks themselves aired segments of the techniques by which they, and indirectly their viewers, had been manipulated. Most notable, perhaps, was a carefully prepared 6-minute news segment on CBS in 1984 featuring White House correspondent Lesley Stahl showing how Reagan's handlers had staged-managed video events with the same attention to detail that they might in the making of a movie. Stahl's message, in effect, was that the American people had been gulled and lulled by these video images. She pointed out how visuals were used to distance Reagan from bad news while placing him at the center of good news. She showed how clips of Reagan exercising vigorously at his ranch effectively offset fears that he was too old. And she demonstrated how visuals were also used to counter the memory of unpopular policies or practices. "Look at the handicapped Olympics, or the opening ceremony of an old-age home. No hint that he tried to cut the budgets for the disabled and for federally subsidized housing for the elderly . . ." (quoted in Jamieson, 1988, p. 60).

All the while that Stahl talked about these manipulations, she presented visuals from Reagan's four years in office as evidence: Reagan sharing concerns with farmers, Reagan lifting weights, Reagan tossing a football, Reagan in bathing suit, Reagan doing his Marlboro walk, Reagan celebrating a birthday with Nancy, Reagan honoring D-Day veterans at Normandy, Reagan greeting senior citizens, Reagan surrounded by flags.

Years later, Jane Mayer and Doyle McManus (1988) wrote about how three Reagan handlers, Stuart Spencer, Kenneth Khachigian, and Robert Teeter, had effectively scripted the 1984 Reagan campaign. Aware that the Reagan administration had run out of ammunition—as Spencer put it, "they don't have a goddamn thing in the pipeline"—the campaign advisors elected to run on the record, claiming through testimonials, and evidencing through visuals, that the Reagan administration had brought about "a new beginning." Some of the video clips that Stahl featured in her news segment appear in the film by that name.

Network Response to the New Video Politics

We have seen that the new video politics is a politics of control, of pretty pictures, of market-tested ads and free video moments that reinforce positive images while undermining negative ones. We have seen, too, that the Republicans have been far better than the Democrats at the game of video politics, particularly at the presidential level. At first it was assumed that the machinations of the Republican media advisors required a Reagan to be effective. Reagan the folk hero; Reagan the actor; Reagan the teflon president; Reagan the great communicator; Reagan the Dr. Feelgood President: these ascriptions were among those used to explain the Reagan fortunes as being one-of-a-kind. But it is becoming increasingly clear that Messrs. Baker, Ailes, Atwater & Co. can get along quite well, thank you, with George Bush as the Republican standard-bearer. The Democrats, meanwhile, continue to shoot themselves in the foot.

For the networks, the new video politics has presented excruciating dilemmas. The first dilemma was whether to risk professional debasement by showing any and all ads the candidates pay them to run, or to exercise discretion in deciding what political spots to air, albeit at the risk of losing potential revenues and alienating the politicians whose ads they refuse. There was considerable talk of further regulation of political spots in the course of the 1988 presidential contest, and there is likely to be a good deal more in the near future (see Richards & Caywood, chapter 13, this volume).

The second dilemma concerns the question of how the networks should cover the presidential campaigns: whether, for example, to give air time to events like President Reagan's appearance at the Daytona stock car race, as opposed, say, to coverage of candidates' statements about policy issues. As early as 1976, CBS News president Richard Salant was expressing concern that his network had provided two hours of strategy stories about the campaign on its evening news program for every hour that it had spent on issues stories (Schram, 1987). This, he acknowledged, was a rather generous estimate, and it did not include pieces driven primarily by compelling video footage. It was mounting opposition to this third category of coverage that may have eventuated in what by 1984 CBS news people were calling the "Plan," a loosely formulated understanding that, henceforward, CBS would refrain from covering video moments that were not in some sense newsworthy (Schram, 1987). From the very first, however, there was resistance to the Plan from within CBS. Moreover, it was difficult to execute such a plan without cooperation from the other networks. Critics argued that it was the networks' obligation to cover the candidates come what may; moreover, it was believed that how a candidate and his staff executed a video event was revealing of the candidate's leadership ability and managerial competence.

Probably the biggest obstacle to fulfillment of the Plan was that it ran counter to increasingly salient financial concerns.[3] The major television networks have been under pressure for some time now from cable, VCR, and independents, and from their own corporate superiors, to cater to public tastes.[4] Said Paletz and Entman (1982), "Fear of missing stories

---

[3]With the coming of age of subscription TV, cable, pay TV, satellites, superstations, and other technological and corporate broadcasting developments, broadcasters and their news operations discovered that they could no longer take for granted the large numbers of viewers to which they had become accustomed. The new "gadgets and gimmicks" that accompanied the communication revolution have taken their toll in the 80s on the traditional information/entertainment/advertising marketplaces. Prophetically, the *New York Times Magazine* reported on August 19, 1979, that the kind of storm that "swept Dorothy off to Oz is (was) about to hit the old broadcasting industry," and that "storm" has taken a financial toll on the broadcasting industry and altered approaches to network news and entertainment programming. For a more detailed analysis of the constraints, as well as the opportunities for response to new technologies by broadcasters see Barrett & Sklar (1980) and Wattenberg (1984).

[4]The inclination of the networks to cater to public tastes is said by some to be a relatively new phenomenon. It certainly seems to be a more pressing consideration in these days of cable and VCR. "It's the job of prime-time entertainment," wrote CBS News president Richard Salant (cited in Polman, 1988) over a decade ago, "to give most of the people what most of them want most of the time. But we in broadcast journalism cannot, and should not, and will not base our judgments on what we think the viewers and listeners are most interested in" (p. 5C).

Contrast Salant's statement with that of CBS News' current president, David Burke (cited in Polman, 1988), who told reporters that CBS News must become "a full corporate player in the corporate environment" (p. 5C). "The big three networks are hurting," said media analyst Dick Polman (Oct. 21, 1988), "which means that the news divisions—once exempt from bottom-line concerns—must now pull their own weight financially."

that competitive media cover, unwillingness to risk boring TV viewers by giving them words instead of pictures, insufficient space to go into sufficient detail: all exist in substantial measure because of profit considerations" (p. 52).

The consequences of pay-as-you go journalism were particularly manifest in the 1988 presidential contest. Apparently the financial pressures being felt by the news divisions were exacerbated. And apparently they became further convinced that the public would switch channels unless they were provided with the "pretty pictures." CBS News current president, David Burke, is reported to have said that CBS must become "a full player in the corporate environment" (Polman, October, 21, 1988, p. 5C). Burke added that what the public apparently does not want is "quality." "I sort of sense an unwanting to know (about critical issues). The public is buying the flag factories and the Pledge of Allegiance and card-carrying-this and card-carrying-that."[5]

When things went swimmingly for the Republicans, as they generally did in September and October, the news coverage of the Bush campaign worked in tandem with the ads to produce a single coherent image. On October 18th, for example, CBS showed Bush speaking up for "peace through strength" at a defense plant, with a huge missile component serving as his backdrop. Following Bush's pledge that he would "not leave America defenseless," the network cut to a Bush commercial showing Bush reviewing the troops in slow motion. Then on to another Bush advertisement, this one ridiculing Dukakis's inglorious ride in a military tank. Said media analyst Dick Polman (October 21, 1988), "This surreal moment may have been a milestone in campaign coverage: 'free media' giving air time to a paid ad that replays an event that was contrived to attract the free media" (p. 1C).

Of particular interest to us in 1988 was what the networks would choose to say about the ads that they carried and the video moments that they showed. Would they join in criticisms of deceptive candidate advertising, for example, or would they stand outside the fray? Conflicts between journalistic norms of balance and accuracy have often been noted (Hackett, 1984). Typically the media choose between them on an issue-by-issue basis. Fires tend to be reported with a view toward accuracy, while firings—say, of controversial political appointees—tend to be reported with a view toward balance (Hackett, 1984). Not always, however, is it possible to choose between them so easily. Skirrow provides the example of the BBC program that argued "that there could be a

---

[5]But this pronouncement of "what the public wants" comes on the heels of the Fowler Commissions' deregulatory initiatives, which increase the amount of commercial spots available for sale to advertisers and drastically reduce the regulatory pressure to present "public service" type programs that might be associated with "quality programming" (Ferrall, 1989).

neutral stand on exploitation and racism." The BBC program "balanced" a hard-hitting documentary on racial oppression in South Africa with a South African production "which showed black people driving around in cars in the apparently affluent and happy township of Soweto" (quoted in Hackett, 1984, p. 233).

For the most part, the news media strive for balance in their reporting of political campaigns. They claim to leave for the candidates and their advisors and surrogates the task of combatting the opposition. And they call upon political analysts of varying shades of opinion to interpret the news. When they present criticisms, it is typically by way of indirect source attributions (e.g., citing critiques of the Bush campaign by members of his own party or by alledged "experts"). When they dare criticize campaign tactics directly, they tend to confine their criticisms to claims that can be readily documented (i.e., questions of accuracy in the narrow sense, rather than to charges of false innuendo, deliberate ambiguity, pictorial bias, and the like). And they look for ways to cast blame evenhandedly (e.g., comparing the Bush attack commercials with the attacks on Bush at the Democratic convention), or to combine praise and blame (e.g., pairing Bush criticism of the Bush campaign's advertising tactics to simultaneously evincing admiration and even awe for these same tactics).

Yet difficult cases do present themselves—cases, for example, in which one candidate distorts matters repeatedly in a debate while the other does not; other cases in which one side has shown its side to be far more capable of managing the news; still other cases in which there simply is no neutral ground.[6] What to do?

---

[6]Simons, 1986, pp. 106–107. More often than not, the journalist strives at least for the appearance of evenhandedness in campaign reporting, so great is the pressure to avoid seeming partisan. Thus, for example, the *New York Times* (Rosenthal, A (9/27/88), p. 14A) ran an article on distortion in the first presidential debate of 1988 alongside its version of the text of the debate. Its title seemed evenhanded enough and not terribly critical: "Like Others Before Them, Debaters Stretched the Truth at Times." Likewise the lead paragraphs:

Vice President Bush and Gov. Michael S. Dukakis hurled piles of complicated figures, obscure names, tongue-twisting acronyms, and seemingly irrefutable facts at each other in their debate Sunday night.

Much of what they said was at least arguable. Some of it was distorted to put themselves in a good light or their opponent in a bad light. Some of it was simply wrong.

This is a time-honored political technique, offering information in the expectation that listeners will not have the resources or the interest to check them, and accept them. (p. 14a)

But was this evenhanded treatment itself a distortion of sorts? Only in the eleventh paragraph did we learn that while there were cases "when Mr. Dukakis was not telling the entire story, or misstated things . . . an examination of the transcript indicates that Mr. Bush said more that was inaccurate than Mr. Dukakis did" (p. 14a).

The 1988 presidential campaigns proved difficult for the news media to cover in part because they remained committed to the journalistic norm of balanced news coverage at a time when the Republicans were so much more willing to trespass on established conventions of presidential campaigning in running what one critic called a "down-and-dirty" campaign (Polman, 10/23/88). It was the Bush campaign, after all, that set the essentially negative tone of the campaign, initiated the practice of keeping its candidates away from the press except during controlled photo opportunities, and repeatedly risked attacking its Democratic opponent with claims that were inferentially false if not manifestly inaccurate (Katz, Oct. 27, 1988; Lewis, Jan. 19, 1989).[7] Aware of the journalistic commitment to balance, the Republicans effectively exploited the norm, knowing full well that the news media would refrain from one-sided criticism lest they risk the charge of partisanship.[8]

Among the criticisms of the news media in 1988 was that they were insufficiently critical of misleading or otherwise deceptive campaign messages.[9] Asked by Evans and Novak whether a Bush ad claiming that Dukakis opposed virtually every weapons system had "gone a little too far," admaker Roger Ailes went unchallenged when he responded, "That's the first time we've seen a pacifist sit on a piece of military equipment since Jane Fonda sat on an anti-aircraft gun in Hanoi." Yet Dukakis had supported virtually every controversial defense system, including the Stealth bomber and the Trident II submarine (Polman, Oct. 21, 1988).[10]

---

[7]Anthony Lewis (1989), writing in the *New York Review,* cited several instances of the press's ability to deal with lies and distortion in the ads of the 1988 campaign. For example, Lewis reported that the ad that showed the polluted Boston Harbor was actually shot at an abandoned nuclear submarine repair yard. A sign that appeared in this ad read, "DANGER/RADIATION HAZARD/NO SWIMMING." Lewis feels that the desire to appear "objective" has become a "dangerous obsession" in American journalism and chides the press for not commenting on distortion, like the aforementioned that surfaced during the 1988 general election campaign.

[8]How likely is it that political handlers are aware of the accuracy problem? Aware enough not to let it interfere with the need for getting out a campaign message. Said Doug Bailey of the Graduate School for Political Management at Baruch College, New York, "If you need to be technically correct, absolutely accurate in every t.v. spot you'll never put a spot on the air" (Rowe, Aug 30 1988, p. 1).

[9]Roger Ailes, as reported by Marvin Kalb (1988), was well aware of what gets the media's attention: "There are three things that get covered: visuals, attacks and mistakes. You try to avoid mistakes and give them as many attacks and visuals as you can" (p. 4d). Note that there is no mention or apparent concern with the accuracy of claims made— only campaign mistakes.

[10]In fact, because of their very similar views on defense, one Knight-Ridder news service feed (*Augusta Chronicle,* September 11, 1988) proclaimed, "They're (Bush/Dukakis) closer than they sound" with the main difference focused on "whether to build new types

Not infrequently during the period in which Bush was erasing a 17-point deficit to take a 10-point lead, the news media combined criticism of the Bush attack commercials with criticism of the Democrats for failing to respond quickly enough in kind (Fiedler, Sept. 12, 1988).[11] The chiding of the Democrats for failing to counterpunch effectively surely had point, and some in the media used it to justify their passivity, claiming that it was not the news media's responsibility but the Democrats' responsibility to rail at the Republicans for their questionable media manipulations (Polman, Oct. 21, 1988). Others maintained, however, that responding in kind would only serve to further corrupt the campaign process. They argued that the situation already had gotten out of hand and threatened to get worse unless the news media asserted themselves more forcefully, not on the side of the Democrats, but on the side of fairness and accuracy (Lewis, Jan. 19, 1989).

Some of the Bush attack commercials were inferentially false, if not downright inaccurate. The furlough ad, asserting that "the Dukakis furlough program gave weekend furloughs to first-degree murderers" provides an example. Subtitles announced that "268 escaped" and that "many are still at large." But the so-called "Dukakis furlough program" was begun by his Republican predecessor, Frank Sargent. Dukakis himself did not decide who got furloughs. Counted as "escapees" were prisoners who overstayed their furlough by two or more hours. Of the 268 prisoners said to have "escaped," only four were murderers and all were eventually caught and returned (Lewis, Oct. 27 1988). A.27

This much can be said about what might be called the "propositional logic" of the furlough ad—its use of evidence and argument to support explicit claims. But what carries the message, at least as much as its misleading statistics and causal attributions, are its stark and shadowy, black-and-white depictions of the prison and revolving gates and the menacing sounds and sights of multiple "Willie Hortons" being permitted to leave those gates to kidnap, murder, and rape. The ad works through visual and auditory associations. It is allusive and elusive for that reason. Its opening, slow-motion pan of a prison tower set against two mountains conjures up nightmaric images of imminent danger. The next visual, of a lone prison guard patrolling stealthily with rifle, plays further on our preexistent fears, and these are reinforced by the metallic drone of the synthesizer in the background. Then comes the revolving

---

of land-based missiles and how fast to develop a space-based missile defense shield (SDI)" (p. 14A).

[11]According to a poll in the October 31, 1988, issue of *Newsweek,* 40% of the people polled blamed the news organizations for the negative aspects of the 1988 campaign. Even though network news was also perceived favorably (81%) in a report by Ornstein (1988), only 52% of the interviewees felt that media reports of the campaign were accurate.

gate scene, the prisoners silent, depersonalized, heads bowed, shot exiting the prison to the grating and rhythmic sound of their own shuffle, as a voiceover intones about the consequences of electing as president the permissive governor of Massachusetts.

There remains the question of whether the networks are *capable* of undercutting deceptive or otherwise misleading campaign hype with the critical tools at their disposal. This was the question we found so fascinating in our study of network responses to ANB. To those readers who shared with us an initial confidence in the power of journalistic criticism, we should point out something we learned later: the White House was apparently overjoyed by Lesley Stahl's scathing critique of its video politics; they realized apparently that Lesley Stahl was no match for those pretty pictures, and that their reappearance on television might only serve to reinforce their initial effectiveness!

Indeed, Schram (1987) recently provided evidence in support of the White House hypothesis by way of his study of a focus group of 16 friends and neighbors in a fairly affluent Chicago suburb who together viewed the Stahl segment with the sound off, along with a few Mondale ads. The Schram study was not scientific by any means, but it is instructive. The assembled group spoke as though they had just been watching Reagan ads; and what they saw they liked—far better than the Mondale ads, which seemed a downer by comparison. Later, when the group was shown the Stahl clip with the sound on, they erupted with laughter at having been duped. But they reported that their favorable attitudes toward the Reagan visuals had not changed. Indeed, the main effect of the Stahl piece was to increase viewer admiration for the Reagan team's marketing acumen.

THE STUDY OF "A NEW BEGINNING"

ANB was shown at the Republican National Convention on August 23, 1984, in place of the traditional introductory speech for the nominated presidential candidate. Produced by a syndicated advertising group known as the Tuesday Team, the 18-minute film is a visually arresting, seamlessly edited, emotionally powerful retrospective on Reagan's first term in office. Viewed as a promotional effort, the film was widely acclaimed as one of the best and most creative advertisements ever made (Clendinen, 1984; Dougherty, 1984; Raines, 1984). Indeed, when historians look back upon the Reagan years, it may well be that they will single out ANB as the quintessential expression of the first four years and a harbinger of both the 1984 and 1988 fall campaigns. Narrated by the president, it exploits Mr. Reagan's exceptional self-presentational skills while also making extensive use of testimonials by ordinary folk and film footage of previously televised video events, such as Reagan's speech to an audience of teary-eyed D-day veterans assembled at Normandy to commemorate the assault on Normandy Beach during World War II.

The showing of ANB at the Republican convention illustrates the problem of network coverage of campaign hype with which we have been concerned in this chapter. Moreover, our study of variations in perceptions of the film as a function of differences in network treatments of it illustrates dramatically the difficulties that television commentators have had and are likely to have in the future in responding to campaign hype of this kind.

For the networks, ANB posed problems on at least two counts. First, there was the question of whether to show the film. Campaign films no less one-sided had previously been shown by the networks as part of their gavel-to-gavel coverage of political conventions, but in 1984 all three major networks had made it a policy to truncate their live coverage, reserving it for "newsworthy" events. Was ANB newsworthy, or was it, as one ABC spokesperson put it, "symbolic of the attempt to use the coverage of a news event for a non-news activity?" (Kaplan, 1984, p. 19). The substitution of ANB for the introductory speech was, by the Republicans' own admission, a calculated attempt to ensure network coverage of the extensive, $425,000 project. They argued that since the networks had aired the Democrats' introductory speech for Mondale, their party's introduction should also be shown. Yet Charles Manatt, chairman of the Democratic National Committee, countered that it was unfair to broadcast the film since the Democrats' film showing candidate Walter Mondale had not been shown by any of the three major networks. Thus the networks were forced to decide whether ANB was an unpaid commercial that they should not air, or a newsworthy documentary that they could accept as a legitimate alternative to traditional political oratory.

The second issue confronting the networks was how to talk about the film. One impulse was to call attention to the propagandistic nature of the film—to the subtle and not so subtle ways, as Bill Moyers put it, that "it exaggerates, accentuates, and manipulates" (*Broadcasting*, August 27, 1984, p. 31). Yet the inclination to "tell it like it is" ran counter to the other conceptions of objective news coverage emphasizing balance, neutrality, and evenhandedness. Had the networks done nothing more than lambast the Republicans for substituting a slick but insubstantialp-seudodocumentary in place of the traditional nominating speech, they might well have evoked charges of favoritism, and not just from the Republicans.

In the face of these conflicting pressures, the networks elected very different treatment strategies. All three major networks remained on location during the showing of the film to the convention delegates, but only NBC aired the film in its entirety. Dan Rather of CBS interspersed brief clips of the film with summaries of its contents, then turned to White House correspondent Bill Plante for a discussion of the controversy surrounding the film and a defense of CBS's decision not to show it in its entirety. The two commentators offered little in the way of criticism of the film, other than their general characterization of it as an extended campaign commercial. Even as they spoke, viewers could overhear sounds of the delegates responding enthusiastically to the showing of the film in the convention hall.

Apart from noting that the Reagan documentary was "controversial," ABC's treatment of the film was essentially uncritical. The centerpiece of their treatment was a comparison by media analyst Jeff Greenfield of clips from the Reagan film with segments from the previously untelevised Mondale documentary. The films were characterized as together comprising a "political debate, a debate fought out not in face to face argument, but with the weapons of the media age—aimed at our hearts more than our heads." Having concluded its comparison of the Reagan and Mondale films, ABC shifted to a general discussion of the two candidates.

Although NBC was alone among the three networks in showing the entire film, it prefaced that presentation with what by virtually all accounts was the most critical commentary on the film. Tom Brokaw warned the viewers, for example, that while "they call it a documentary, it is not a documentary, it's a commercial for Ronald Reagan. I suppose some Democrats and other commentators may even call it propaganda at some point." Rodger Mudd said of the Republican production that it "will not tax your mind, it will not challenge your intellect, but it will assault your emotions head on." The film, he said, would include "references to God, quotes from the Bible, and lots of crying." About half way, viewers would forget they were watching a masterful piece of propaganda "and you will begin to think you are watching a television commercial for Leisure World or one of those lumber companies that is always replenishing the earth." While Mudd detailed the references to God and country in the film ("you will see the American flag by actual count at least 26 times in different scenes"), John Chancellor was enumerating significant omissions from the film— the failure of the Reagan administration to reduce the federal deficit, for example, as well as the sensitive subjects of Beirut, El Salvador, and Nicaragua. Overall, suggested NBC, the Reagan film was slick and powerful, but worrisome for just that reason; it was, said Brokaw, "one of the most effective communications that any campaign has ever produced.''

Research Questions

How would comparable viewers react to these alternative network treatments of ANB, and how, as a consequence, would they assess the film itself? How would prior predispositions for or against Ronald Reagan influence perceptions of both the media commentaries and the film? Specifically, as regards NBC, how would their critical preview of the film influence perceptions of its accuracy, power, and value, as compared with perceptions of viewers who watched ABC and CBS during the same time period or who saw the film without any network commentary?[12]

These were the major research questions in this study, and they raised in turn the larger questions about the uses and limits of criticism by television commentators to which we referred earlier. Should critical previews be expected to make a difference? Should they prompt viewers to think less of campaign messages like ANB, or should these critiques only heighten interest and enthusiasm for the presentation without necessarily diminishing trust in the presentation's truthfulness or accuracy?

There is a fair amount of behavioral research literature that indicates that forewarnings of a persuader's propagandistic intent as well as critical precommunications about the contents of the persuasive message are likely to produce resistance to the message, except among persons initially committed to positions endorsed in the subsequent message (Petty & Cacioppo, 1977, 1981).

For those not fully enamored with Reagan, then, NBC's preview of ANB might well have provided the ammunition for a reasoned rejection of the Reagan message. Even for pro-Reagan viewers, one might have predicted, the NBC preview would be disturbing and perhaps dissonance-producing; hence, in order to convince themselves of the trustworthiness of ANB, they would have to discount the value of NBC's commentary on the film (Festinger, 1957; Petty & Cacioppo, 1981).

But what now of the fact that ANB relied in large measure on verbal and visual depictions to carry its message? Would its nonpropositional logic be corrigible to the propagandistic logic of the NBC commentary? What, too, of the possibility that in bestowing unusual attention on the film and also attesting to its great power, the NBC network treatment

---

[12]Transcripts of the three network commentaries are available upon request.

might actually enhance perceptions of the value of the film in the eyes of the viewers?

Method

The subjects of this study were 148 undergraduates at Temple University, who were randomly assigned by sections of lower-level speech courses to one of four treatment groups.[13] Three of the four groups each saw one of the network treatments of the film, exactly as it appeared on television. One group each saw the ABC and CBS treatments, whereas the group we have labeled NBC/Pre saw the network's critical preview of the film and then the entire film. For the fourth group, which we have called NBC/Post, the commentary/film sequence was reversed. These viewers first saw and evaluated the Reagan film, then saw and evaluated the NBC commentary. All other subjects (Ss) rated the film and then the commentary after they had seen both.

The study was introduced to the respondents as follows:

> On August 23, 1984, at the Republican National Convention held at Dallas, Texas, a film about President Reagan was shown to the delegates just prior to the President's nomination acceptance speech. Major network coverage of the event varied.

> One network aired the film in its entirety, but offered commentary prior to showing it. The other two networks chose not to air the film in its entirety, but instead offered selections or "cuts" from the film interspersed with commentary.

> We are surveying students to determine their reactions to the network coverage of the film and to the event itself. You will be viewing the event as it was broadcast by one of the networks or a special format created for this survey, and then responding to a questionnaire.

The survey questionnaire was in three parts. Part I consisted of six questions designed to secure demographic data and to determine political predispositions. Part II checked for prior exposure to the film and network treatments and asked questions designed to tap perceptions of the film. Respondents were asked to indicate their perceptions of the film on a series of 7-point semantic differential scales. In Part III, respondents were asked to indicate their perceptions of the commentary. Part III of the questionnaire also offered a repeat question about respondents' voting intentions, then asked for assessments of Reagan's

---

[13]Six "regular" classes participated in this study during their regularly scheduled class time, along with a small number of volunteers from other speech courses.

ability as president, and then probed assessments of what the networks should have done with the film.

The 7-point semantic differential scales included in the questionnaires were designed to tap the dimensions of Accuracy, Power, and Value. Factor loadings on the 13 items used in the study are presented in Table 12.1.

Results

Of primary concern in this essay is whether perceptions of the film and network commentary were influenced by exposure to one or another network treatment of the film and also by prior predispositions for or against President Reagan. From responses to the questionnaire an overall picture of the sample emerges. The group was 48% male, 52% female; 76% were White, 24% non-White, of whom by far the largest number were Black. Of the total respondents, only 34% said that they would vote for Reagan in 1984, whereas 52% indicated that they would vote for Mondale. Some 48% reported being neutral-to-negative toward Reagan; about half were approving. Voting intentions and assessments of the president's performance remained fairly stable on the post-questionnaire, with but a few additional respondents now indicating that they intended to vote for Reagan and approximately the same percentage as before registering approval. Only 34% said they had previously seen ANB; 20% reported seeing it aired during coverage of the Republican convention, 11% subsequent to the convention, and 3% more than once.

Table 12.1 Factor Loadings (Varimax Rotated Principle Components Matrix)

	Dimensions		
Components	*Accuracy*	*Power*	*Value*
Truthful—untruthful	0.84		
Informational—propagandistic	0.61		
Accurate—inaccurate	0.52		
Exciting—dull		0.83	
Vigorous—lethargic		0.78	
Energetic—tired		0.76	
Dynamic—static		0.72	
Interesting—boring		0.68	
Strong—weak		0.61	
Wise—foolish			0.74
Valuable—worthless			0.68
Beneficial—harmful			0.68
Good—bad			0.65

The major findings from the study may be summarized as follows:

(a) Mean ratings of the film and the network treatments of the film were generally high (see Table 12.2). Only film accuracy ratings tended to fall below the 4.0 midpoint on the 7-point semantic differential scales.

(b) Both network treatment and prior attitudes toward the president had substantial influences on perceptions of the film. Effects of the predispositional variable were even greater. Those who thought well of the president to begin with were far more likely to think well of the film, irrespective of which group they had been assigned to. But for the Value dimension, interaction effects of the treatment group and predispositional variables were not significant.

(c) In terms of ratings of the commentaries, there were significant main effects for the treatment group variable on the dimensions of Accuracy, Value, and Power. The effects of respondents' prior attitudes toward Reagan were consistently in the predicted direction but failed to achieve significance at the 0.05 level. There were no significant interaction effects. Apparently, attitudes toward Reagan did not play as decisive a role in ratings of the commentaries as they did in ratings of the film.

(d) NBC's critical preview of the film apparently did indeed make a difference, but not in the direction one might have predicted. The NBC/Pre treatment group rated the film as most accurate, most powerful, and most valuable, even though it was the group that had heard the

Table 12.2   Means and Standard Deviations

	Treatment Group			
	CBS (M/SD)	*ABC (M/SD)*	*NBC/Pre (M/SD)*	*NBC/Post (M/SD)*
*Perceptions of the Film				
Accuracy	3.40/1.26	3.91/1.49	4.73/1.63	3.64/1.40
Power	4.75/1.34	4.99/1.31	5.79/1.40	5.25/1.35
Value	4.59/1.46	4.72/1.26	5.09/1.56	4.46/1.34
**Perceptions of the Commentaries				
Accuracy	4.60/1.06	5.13/1.10	5.66/1.18	5.92/1.25
Power	4.05/1.22	4.50/1.18	4.79/1.38	4.88/1.04
Value	4.39/1.22	5.16/1.10	5.56/1.24	5.57/1.30

*Note tht NBC/Pre ratings are higher than ratings of all other groups on all three dimensions. Film ratings are significantly higher $p < 0.05$) than all other groups on the Accuracy dimension and than CBS and ABC on the Power dimension. Differences tend toward statistical significance ($p < 0.10$) compared with NBC/Post on the Power and VAlue dimensions. All other differences in mean ratings by treatment groups are not significant.

**Note that ratings of the commentaries are consistently higher for NBC viewers. Differences between NBC/Pre and NBC/Post were not significant.

film most roundly criticized. (Recall that the NBC/Post group had not heard the NBC commentary at the point at which they rated the film.) Differences between NBC/Pre ratings and those of the other treatment groups verged on being statistically significant ($p < 0.10$) on all three dimensions and were significant on the Accuracy dimension ($p < 0.001$).

Warranting special attention is the finding that mean ratings of the film's accuracy by the NBC/Pre group were more than a *full* point higher than those by the NBC/Post control group that had seen only the film. NBC/Pre ratings of the accuracy of the film likewise were significantly higher than those by CBS and ABC viewers. The NBC/Pre group also assigned significantly higher ratings to the film on the Power dimension than did CBS and ABC viewers. They tended, in other words, to regard the film as more exciting, vigorous, dynamic, interesting, and the like. Differences between means were not significant on the Value dimension.

(e) Were the higher ratings of the film by those in the NBC/Pre group due to a discounting effect? Did most viewers in that group, and especially the pro-Reagan viewers, judge NBC's own criticism of the film to be untruthful, inaccurate, even propagandistic?

Quite the opposite turned out to be the case. Whether presented before or after the film, the NBC commentary was rated as highly accurate—far more accurate than the CBS and ABC commentaries. Moreover, it did not seem to matter terribly much whether the viewer was pro-Reagan or anti-Reagan. As indicated earlier, viewers apparently rated the commentaries in a fairly nonpartisan manner, with attitudes toward Reagan approaching but not achieving statistical significance. NBC/Pre and NBC/Post also came out highest on the Power and Value dimensions, with but small differences between them. Apparently the order of the appearance of the film and commentary were not a factor in NBC viewers' appreciation of both. CBS earned the lowest ratings on all three dimensions. ABC scored significantly higher than CBS on the Value dimension.

Discussion

We asked earlier in this essay whether NBC's critical preview of ANB would prompt viewers to react more negatively to the film than viewers who either watched ABC or CBS during the same period or who rated the film before seeing any network commentary. Barring that, would there be evidence of a discounting of the NBC commentary, especially by pro-Reagan viewers?

Our findings provided no support for these hypotheses, and, in fact, quite the opposite seems to have occurred. Admittedly, the subjects in this study were disproportionately unsympathetic to Reagan relative to the population as a whole, and some of them had seen all or a portion of the film before. But these subjects were distributed nearly equally across treatment groups. The fact is that NBC/Pre viewers rated the film more favorably than did all other viewers, including their counterparts in the NBC/Post group. Far from discounting the NBC commentary, the NBC viewers—among them many pro-Reagan viewers—gave NBC's handling of the film the *highest* ratings. Conceivably, these viewers were influenced more by the opportunity to see the entire film than by the NBC commentary. Yet, this would not explain the higher ratings of the film by the NBC/Pre group over those who saw only the film—a full point difference, as previously noted, with respect to the Accuracy dimension. Nor would it explain the fact that the accuracy of the NBC commentary was not called into question by the respondents and was indeed rated higher than the CBS and ABC commentaries. *NBC viewers clearly liked the commentary they saw. They also liked the film; and they evidently had no difficulty reconciling these seemingly inconsistent attitudes.*

Why, then, did viewers respond as they did? Why in particular did NBC viewers evince so little apparent difficulty in liking the film? We have no definite answers to these questions, but our assessments of the situations confronting the respondents may help to explain the findings. Indeed, they may not only help explain why journalistic criticism did not make an anticipated difference as applied to ANB, but why similar criticism by television commentators of comparable campaign materials in 1988 apparently did not make a difference. Here we expand on three arguments put forth in our initial report: (a) that the genre of political campaign rhetoric, (b) the modality of the nonpropositional rhetorical depictions, and (c) the contextual frame of television culture, all operating together, are potent forces in blunting the effects of rhetorical criticism's linear, calculative logic.

Consider first that viewers may have held the Reagan film to a different standard of accuracy than they did the network's treatment of the film. If so, they could appreciate the accuracy of NBC's critique of the film while simultaneously believing that the film itself was reasonably accurate for campaign films of its kind. Correspondingly, they may have held the film to a different and less demanding standard than was implied in the NBC critique of the film.

To the charge, for example, that the film was not a documentary in the usual sense, but should more accurately have been labeled "propaganda," the viewer might have responded, "Yes, but so what?"

Put another way, the film network commentary may well have belonged to different rhetorical genres (Simons & Aghazarian, 1986), each with its own viewer expectations and standards. And it is possible, as Van Gordon Sauter has suggested, that viewers discount political campaign hype as mere hype even before it is commented on, just as they do sales and advertising hype (Schram, 1987). Nimmo and Combs (1980) and others have noted that although there are clearly limits on how far we will allow politicians to go, we tend in our culture to make contradictory demands upon them. Thus, for example, we demand that they be honest and sincere but also smooth and calculating. We deplore in the abstract their tendency to pander to public taste, but we also want them to tell us what we want to hear. Spero (1980) has observed that even though media commentators periodically decry the tendency to sell politicians as if they were soap, the fact is that there are far more strictures on soap advertisers than there are on promoters of politicians. It is generally recognized that even the most statesmanlike politicians are not averse to using exaggerated, one-sided arguments as well as strong emotional appeals. That a campaign message plays effectively on voters' emotions may be regarded as cause for concern, but also for admiration and even awe. Once having come to regard the message as emotionally powerful, we may come to see it also as valuable and accurate, this so as to achieve cognitive consistency. Ironically, then, in criticizing ANB as powerful propaganda, NBC may have effectively increased viewers' admiration of it on other counts as well.

Our second point, closely related to the first, is that viewers of the film may have been largely impervious to NBC's criticisms of it because the film and its critique represented different modes of rationality. Recall our discussion of rhetorical criticism. Said Osborn (1986):

> Electronic images now come to us more easily, directly, with disarming innocence and a presumptuousness that may bluff us into accepting them as clear and favored widows upon reality. . . . We have no traditional theory that deals with this complex and often subtle form of rhetoric. The theory we do possess equips us primarily to detect the sound and the spurious in arguments that display their proofs and inferences in linear development from proposition to conclusion. Attempting to apply the quasi-logical theoretical equipment to powerful new synchronic forms of communication is likely to produce a quaint and curious criticism that baffles at least as much as it enlightens. (p. 89)

Recall, too, our earlier references to the Lesley Stahl piece. It may well be that journalistic criticism works best in assessments of discourse like its own—discourse that puts forth clearcut arguments and defends them with evidence. But visuals, like those Stahl was commenting on, are not of that sort. The NBC commentary was heady and incisive in its enumerations of the film's omissions and exaggerations, but it could not effectively deny or refute the experience of having been moved by film images that were heart-warming, gut-wrenching, and visually as well as aurally arresting, and it may well have inadvertently reinforced those experiences. Whereas NBC showered viewers with facts and statistics, ANB bathed them in the warm afterglow of comforting images.

When the facts and the images are discrepant, as we have noted, viewers are apt to be more influenced by what they see. Indeed, it may be that verbal commentaries on visual messages have so little effect in part because they initially activate different hemispheres of the brain. Tom Brokaw has acknowledged that commentaries by him and his fact-oriented correspondents are probably no match for well-crafted video images (Schram, 1987). Regarding electronic images in particular, Tony Schwartz (1973) has gone so far as to suggest that traditional standards of clarity, truthfulness, and rationality are largely irrelevant.

Our final point is that television provides an inhospitable context for journalistic criticism. Viewers have been conditioned to treat television news as yet another form of entertainment. Above and beyond the formidable problems of combatting the filmmakers' electronic amalgam of words, music, and actions with mere words is the problem of adapting journalistic criticism to a culture of unseriousness. Journalistic criticism, to make its point, must be heady and challenging, and in the process it must risk seeming unpleasant, offensive, and antagonistic by calling into question the reality presented by the rhetor and perhaps counterposing another, less agreeable reality.

Consider now the problems of getting viewers to take serious criticism seriously over television. Neil Postman (1985) has argued that television's overriding frame of frames is entertainment. The problem, he says, is not just that television presents us with entertaining subject matter, but that the subject matter must be presented and processed as entertainment, including the news. Indeed, suggests Robert Stam (1983), television aggravates that problem, encouraging us to view news events as miniature dramas and news celebrities as soap opera characters. These extend to the anchors and reporters themselves. The former are often seen as superheroes, but of a sort that populate the world of cinematic fiction. The "top stories" that they bring us have all the earmarks of fiction, and we are invited in turn to gain pleasure from them, even at their most morbid. Said Postman (1985) of the television news:

> No matter what is depicted or from what point of view, the overarching presumption is that it is there for our amusement and pleasure. Everything about a news show tells us this—the good looks and amiability of the cast, their pleasant banter, the exciting music that opens and closes the show,

the vivid film footage, the attractive commercials—all these and more suggest that what we have seen is no cause for weeping. (p. 87)

The same is true for the commentaries we hear on news specials, like NBC's coverage of ANB. The entertainment theme undercuts seriousness, maintained Postman, leading newscasters to avoid it where possible and viewers to dismiss it or become inured to it. We would add that the problem is a progressive one. Entertainment drives out seriousness, making it increasingly unlikely that viewers will clamor for careful journalistic criticism when they can be entertained.

IMPLICATIONS: WHAT IS TO BE DONE?

This chapter has presented a summary of our research on ANB in the context of a larger exploration of the networks' role in delivering and responding to the new video politics. In seeking to account for the failure of NBC's much-esteemed critical preview to impact negatively on perceptions of the film, we looked especially at structural variables, factors that might apply not just to these networks' treatment of ANB, but to comparable coverage of comparable campaign materials. It was suggested that (a) viewers expect and demand less of political campaign rhetoric in the way of balance, accuracy, and the like than they do of campaign coverage by the news media, and thus could have regarded ANB as reasonably accurate for campaign rhetoric of its type while simultaneously thinking well of NBC's critique of it; (b) rhetorical criticism's calculative rhetoric of argumentation is relatively powerless to counteract the largely nonverbal, nondiscursive rationality of campaign films; and (c) television's dominant contextual frame undercuts serious criticism, rendering it into another form of entertainment.

Together these factors should blunt the effects of televised rhetorical criticism, especially as it bears on political campaign rhetoric. It should be emphasized, however, that we have no direct evidence that these factors were operative in this study, or that they were the only factors. It may be that NBC's criticisms would have been more telling were it not for the fact that ANB was narrated by and about the "Great Communicator" (as Ronald Reagan was called). It may be as well that something so simple as shutting out the noise from the convention floor would have gone a long way to getting viewers to take NBC's forewarnings more seriously.

In light of widespread dissatisfaction with the conduct and coverage of the 1988 campaign, there has been a good deal of talk about campaign reform. One possible policy implication, given the problems of effectively countering videos like ANB, is that the networks should resist broadcasting televised campaign hype of this kind. There have also been proposals to prohibit various forms of political advertising, including such miniature ANBs as the Reagan "Morning in America" ads and the Bush "Granddaughter" ads. Columnist William Pfaff (1988) observed that there is nothing extraordinary about banning or restricting political advertising; every other democracy in the Western World either bans or strictly controls it, preferring instead to grant equal time to each party or candidate for extensive interviews, staged discussions, formal speeches, and the like. Traditionally, political advertising has been accorded first amendment protections, but there is apparently some movement in Congress to work with the National Association of Broadcasters in devising ways to restrict political advertising formats (Caywood, 1989; see also Richards & Caywood, chapter 13, this volume).

A second implication, given the marked similarity in recent years between paid advertising and free TV, is that the networks ought to join together in specifying rather narrowly what sorts of video moments they are likely to consider newsworthy, possibly adapting something like the CBS "Plan" of 1984 as a guide to coverage by all responsible television newscasters. This might reduce the risks of lowered ratings of any one network attempting to implement such a plan on its own.

Still, the chances of any of these suggestions coming to fruition seem fairly low as long as the networks are hurting financially, as long as a lobotomized public clamors for more news that entertains, and as long as one party, the Republicans, remains so much more adept at video politics in going after and holding on to the grand presidential prize.

There is yet a third implication, and that concerns the way newscasters cover and comment on video events. Insofar as events of this kind are staged for the viewer, it might be both entertaining and instructive to educate viewers on a regular basis about the techniques used to win their fair and favorable attention. Such an in-depth approach to the making of video moments might devote considerably more time to visuals of back-stage activities by advance men, backdrop designers, sound specialists, and the like than to clips of the actual staged event. It might be part of a larger effort to increase viewers' sophistication at processing video politics.

Along similar lines, it has elsewhere been suggested that presidential candidates and others running for high office be encouraged to hold debates toward the conclusion of their respective campaigns about the way they have campaigned (Simons, 1988). Debates of this sort might well feature the candidates holding up their opponents' ads and videos to ridicule while defending their own. This could again be both an informative and an entertaining way of rendering rhetorical depictions more accessible to criticism.

At the risk of appearing banal, we must conclude with a call for more research on the possibility for more effective critical response to the new video politics. The news from this research study is glum indeed, but hope for effective response strategies should not be abandoned. The problem is a progressive one, an extension of a long-standing public tendency to treat reports of news events as a kind of parasocial play.[14]

REFERENCES

Augusta Chronicle (1988 Sep. 11,). Biggest difference: Rhetoric, p. 14A.

Barrett, M., & Sklar, Z. (1980). *The eye of the storm.* New York: Lippincott & Crowell.

Brockriede, W. E. (1974). Rhetorical criticism as argument. *Quarterly Journal of Speech, 60,* 165–174.

Broder, D. (Oct 20, 1988). Presidential politics now comes down to instant replays. *Philadelphia Inquirer,* 16A

Caywood, C. (1989, Feb. 6). Political ads in jeopardy. *Advertising Age.* p. 17

Clendinen, D. (1984, Sept. 14). Actor as president: Half-hour commercial wrapped in advertising's best. *New York Times,* p. 18.

Dougherty, P. H. (1984, Aug. 8). Reagan's emotional campaign. *New York Times.,* p. D. 29.

Edelman, M. (1964). *The symbolic uses of politics.* Chicago, IL: University of Chicago Press.

Ferrall, V. (1989). The impact of television deregulation on private and public interests. *Journal of Communication, 39,* 8–38.

Festinger, L. (1957). *A theory of cognitive dissonance.* Evanston, IL: Row, Peterson.

Fiedler, T. (1988, Sept. 12). In campaign ads every picture sells a story, critics say. *Philadelphia Inquirer.* p. 13A

Hackett, R. A. (1984). Decline of a paradigm? Bias and objectivity in news media studies. *Critical Studies in Mass Communication, 1,* 229–259.

Jamieson, K. H. (1988). *Eloquence in an electronic age: The transformation of political speechmaking.* New York: Oxford University Press.

Kalb, M. (1988, Nov. 6). How the media distorted the race. *Atlanta Journal Constitution,* p 4D.

Kaplan, P. (1984, Aug. 21). Introducing Reagan: Images and a theme song. *New York Times,* p 19.

Katz, G. (1988, Oct. 27). Memories made of campaign negatives. *USA Today,* pp. 6A–7A.

Lewis, A. (1988, Oct. 27). What is a man profited? *New York Times.* p. A.27

Lewis, A. (1989, Jan. 19). The intimidated press. *New York Review,* pp. 25–28.

Media the message at GOP convention (1984, Aug. 27). *Broadcasting,* p. 31.

Miller, G. R., Burgoon, M., & Burgoon, J. K. (1984). The functions of human communication in changing attitudes and gaining compliance. In C. Arnold & J. Bowers (Eds.), *Handbook of rhetorical and communication theory* Boston, MA: Allyn and Bacon. (pp. 400–474).

---

[14]See Murray Edelman, *The Symbolic Uses of Politics* (Chicago: University of Chicago Press, 1964).

Nimmo, D., & Combs, J. E. (1980). *Subliminal politics*. Englewood, NJ: Prentice Hall.

Ornstein, N. (Oct. 31, 1988). Issues and Answers. *Newsweek*.

Osborn, M. (1986). Rhetorical depiction. In H. W. Simons & A. A. Aghazarian (Eds.), *Form, genre, and the study of political discourse*. Columbia, SC: University of South Carolina Press, p. 89.

Paletz, D., & Entman, R. (1982). *Media, power, politics*. New York: The Free Press.

Petty, R. E., & Cacioppo, J. T. (1977). Forewarning, cognitive responding, and resistance to persuasion. *Journal of Personality and Social Psychology, 35,* 645–655.

Petty, R. E., & Cacioppo, J. T. (1981). *Attitudes and persuasion: Classic and contemporary approaches*. Dubuque, IA: Brown.

Pfaff, W. (1988, Oct. 16). Political TV ads should be limited. *Philadelphia Inquirer*, p. 2F.

Polman, D. (1988, Oct. 21). Is sound-bite politics what viewers want? *Philadelphia Inquirer*, 1C, 5C.

Polman, D. (1989, Feb. 2). *Philadelphia Inquirer*.

Postman, N. (1985). *Amusing ourselves to death*. New York: Viking Penguin, Inc.

Raines, H. (1984, Aug. 24). Reagan sees clear choice. *New York Times,* A.13.

Rosenthal, A (Sept. 27, 1988) Like others before them, debaters stretched the truth at times. *New York Times,* p 14A.

Rowe, J. (1988, Aug. 30). Getting a degree in political nuts and bolts. *Christian Science Monitor*, p. 1.

Schram, M. (1987). *The great American video game*. New York: William Morrow and Company.

Schwartz, T. (1973). *The responsive chord*. New York: Anchor Books.

Simons, H. (1986). *Persuasion: Understanding, practice, and analysis*. 2nd ed. New York: Random House.

Simons, H. (1988, May 30). *Disk-assisted political debate*. Paper presented at the 1988 ICA convention in New Orleans, LA.

Simons, H., & Aghazarian, A. (1986). *Form, genre and the study of political discourse*. Columbia, SC: University of South Carolina Press.

Simons, H., Stewart, D., & Harvey, D. (1989). Effects of network treatments of a political campaign film: Can rhetorical criticism make a difference? *Communication Quarterly, 37,* 184–198.

Spero, R. (1980). *The duping of the American voter*. Philadelphia, PA: Lippincott & Crowell.

Stam, R. (1983) Television news and its spectator. In E. A. Kaplan (Ed.) *Regarding television* (pp. 23–43). Greenwood Press.

U.S. News and World Report. (1988, Sept. 12). The handlers take over, p. 14.

Wattenberg, B. (1984). *The good news is the bad news is wrong*. New York: Simon and Schuster.

IV

Regulating Signs and Images

13

Symbolic Speech in Political Advertising: Encroaching Legal Barriers

Jef I. Richards
University of Texas at Austin

Clarke L. Caywood
Northwestern University

INTRODUCTION

Law may seem unrelated to semiotics and political advertising. As fields of study, law and semiotics appear to be separated by a chasm of intellectual origin. However, Kevelson (1977, 1986) has written extensively about "legal semiotics," revealing the underlying semiotic nature of legal decisions and policies. This chapter takes a somewhat different approach to integrating these fields, by showing how semiotic analysis can be applied to assist legal policy-making, especially in the regulation of speech. This chapter uses political advertising as a volatile platform to illustrate that application. Although semiotic analyses could certainly contribute to legal understandings of many aspects of political advertising, visual or verbal, our discussion focuses primarily on the visual and structural features of these ads.

Although judges and many legislators have legal training and are adept at gleaning the ambiguities and multiple meanings inherent in words, they are inexperienced at dealing with nonverbal communications, as represented in legal decisions dealing with pictorial expressions (Richards, 1986; Richards & Zakia, 1981). Although there are instances where the law has acknowledged a citizen's right to communicate without words, such as burning a draft card (United States v. O'Brien, 1968) or a flag (Texas v. Johnson, 1989) in protest, courts have found it difficult deciding how to handle most instances of nonverbal expression. For example, where a detailed semiotic analysis of pictures (or even cuts, sweeps, zooms, and timing) in a political commercial might unearth iconic, indexic, or symbolic meaning, the legal system historically has interpreted verbal content only (Richards, 1986; Richards & Zakia, 1981).

Despite First Amendment protection of political advertising, legislative measures have been proposed to regulate the format or structure of political advertising (Laczniak & Caywood, 1987; National Association of Broadcasters 1989). Should these proposals be acted upon, the legal system's unfamiliarity with nonverbal meaning attribution may result in an unintentional jeopardizing and narrowing of free speech rights during a political campaign (Caywood, 1985; Caywood & Preston, in press). Through a careful semiotic analysis, it may be possible to educate lawmakers and interpreters to protect political speeches from a novel form of infringement.

Just as lawmakers seldom hold any expertise in semiotics, it is likely that few semioticians have significant knowledge of the practice of law. The material that follows provides some rudimentary understanding of law as it applies to political advertising. It outlines the proposals made, to date, to regulate political ad structure and content. It also explains the legal theory supporting the proposals and shows how semiotics might be used to reinterpret those proposals as unintentionally jeopardizing free speech.

THE PROBLEMS IN POLITICAL ADVERTISING

Prevalence of Negative Campaigning

National and regional elections during the 1980s attracted a great deal of public and popular media attention. However, the attention was directed as much (or more) to candidates' advertising as to their qualifications or positions on the issues (Boot, 1989; Fialka, 1986; Goldsborough, 1984; Grady, 1988; Murphy & Zeppos, 1987; Reston, 1983; Taylor, 1985; Tolchin, 1984). It was not the high quality of the ads, their entertainment value, or even the huge expenditures consumed in the promotional process that attracted the lion's share of this attention. Rather, the preeminent topic in the 1980s was the muckraking character of many political ads, the so-called *negative advertising* (Caywood, 1989; Cohen, 1989; Colford, 1986, 1988; Dionne, 1988a; Homan, 1987; Horton & Chase, 1988; Laczniak & Caywood, 1987; Merritt, 1984; Rosenstiel, 1988; Rosenthal, 1988; Will, 1986, 1988).

Negative or "attack" campaigning is nothing new to American politics. Even our earliest and most revered statesmen were subjected to smear campaigns. It was alleged, for instance, that George Washington was an unfit leader because of latent monarchical aspirations (Winsbro, 1987). Thomas Jefferson stood accused of everything from keeping a slave mistress to defrauding a widow and her children (Neel, 1985). Abraham Lincoln was labeled everything from a fiend, to a robber, to a traitor (Winsbro, 1987). And these attacks are not confined to presidential campaigns. They have included congressional candidates (Winsbro, 1987) and probably every other office, including dog-catcher (Cohen, 1989). Such attacks have even been published anonymously (Commonwealth v. Acquaviva, 1959).

The recent flurry of negative advertising has raised the ire of voters (Dionne, 1988a), candidates (Rosenthal, 1988), and even the advertising industry (Altschiller, 1988; Horton & Chase, 1988; Matthews, 1984). A consensus has developed that these reputation-bashing ploys have gotten out of hand and need to be tempered. Because voluntary temperance has not come to the fore, a succession of congressional bills proposing legal solutions is inevitable (Caywood, 1989; Caywood & Preston, in press).

Reliance on Image over Substance

A related concern is the growing reliance by candidates on "image" appeals (Lustig, 1986). Image advertising promotes the candidate's good looks, family orientation, and other emotional qualities in lieu of addressing campaign issues. Shyles, (1986) uniquely differentiated between image as a "graphic representation" or as "candidate's character." In the former he credited Wychoff for defining image as "clearly linked to selected methods of presentation used by the candidate's production team" (p. 113). For example, ads project an image if they use "still pictures, fast cutting and music" versus "straight-talk-to-the-camera-formats" (p. 113). More traditionally, image is used by most authors to refer to the character traits of the candidate (Cundy, 1986; Shyles, 1986).

In Gore Vidal's "The Best Man," Henry Fonda (as Secretary of State) made a comment that is revealing in the present context. "I'm afraid I don't know much about images," he said. "That's a word from advertising where you don't sell the product, you sell the image of the product. And sometimes the image is a fake" (Houghton, 1987). Critics claim that politicians and their political communications advisors, or "handlers," have chosen form over substance, in an arena where substance proscriptively should be the only consideration of the audience (Ailes, 1988; Dionne, 1988b; Reston, 1983).

Laczniak & Caywood (1987) attribute this pervasive use of imagery to a concomitant dependence on television as the political medium of choice. Oreskes (1988) notes that in the last presidential campaign the "managers are children of the television age . . . who hold the attitude that television is the central fact of political life" (p. 1). Winsbro (1987), apparently agreeing that television is a major culprit, reflects the dominant concern of many critics:

> The problem with television advertising seems not so much to lie with misrepresentation and distortions respecting factual matters, as with its general lack of content and its inherent manipulativeness. Of course . . . campaign speech has never been distinguished for its intellectual cogency or analytic rigor. But, even granting that much political rhetoric is relatively meaningless anyway, the fact remains that television ads that rely primarily on imagery and 'mood advertising' have a unique potential for being *absolutely* uninformative. (p. 909)

In addition to being generally uninformative about campaign issues, image appeals have been integrated effectively into negative advertising. Reflecting on the 1988 Bush-Dukakis campaigns, one commentator argued:

> The images are scary: prisoners marching in slow motion, polluted water, an empty Oval office, the fragility of human life implied by the sound of a beating heart.

> And the message—in a new round of ads and on the stump in the presidential race—is turning from what many already bemoaned as negative to threatening and frankly nasty. (Rosenstiel, 1988, p. A4)

Given this confluence of imagery and negativity, and the general distaste held for each, it is likely that both will be subject of future regulatory proposals. In fact, as we discuss later, recent attempts to control political advertising have been directed at both. Before addressing those proposals, however, we will review the laws that presently impinge on political promotions.

REGULATING POLITICAL ADVERTISING

Federal Regulation

Before describing proposed regulatory options for political advertising, it is valuable to understand what laws already exist to limit campaign advertising. Although some restrictions exist at both the state and federal levels, it is clear that for the moment that they present few barriers to current political ad tactics.

Only a handful of national laws have been enacted that directly affect political advertising. Some have attempted to expand, rather than contract, the rights of politicians. One of the laws initially designed to improve speech is the "equal access" law, requiring that broadcasters who provide station time to one candidate must also provide equal opportunities to all other candidates for that office (FCC Act 1989, Sect. a). In the name of more speech, limits are also placed on the prices broadcast stations (FCC Act 1989, Sect. b) and print media (FECA 1985, Sect. b) can charge for political advertising. The purpose of these laws is to ensure all candidates for an office have equivalent access to the mechanisms of free speech, so that none are given unfair advantage over others. In the short run, at least, these laws do not serve as impediments to negative advertising, but rather facilitate it. They have, however, whetted the appetite of election reformers for changing campaign dynamics—especially with regard to communications.

Even the Supreme Court has recognized the importance of media-based communications—and the money necessary to purchase media time—in a political election:

> A restriction on the amount of money a person or group can spend on political communication during a campaign necessarily reduces the quality of expression by restricting the number of issues discussed, the depth of their exploration, and the size of the audience reached. . . . The electorate's increasing dependence on television, radio, and other mas media for news and information has made these expensive modes of communication indispensible instruments of effective political speech. (Buckley v. Valeo, 1976, p. 635)

Thus, the Court decried campaign expediture limits as "direct and substantial restraints on the quality of political speech" (Buckley v. Valeo, 1976, p. 644).

Congress did attempt to viscerate corruption and appearance of corruption in political campaigns by enacting the Federal Election Campaign Act of 1971 (FECA 1985, as amended). This law requires anyone paying for a political ad to place their name on the ad and to disclose whether or not the ad has been authorized by a candidate (FECA 1985, Sect. 441d[a]). Also, it declares that political ad expenditures exceeding $250 be reported to the Federal Election Commission (FECA 1985, Sect. 434[c]). This provision may minimally restrict negative advertising by requiring advertisers to admit their participation. It can be assumed that laws prohibiting anonymous political messages limit the freedom of those who might attack a candidate. However, given our moral and legal tradition of "the right to confront our accuser," such statutes are seldom challenged as abridgments of free speech despite some restrictive contemporary efforts reported below.

State Regulation

States also exercise some authority over federal campaigns within their boundaries, so long as they do not conflict with federal laws (Friends of Phil Gramm, 1984, p. 776), and have complete authority to regulate state and local campaigns. Table 13.1 provides a state-by-state summary of the laws affecting political advertising in each. It can be seen that many states have laws similar to those applied to federal elections. For example, most states prohibit publishing the ads anonymously, and 12 states have statutes forbidding owners of the advertising medium from charging excess rates for political ads (though Kentucky expressly *permits* that practice). Many states, however, have specific requirements not existing at the federal level, such as stipulating that the ads bear captions like "Paid Advertisement" (Alabama) or "Paid Political Advertisement" (California, Florida), or some longer disclosure (Indiana). Several states prohibit either false or deceptive statements in the ads (California, Minnesota, Ohio, Oregon). However, none of these state laws appears to directly address the more current phenomenon of negative advertising.

California laws actually specify the font and size of type used for identifying the ad source. Restricting the use of certain symbols, Kentucky forbids the use of the American flag in ads. The state of Washington requires candidate photos to be current, within five years, and Oklahoma prohibits some state officials from offering endorsements. Although not common, these laws are indicative of legislative thinking about the power of nonverbal, and to a lesser degree verbal, communications.

Another legal intrusion on political advertising at the state level, although generally not a statute, is the law of libel. Where political candidates are defamed by statements published during a campaign, it is possible for them to win a private suit against the party who published the statement(s) (Albert, 1986). However, such cases are difficult to win because candidates are "public figures" (Monitor Patriot Co. v. Roy, 1971, p. 271) and must prove the libel was done with knowledge of, or reckless disregard for, its falsity (New York Times v. Sullivan, 1964). Perhaps more important to the public interest is the fact that by the time the maligned candidate prevails in court, the election is typically a historical fact (Winsbro, 1987).

Table 13.1 State Statutes Regulating Political Advertising

State	Statute	Subject	Explanation
Alabama	17-22-13	Anonymity	• "Bear name of committee."
	17-22-14		• "Political ads in newspapers shall say 'Paid Advertisement.' "
	37-1-140	Rates	• Political advertising is not operating expense and cannot be considered when setting rates.
Alaska	15.13.090	Anonymity	• Include sponsor name.
	15.56.010	Anonymity	• Include disclosure "paid for by" within advertisement.
	Same	Falsity	• Prohibits knowingly circulating false information that would provoke a reasonable person to alter attitudes toward a candidate.
Arizona			
Arkansas	7-1-103	Anonymity	• Include sponsor name.
	23-4-207	Rates	• Media rates limited.
California	Elec. Code 11701		• The voting public is entitled to the same protection from deception as form advertisers of commercial products.
	Elec. Code 11708		• Political ads in newspapers shall bear "in 10-point roman type" the words "Paid Political Advertisement."
	Elec. Code 11709		• Simulated ballots shall not bear official seal or insignia of any public entity.
	Gov. Code 15355.7		• Funds targeted for industrial marketing programs cannot be used for political advertising.
	Pub. Util. Code 453	Rates	• Media rates limited.
	Veh. Code 1656.5	Medium	• No political ads in driver's handbook.
Colorado	1-13-108	Anonymity	• Include sponsor name.
	1-13-119	Falsity	• False statements prohibited.
Connecticut	Gen. 9-236	Location	• Regulates advertising near polling place.
	Gen. 9-333w	Anonymity	• Include sponsor name.
Delaware	Gen. 8005	Anonymity	• Include sponsor name.

(continued)

Table 13.1 *(Continued)*

State	Statute	Subject	Explanation
Florida	Gen. 229.805	Medium	• No use of educational TV to directly or indirectly promote candidates.
	103.081	Association	• Protects use of party name/symbol.
	106.143	Anonymity	• Ads shall be marked ''Paid Political Advertisement'' and include name of party.
	106.16	Rates	• Equal ad rates for all candidates.
Georgia	None		
Hawaii	11-215	Anonymity	• Name of sponsor.
Idaho	67-6614A	Anonymity	• Include sponsor name.
Illinois	C. 46, P. 9-9	Disclosure	• Political communications on fund-raising materials must include required statement.
	C. 46, P. 29-14	Anonymity	• Include sponsor name.
	C. 111 2/3, P. 9-112.3	Medium	• No ads on highway shelters.
	C. 111 2/3, P. 9-225.3	Rates	• Media rates limited.
Indiana	3-9-3-2	Anonymity	• Specific disclosure required, regarding sponsorship and authorization.
	8-1-2-6	Rates	• Media rates limited.
Iowa	56.14	Anonymity	• Include sponsor name.
Kansas	Gen. 14-2-11	Location	• No political ads on liquor stores or in bars.
	Gen. 21-3739	Medium	• Cannot stick ads on utility poles.
	Gen. 25-2407	Anonymity	• Any paid matter in a newspaper or periodical must be followed by ''Advertisement'' or ''Adv.'' and the name of the sponsor.
	Gen. 25-4156	Rates	• Media rates limited.
	Gen. 25-2407	Anonymity	• Statute broader than most
Kentucky	2.060	Contents	• United States flag not to be used in ads.
	121.065	Rates	• Media *can* charge excess rates for political ads.
	121.190	Anonymity	• Include sponsor name.
Louisiana	18:1334	Location	• No ads in nursing homes.
	18:1462	Location	• No ads in polling place.
	18:1464	Rates	• Media rates limited.
Maine	21-1394	Anonymity	• Clear and conspicuous statement of authorization (or not) by candidate, with name and address of sponsor.

(continued)

Table 13.1 *(Continued)*

State	Statute	Subject	Explanation
Maryland	Art. 33, 26-9	Anonymity	• Include sponsor name.
	Art. 33, 26-17	Rates	• Media rates limited.
Massachusetts	56-39	Anonymity	• *Signature* of sponsor required.
	56-42	Disclosure	• The word "advertisement" must appear on the ad in print no smaller than the type of the text.
	56-43	Content	• Limits on use of thw word "veteran" in ads.
Michigan	169.247	Anonymity	• Include sponsor name. Secretary of State has power to specify size and location of sponsor's name.
Minnesota	10A.17	Disclosure	• Ads placed independent of candidate must state that they were not approved by candidate.
	211B.05	Anonymity	• Include sponsor name.
	211B.05	Rates	• Media rates limited.
	211B.06	Falsity	• Makes it a misdemeanor to intentionally publish false information in political ads.
	256B.47	Payment	• Cannot include cost of political ads into nursing home rates.
Mississippi	23-3-37	Special	• Candidates must approve *all* advertising.
	23-3-39	Exception	• Newspaper editorials and newsmatter need not be approved by the candidate.
Missouri	115.637.05	Anonymity	• Include sponsor name.
Montana	13-35-225	Anonymity	• Include sponsor name, clearly and conspicuously.
	13-35-233	Time	• No ads on election day.
Nebraska	49-1474.9	Anonymity	• Include sponsor name. State commission given power to specify size and placement of name.
Nevada	294.050	Media	• Media agencies keep copies of ads for 30 days after election.
New Hampshire		Anonymity	• Must be signed by sponsor, with print large enough to be "clearly legible." TV and radio ads must also identify sponsor, but bumperstickers and buttons are exempt.

(continued)

Table 13.1 *(Continued)*

State	Statute	Subject	Explanation
			• Political ads must be marked as such, in print media.
New Jersey	1934.38.1	Anonymity	• Include sponsor name, but only in printed matter.
New Mexico	1-19-16	Anonymity	• Include sponsor name.
New York	None		
North Carolina	163.278.16	Anonymity	• Does not apply to print ads smaller than 2 × 2 inches or to radio/TV ads less than 20 seconds.
	163-278.18	Rates	• Media rates limited.
North Dakota	16.1-10-04	Falsity	• Deliberately calculated falsehoods prohibited.
	16.1-10-04.1	Anonymity	• Include sponsor name on printed matter only.
Ohio	3517.13	Rates	• Media rates limited.
	3599.09	Anonymity	• Include sponsor name.
	3599.091	Falsity	• False statements prohibited.
Oklahoma	4242	Endorsing	• Employees of Oklahoma Bureau of Investigation or Bureau of Narcotics cannot endorse candidates.
Oregon	254.205	Content	• No political ads on same page as simulated or facsimile ballot.
	260.522	Anonymity	• Include sponsor name.
	260.532	Falsity	• False statements prohibited.
	260.542	Content	• Restrictions on use of term "reelect" in ads.
Pennsylvania	25-325	Anonymity	• *Paid* ads must disclose sponsor and authorization.
	same	Timing	• Restrictions on *when* ads can run.
Rhode Island	17-23-1	Anonymity	• Include sponsor name.
	17-23-2	Anonymity	• Also applies to posters, fliers, and circulars.
	17-23-14	Rates	• Media rates limited.
South Carolina	7-25-180	Anonymity	• Include sponsor name.
South Dakota	12-25-4.1	Anonymity	• Include sponsor name.
	12-25-5	Disclosure	• Political ads must be labeled as such.
Tennessee	2-19-120	Anonymity	• Include sponsor name, *except on communications with one face,* i.e., billboards.
	2-19-206	Location	• No use of state property.
Texas	Elec. Code 255-001	Anonymity	• Include sponsor name.
	Elec. Code 255-002	Rates	• Must charge lowest rates.

(continued)

Table 13.1 *(Continued)*

State	Statute	Subject	Explanation
Utah	20-14-27	Anonymity	• Include sponsor name, in *paid* ads.
	20-14-28	Falsity	• Prohibits knowlingly making a false statement regarding a candidate.
Vermont	None		
Virginia	24.1-277	Anonymity	• Include sponsor name.
Washington	42.17.510	Anonymity	• Include sponsor name.
	42.17.520	Content	• If ad contains picture(s) of candidate, at least one shall have been taken in the past five years, and it shall be the largest picture.
	65.16.095	Rates	• Media rates limited.
West Virginia	59-3-6	Rates	• Media rates limited.
Wisconsin	11.30	Anonymity	• Include sponsor name.
Wyoming	22-25-110	Anonymity	• Include sponsor name.
	22-25-112	Rates	• Media rates limited.

Libel law does little to dissuade either negative or questionable image ad appeals *during* the campaign, even those that include knowingly false statements. Although the threat of losing a libel suit at some later date might discourage some false statements, it is very difficult for candidates to win such cases (e.g., Manasco v. Walley, 1953; Monitor Patriot Co. v. Roy, 1971). For example, in a particularly bitter 1986 U.S. Senate race in Wisconsin the Democrat challenger, Ed Garvey, filed a libel suit against the incumbent, Bob Kasten (Lieffers, 1986). The suit was later settled out of court, with sealed documents. The outcome of the suit seemed to favor Garvey, but the election was lost. In one analysis prior to settlement of the case, it was noted:

> The Garvey case could be labeled a classic libel lawsuit with a new twist: The media is not a defendant. According to James Doyle, Garvey's attorney, the question the suit poses is: "Should those people who are producing a political ad be required to make some kind of check on the facts?" (Lieffers, 1986, p. 13)

Even if libel law were to act as a major impediment to libelous remarks, it does not affect negative or image appeals that are *not* false. And, for those few that are false, the use of image appeals that rely on subtle innuendo and symbols rather than explicit declarations can make it much more difficult to prove that any false statement was even *made* by the advertiser.

Existing state and federal laws do little to directly control either negative or image advertising. As a consequence, over the past five years, proposals have been offered to give the not-so-long arm of the law a grip on these disliked practices.

PROPOSALS FOR REFORM

Laczniak and Caywood (1987) addressed the perceived problems of negativity and imagery, as well as the broader concern of ethically dubious practices in political television advertising and the resultant alienation of voters (see also Caywood & Laczniak, 1985). Their research identified eight different public policy options to reform broadcast advertising in political campaigns. Those options are summarized in Table 13.2.

From a semiotic perspective, one of the most interesting of these options is regulating the style (i.e., format) of the advertisements (Option B). This could take the form of mandating the sequence of material presented, the tone and manner of the announcer, whether it is presented in color or black-and-white, controlling the modality of the presentation, or a plethora of other specific requirements not directly related to the *explicit verbal message*. One variation of this approach was supported by Winsbro (1987): "Political ads *could,* as in France, be restricted to a straightforward, 'talking head' format, where the candidate herself or an individual supporter addresses voters directly, unaccompanied by any form of special effects" (p. 912).

In 1984 this method of regulation was advanced at the national level by Senators Rudman and Inouye and Congressmen Conable and McHugh in sister bills submitted to both Houses of Congress. The so-called "Fairness in Political Advertising Bills," in salient part, would have dictated:

Sec. 324.(a) No person may make any expenditure for the broadcast of any televised paid political advertisement, unless such advertisement meets the following requirements:

(1) The advertisement may not contain any visual or auditory material other than—

(A) the voice and image of the candidate or alternative speaker speaking into the camera for the duration of the advertisement. . . .

(4) The background or backdrop for any such advertisement—

(A) shall be filmed, televised, or taped at the same time and with the same camera as that filming, televising, or taping the candidate or

Table 13.2 Public Policy Options for Political Television Advertising Reform

Option	Description	Advantage
A: Federally Funded Broadcast Advertising Model	A public fund would underwrite broadcast ads for campaigns, and would stipulate that no other money be spent for broadcast ads.	This would alleviate influence of political action committees, and equalize the amount spent by each candidate.
B: Regulate Advertising Style Model	Style or form of political TV ads would be regulated, without restricting the "content."	This could be used to eliminate use of imagery in the ads, by requiring "talking head" or "tombstone" type ad format.
C: "Time equals Substance" Model	Would require political TV commercials to be a minimum of 120 seconds in length.	It would be difficult to sustain an image, emotional, or nonfactual appeal or an unsubstantiated attack on one's opponent for that length of time.
D: National Political Advertixing Review Board Model	A *voluntary* regulatory group would be established to screen political ads for general ethical propriety.	Unfair, unethical, misleading, or deceptive ads would not be permitted for broadcast.
E: Lincoln-Douglas Model	Each candidate would be required to purchase commercial time in 90-second blocks, using the first 60 seconds for their message and the last 30 seconds would be given to their opponent for rebuttal.	Promotes political debate, and use of imagery or negative smears could be addressed by the opponent immediately.
F: United Kingdom Model	Strict limits imposed on amount of TV political advertising each candidate could purchase.	Would force candidates to make better use of ad time, because of it being so limited.
G: Brazilian Model	Strict limits imposed on amount of TV political advertising each party could purchase, as above but more severe.	Same as above.
H: Australian Model	Would require a 72-hour cooling-off period prior to voting, during which time no ads would be allowed.	Avoids last-minute negative advertising, which gives opponent insufficient time to broadcast a rebuttal. Also, less opportunity to sway voters' emotions at last minute with image ads.

> alternative speaker, and
> (B) must be the filming, taping, or televising of an actual scene or an
> actual event at the time of such scene or event, and may not include
> any staged production of any event or scene.
> (Fairness in Political Advertising Bills, 1984)

The apparent rationale behind these bills was that television advertising, as the primary mode of political campaigning, obscures rather than provides full, fair, and rational debate on the merits of the issues and candidates. Such ads are believed to have contributed to declining political involvement of the public. More specifically, the bills state that "television advertising is unique in its effect and emotive content, being virtually unanswerable and less susceptible to the usual constitutional remedy of more, or more diversified speech" (Fairness in Political Advertising Bills, 1984). It should be noted that this same logic has been proffered for proposals to limit nonverbal aspects of attorney advertising (In re Felmeister & Isaacs, 1986).

The mention of "emotive content" reveals an explicit concern with image appeals. A similar bill was proposed in 1987 by the late Representative Claude Pepper of Florida. Acknowledging a concern over negative appeals, Pepper's legislative assistant, Dave Erlich, justified such a measure, stating, "There have been more and more instances of candidates running slur campaigns against their opponents without attribution" (Homan, 1987 p. 55). It should be noted that the "opponents" referred to by Erlich are usually challenging incumbents, who return to Congress 98 percent of the time.

Importantly, none of these bills has ever been enacted as law. However, they indicate an ongoing and persistent consideration of controlling political ad format in lieu of regulating "content," in the traditional (verbal) sense.

CONTENT-BASED RESTRICTIONS

A Hierarchy of "Free" Speech

Although the first amendment of the U.S. Constitution guarantees "Congress shall make no law . . . abriding the freedom of speech, or of the press," the courts have managed to interpret the words *abriding* and *speech* to admit to several exceptions. The exceptions, which include libelous remarks (New York Times v. Sullivan, 1964), "fighting words" (Hess v. Indiana, 1973), limits on the time, place, and manner of the speech (Walker v. City of Birmingham, 1967), and obscenity (Miller

v. California, 1973), for many years also included advertising (Richards & Zakia, 1981). If Congress found a particular type of ad offensive, there was little to stop it from barring or otherwise regulating such ads.

The status of advertising changed in 1976, with the U.S. Supreme Court's pronouncement that advertising, in fact, was protected under the first amendment (Virginia Board of Pharmacy, 1976). However, unlike most other types of speech, advertising has been declared to reside lower in a hierarchy of protected expression (Central Hudson Gas, 1980). Because the purpose of advertising is to promote a mere marketplace transaction, the Court considers there to be a "common-sense distinction" between advertising and other forms of speech (Central Hudson Gas, 1980), making it somehow less desirable in our set of social values. Consequently, some restrictions are permitted on advertising that would be considered abhorrent if applied to truly valuable speech (Richards, 1987).

Some scholars are concerned that giving First Amendment protection to commercial ads will weaken the protection of more traditional political speech (Baldesty & Simpson, 1982; Shaw, Hurd, & Bader, 1984). Alderman (1982) stated, "The present practice of narrowly defining commercial speech will cause a dilution of traditional first amendment values" (p. 760).

While advertising resides on the bottom rung of this constitutional hierarchy of valued expression, political speech sits at the top (Buckley v. Valeo, 1976; Monitor Patriot Co. v. Roy, 1971). The Supreme Court, in *Mills v. Alabama* (1966), reflected that view:

> Whatever differences may exist about interpretations of the First Amendment, there is practically universal agreement that a major purpose of that Amendment was to protect the free discussion of governmental affairs. This of course includes discussions of candidates, structures and forms of government, the manner in which government is operated or should be operated, and all such matters relating to political processes. (pp. 218–219)

Stated another way, "speech concerning public affairs is more than self-expression; it is the essence of self-government" (Garrison v. Louisiana, 1964, pp. 74–75).

The reason behind this preferential protection of politically related speech is the philosophy that only by permitting the freedom to fully support or criticize every aspect of our government can we hope to achieve a form of government that truly represents the desires of the populace. As John Stuart Mill (1859) argued, only by allowing every view to be expressed, no matter how unpopular, can we ever hope to approach the truth. To this end the Supreme Court has recognized:

The constitutional right of free expression is powerful medicine in a society as diverse and populous as ours. It is designed and intended to remove governmental restraints from the arena of public discussion, putting the decision as to what views shall be voiced largely into the hands of each of us, in the hope that use of such freedom will ultimately produce a more capable citizenry and more perfect polity and in the belief that no other approach would comport with the premise of individual dignity and choice upon which our political system rests. (Cohen v. California, 1971, p. 24)

A few constitutional law scholars have gone so far as to suggest that the First Amendment protects *only* political speech (Bork, 1971; Meiklejohn, 1948). There is a strong presumption under the law that political speech is protected by the Constitution, making it very difficult for a legislature to adopt any law that interferes with that speech.

Is It Political Speech, or Advertising?

Clearly, political advertising is protected by the First Amendment. But is it *advertising* or is it *political speech?* If the former, it gets much less protection than the latter. The protections afforded advertising fall under the "commercial speech" doctrine (Virginia Board of Pharmacy, 1976). That term is used, instead of *advertising,* because the Supreme Court has distinguished between ads that have a commercial function and those that do not (*New York Times,* 1964).

What this means, in the present context, is that political advertising is protected to the same extent as other political speech. At least one federal court has specifically noted that distinction (Friends of Phil Gramm, 1984). Consequently, former ad industry spokesman John O'Toole (1988) is ostensibly accurate in stating, "The public's outrage over the tactics and techniques of political messages—a biennial occurrence—stems from its belief that those messages are advertising [which they aren't] and that they're constrained by the same rules as advertising [which they aren't]" (p. 17).

It is very difficult to impose restrictions on political ads that will pass constitutional muster. Even industry-inspired *self*-regulatory efforts have been aborted. The American Association of Advertising Agencies (4A's), the leading advertising trade association, gave up an attempt to use its powers to review ads—after its members were sued (Matthews, 1984).

Limits on Political Speech

Although political speech deserves the fullest protection of the First Amendment, this does not translate to *no* permissible regulations. The courts have recognized that the government has some interests that are so compelling as to justify a minimal inconvenience on speakers. Indeed, although relatively few of the state regulations listed in Table 13.1 have been tested before the Supreme Court, it is likely that many or most of them would be allowed under the Constitution. For example, one of the more popular restrictions forbids use of false statements in political ads. Supreme Court decisions suggest these limitations are allowed, to serve the government's interest in an informed electorate, so long as the only statements prohibited are those made with knowledge or reckless disregard of their falsity (Garrison v. Louisiana, 1964; Monitor Patriot Co. v. Roy, 1971). This does not, however, give states license to regulate *deceptive* statements in political ads.

This distinction between false and deceptive is an important one. Falsity is objective, whereas deceptiveness is subjective (Preston, 1975). Peirce's model of semiosis (Mick, 1986) is instructive on this point. The term *falsity* results from the object-sign relationship, whereas *deceptiveness* refers to the object-interpretant relationship. Because deceptiveness thus entails both object-sign and sign-interpretant associations, it can arise from *either,* and occur even where there is no falsity (Preston & Richards, 1986). Therefore, laws prohibiting deceptiveness tend to infringe on speech more than those directed at falsity. Although advertising (commercial speech) can be regulated for deceptiveness, because of its lesser constitutional status (Central Hudson Gas, 1980), political advertising can only be restricted for *falsity,* and then only when the statement is made with *knowledge of (or reckless disregard for) that falsity.* For example, in an untried case on negative political ads, the attorney for Senatorial Candidate Ed Garvey noted, ''It's our position that you are protected by the libel laws, that you can't knowingly tell lies against people'' (Lieffers, 1986, p. 13).

The prevalent view, however, is that courts and legislatures have no legitimate role in policing campaign speeches for falsity (Winsbro 1987), so some courts may refuse even to enforce a prohibition of falsity in the political arena (e.g., Rudisill v. Flynn, 1980). If the deceptiveness standard could be applied to political ads, much of the negative and image appeals might be regulated. This is a critical difference between political and commercial advertisements.

Whether we are discussing speech at the top or the bottom of the constitutional hierarchy, there are two basic categories of regulation: antispeech and nonspeech (Nimmer, 1973). An antispeech restriction attempts to protect some governmental interest (e.g., higher voter turnout at the polls) by suppressing speech *content,* that is, the ideas conveyed by the speech. Nonspeech restrictions attempt to protect the interest by controlling where, when, or how the speech is made, without regard for its content. Prohibitions on deceptiveness or falsity are examples of antispeech regulations, because they directly affect the content of the message.

Although there are exceptions, such as in cases of deceptiveness or falsity, antispeech restrictions are presumptively unconstitutional[1] (Minneapolis Star & Tribune, 1983). Any other policy would enable public officials to ban all ideas with which they disagree. Therefore, it has been very difficult for the government to justify regulating speech directed at controlling its content (Greer v. Spock, 1976). The law recognizes that this is especially important for political speech, because of our "profound national commitment to the principle that debate on public issues should be uninhibited, robust and wide-open" (*New York Times* v. Sullivan, 1964, p. 270). However, the courts permit much more latitude when the regulation is aimed at *commercial* speech content (Central Hudson, 1980).

NON-SPEECH REGULATION—OVERVIEW

Nonspeech regulations, on the other hand, are much easier to justify (US v. O'Brien, 1968). This is because the purpose of such restriction is not to suppress one idea in favor of others, that is, the government's interest is "unrelated to the suppression of free expression" (p. 377). Unlike antispeech, nonspeech restrictions are presumptively valid. Restrictions on the "time, place, or manner" of speech are generally considered by the courts to be nonspeech regulations (Consolidated Edison Co., 1980). For example, it is permissible for the government to prohibit use of billboards in certain locations because "the government has legitimate interests in controlling the noncommunicative aspects of the medium" (Metromedia v. City of San Diego, 1981, p. 502).

The transparent intent behind the various format restrictions proposed for political advertising is to adopt a constitutionally permissible nonspeech, or "manner," regulation. It is claimed that a designation of typesize, layout, or restriction on pictorial aspects of the ads would apply equally to all politicians without inhibiting what they "say." Proponents of these regulations are attempting to proffer restrictions that do not significantly affect content, and are therefore presumptively valid. However, if semiotic-based research were to show these restric-

---

[1]"Presumptively unconstitutional" means that the court starts with the assumption that the regulation is unconstitutional, and the government entity wanting to impose the restriction must provide enough evidence to convince the court it should be considered constitutional.

tions to have a substantial impact on a politician's message content, they would be presumed invalid under the Constitution.

Format as Content

It would be perverse for advocates of format restrictions to argue that photographs or illustrations have no communicative powers. Even the earliest civilizations knew of, and used, those powers. The fact that they remain in abundant use in journalism, public relations, and advertising— the communication professions—attests to their ability to convey meaning. In fact, the Supreme Court in *Zauderer v. Office of Disciplinary Counsel* (1985) recently agreed that pictures and illustrations, even in commercial advertising, deserve protection of the first amendment. In *Zauderer,* the State of Ohio prohibited use of illustrations in attorney advertising. One lawyer, nonetheless, used an ad illustrating a Dalkon Shield Intrauterine Device to solicit clients for law suits against the manufacturer. The Court determined that the blanket prohibition of illustrations violated the attorney's rights, noting:

> The use of illustrations or pictures in advertisements serves important communicative functions: it attracts the attention of the audience to the advertiser's message, and it may also serve to impart information directly. Accordingly, commercial illustrations are entitled to the First Amendment protections afforded verbal commercial speech. (p. 647)

The more likely argument by political ad critics is that anything a politician can say in pictures can be said in words. One proponent of "talking-head" type restrictions argued, "Certainly a format restriction on television ads would not suppress 'ideas' in any conventional sense: a candidate could *always* make his point verbally" (Winsbro, 1987, p. 914). Taking this position, it would be arguable that only the manner of speech, not its content, is affected. This, however, assumes either that pictures are denotation without connotation, permitting substitution of another denotational system, or that the connotational impact can be given equal force with words.

The Semiotic Perspective

Barthes (1977) addressed that first assumption, reflecting that a news photograph is denotation without connotation, a message without a code. But, he went on to recognize that this is true only at one level of analysis, and that the photo actually fills a dual role wherein it also lends to connotation: "Connotation, the imposition of second meaning on the photographic message proper, is realized at the different levels of production of the photograph (choice, technical treatment, framing, layout) and represents, finally, a coding of the photographic analogue" (p. 20). Every aspect of a picture, including where it appears in an ad, can connote meaning to the viewer (Williamson, 1978).

That words can connote meaning equivalent to that provided by pictures is an equally weak assumption. Zakia (1987) asserted, "Picture and text each serve a definite purpose and together they provide a gestalt—an alphapictorial statement that is stronger and richer than either alone" (p. 7). Visual and verbal signs have separate functions and are not wholly interchangeable. Indeed, it is arguable that no two signs are interchangeable, even within the same modality.

The reason for this is twofold: (a) most signs are arbitrary, created in an artificial manner by unilateral decision (Barthes, 1968), and (b) each sign can have multiple functions and serve as the expression of several contents (Eco, 1979). Even if the multiple functions of a sign are connotatively linked (e.g., a political ad with an atomic mushroom cloud may mean "War threatens all life" *and* "I should not vote for a candidate who would push the nuclear button"), each sign has a relatively fixed set of meanings. Each element of that set may be represented in a segment of the target audience. And, the arbitrary nature of signs makes it probabilistically unlikely that any other sign would evoke precisely the same meaning for each of those viewers. Although the sets of meanings might overlap, in very few cases would it be an identity. Between visual and verbal signs, the complexity and detail of a typical picture would lead us to expect a much broader set of meanings, too large to be equalled by any manageable verbal sign: a picture is worth a thousand (or more) words (Eco, 1979). This suggests it is impossible, in most instances, for words to equal the connotative effects of a picture.

Regulatory proponents might argue that, of the total set of meanings generated by a picture, only a specific subset is intended by the advertising politician, and that small subset *can* be conveyed by a verbal sign. This, too, is a deficient argument. A politician is constitutionally entitled to convey the meanings he or she chooses, whether or not some of those meanings are intended. The politician is entitled, literally or figuratively, to stick a foot in his or her mouth. If the government was permitted to confine speakers to *only* their intended meanings, the First Amendment would be rendered meaningless. There is some quantity of ineradicable miscomprehension inherent in all communication (Preston & Richards, 1988), so any message could be regulated under such logic.

Winsbro (1987), favoring "talking head" or other format restrictions on political ads, argued:

[T]he candidate who airs pictures of the statute [sic.] of liberty, of gurgling brooks and May weddings, all to the accompaniment of sonorous symphonic music, is not seeking to provide the electorate with additional, pertinent information. He is not trying to "make a point" at all. On the contrary, he is doing no more than inviting the home audience to attach certain pleasing associations to his candidacy, in the same manner that other commercials hint of the high jinks and good times that are somehow ineluctably associated with the consumption of, e.g., beer and soft drinks. The "special effects" in political ads typically do not serve to amplify or to expand upon a point already made, but rather to evade the requirements of rational argumentation altogether. (p. 915)

The behavioral response elicited by some meanings is a level of emotionality. Frequently an emotional response results from a unique *set* of meanings, through an interaction of those meanings. If we cannot replicate precisely the same set of meanings through an alternative sign, the emotion will not be forthcoming. For example, the statement "Many soldiers died in Vietnam" is unlikely to produce the level of emotionality resulting from a picture of dead soldiers. During a 1989 conference sponsored by American University, political consultants noted that they would sometimes edit out certain scenes (including Vietnam bodies) from "packaged" ads produced by the National Democratic Committee because the pictures sent the wrong message or the emotionality created by them was too extreme. Often, it is exactly this heightened emotional response for which the politician's message is tailored. *If only pictures will achieve a certain desired response, the effective content of the message will be severely impaired by limiting the message to words.*

Examples of this occur repeatedly in political ads, such as the 1964 anti-Goldwater ads depicting a little girl disappearing into a mushroom cloud and a Ku Klux Klan meeting in progress (Winsbro, 1987). More recently, Jesse Jackson planned a television spot showing him with the pilot he had arranged to be freed from Syria (Katz, 1988). Each of these are "image" ads, intentionally designed to evoke a set of meanings that would result in a desired emotion (although not always achieved).

Consequently, image ads, by their very nature, involve a unique content that will be impaired by a restriction on expressive modality, and negative ads that rely on image appeals (e.g., the anti-Goldwater ads of 1964, or the "Willy Horton" revolving-prison-door ads of 1988) are equally at risk. Winsbro's argument seems premised on an unfounded assumption: that emotion-evoking attributes of an ad convey no content. The Supreme Court acknowledged the constitutional value of emotion-evoking appeals, although not in the context of visual communication:

[W]ords are often chosen as much for their emotive as their cognitive force. We cannot sanction the view that the Constitution, while solicitous of the cognitive content of individual speech, has little or no regard for that emotive function which, practically speaking, may often be the more important element of the overall message sought to be communicated. (Cohen v. California, 1971, p. 26)

This seems a valid policy for visual imagery, as well.

CONCLUSIONS

Proposed "reform" limits for political advertising are squarely aimed at image appeals, particularly those used in negative or attack campaigning. Although these proposals may be well meaning, and attempt to avoid infringing on the politician's right to speak, they are constructed on a faulty premise: that visual and other nonverbal matter in advertising conveys no meaning that cannot be conveyed verbally.

Semiotic theory suggests this simply is not true. More traditional political communications theory seems to agree. As political communications researchers Nimmo and Combs (1983) noted in their own language, "mediated political realities are symbolic, that is, they consist of a set of symbols purporting to represent the way things are, symbols that people take for granted *are* real" (p. 50). They concluded that much of American political campaigning consists of "seasonal rituals of fantasies, rhetorical vision, and melodramas" (p. 68) and that *content* has very little to do with any of this. Edelman (1964), too, theorized that symbols occupy an important and unique position in the American political schemata. Nonverbal matter seems to hold a special place in campaign appeals, conveying meanings not within verbal reach.

The facts seem to bear this out. In 1988 the Bush campaign was generously basted with rich, negative visual imagery, such as the revolving jail door and a polluted Boston Harbor. The media hailed that these negative ads were effective at winning voters (Dionne, 1988a; Rosenstiel, 1988). Visual imagery was uniquely effective. But such ads do not lose their constitutional protection merely because they are effective (*New York Times* v. Sullivan, 1964).

Theory, however, is not especially convincing as evidence in a court or congressional hearing. The next step is to empirically test this theory. Armed with empirical proof, it is possible for semioticians to contribute to both this body of theory and the legal process, thereby helping to protect our rights of free (nonverbal) speech.

Several new and revived format-related bills are currently pending before Congress. One bill before the Senate proposes to "curtail negative campaign advertising" by permitting use of public funds for media only where "the eligible candidate presents his own program, opinions, and qualifications" (United States Senate, 1989b). Another Senate bill would require candidates to "appear in person" if they "refer, directly or indirectly, to another legally qualified candidate for that office" (United States Senate, 1989c). Yet another bill is directed at requiring a candidate to be "identifiable during 50 percent of the time of any broadcast of a political announcement or advertisement" (United States Senate, 1989a). Each of these proposed laws, like the ones mentioned earlier, is intended to skirt the constitutional impediments by controlling format in lieu of content. Yet, each encroaches on those constitutional barriers if format, as argued here, is "content."

None of these bills has yet been enacted at the federal level. However, even if all of these current reforms die in committee, no crystal ball is required to foresee similar moves in the near future. The risk of not attending to this fertile area of potential speech regulation may be to jeopardize free speech. Caywood and Preston (in press) note that tying public financing to controls on campaigns, the continued excesses in political ads, a governmental emphasis on protecting the listener over the speaker, and other recent trends could result in regulation of political advertising. This is a topic in need of attention now, while there is time to conduct appropriate research.

To date, semioticians have played little or no role in public policy. It can be seen here that there are valuable contributions that can be made in this area. The foregoing is merely one example of possible application of semiotic study. Other areas include deceptive advertising and obscenity. No other field, including psychology, has dedicated as much attention to how meanings are communicated from one person to another. Where the regulation of speech is involved, semiotics promises unique potential for advancing legal insights.

REFERENCES

Ailes, R. (1988, Oct. 2). Isn't there a better way to run an American election? *New York Times,* Oct. 2, Sec. 4, 1.

Albert, J. A. (1986). The remedies available to candidates who are defamed by television or radio commercials of opponents. *Vermont Law Review, 11,* 33–73.

Alderman, R. M. (1982). 'Commercial entities' non-commercial speech: A contradiction in terms. *Utah Law Review, 1982,* 731–761.

Altschiller, D. (1988, March 20). More dollars equal less message. *New York Times,* March 20, F3.

Baldesty, G. J., & Simpson, R. A. (1982). The deceptive 'right to know': How pessimism rewrote the first amendment. In B. F. Chamberlain & C. J. Brown (Eds.), *The First Amendment Reconsidered* (pp. 62–88). New York: Longman.

Barthes, R. (1977). *Image-music-text.* New York: Hill & Wang.

Barthes, R. (1968). *Elements of semiology.* New York: Hill & Wang.

Boot, W. (1989). Campaign '88: TV overdoses on the inside dope. *Columbia Journalism Review,* Jan/Feb, 23.

Bork, R. H. (1971). Neutral principles and some first amendment problems. *Indiana Law Journal, 47,* 1–35.

Buckley v. Valeo, 424 U.S. 1 (1976).

Caywood, C. (1989, Feb. 2). Political ads in jeopardy. *Advertising Age,* 20.

Caywood, C. (1985). *A constitutional jeopardy theory: Toward a novel theory of political advertising regulation under first amendment and commercial speech doctrines.* Unpublished doctoral thesis, University of Wisconsin-Madison.

Caywood, C., & Laczniak, G. (1985). Political advertising: Ethical issues. *Winter Theory Conference Proceedings.* Chicago, IL: American Marketing Association.

Caywood, C. L., & Preston, I. (in press). The continuing debate on political advertising: Toward a jeopardy theory of political advertising as regulated free speech. *Journal of Public Policy and Marketing.*

Central Hudson Gas v. Public Service Commission, 447 U.S. 557 (1980).

Cohen, S. E. (1989, Feb. 2). For a kinder election campaign. *Advertising Age,* 20.

Cohen v. California, 403 U.S. 15 (1971).

Colford, S. W. (1988, Jan. 18). Kemp's bashing ads seem to help. *Advertising Age,* 94.

Colford, S. W. (1986, Dec. 15). Negative label for ads angers political pros: Consultants spurn idea of policing. *Advertising Age,* 90.

Commonwealth v. Acquaviva, 145 A.2d 407 (Penn. 1959).

Consolidated Edison Co. v. Public Service Commission, 447 U.S. 530 (1980).

Cundy, D. T. (1986). Political commercials and candidate image: The effects can be substantial. In L. L. Kaid, D. Nimmo and K. R. Sanders (Eds.), *New perspectives on political advertising* (pp. 000). Carbondale, IL: Southern Illinois University Press.

Dionne, E. J. (1988a, Oct. 26). New poll shows attacks by Bush are building lead. *New York Times,* 1.

Dionne, E. J. (1988b, Oct. 30). The campaign has real issues in spite of itself. *New York Times,* Sec. 4, 1.

Eco, U. (1979). *A theory of semiotics.* Bloomington, IN: Indiana University Press.

Edelman, M. (1964). *The symbolic uses of politics.* Urbana, IL: University of Illinois Press.

Fairness in Political Advertising Bills, S. 2409, H.R. 5307, 98th Cong., 2d Sess., 1984.

Federal Communications Commission Act, 47 U.S.C.A. 315 (1989 Supp.).

Federal Election Campaign Act, 2 U.S.C.A. 431 et seq. (1985).

Fialka, J. J. (1986, Nov. 13). Intense mudslinging in South Dakota senate race provokes many to favor restricting political ads. *Wall Street Journal,* 60.

Friends of Phil Gramm v. Americans for Phil Gramm in '84, 587 F.Supp. 769 (1984).

Garrison v. Louisiana, 379 U.S. 64 (1964).

Goldsborough, R. (1984, Nov. 5). The '84 ads: High gloss, low blows. *Advertising Age,* 3.

Grady, S. (1988, Oct. 13). Campaign a nightmare of negativism. *Wisconsin State Journal,* 15A.

Greer v. Spock, 424 U.S. 828 (1976).

Hess v. Indiana, 414 U.S. 105 (1973).

Homan, R. (1987, Oct. 26). Bill eyes political ad tactics. *Advertising Age,* 55.

Horton, C., & Chase, D. (1988, Oct. 7). Agency Execs Rap Candidates on Ad Tactics. *Advertising Age,* 1.

Houghton, J. C. (1987, March 16). Semiotics on the Assembly Line. *Advertising Age,* 18.

In re Felmeister & Isaacs, 518 A.2d 188 (N.J. 1986).

Katz, G. (1988). No punches pulled in final ad blitz. *USA Today,* 6.

Kevelson, R. (1977). *Inlaws/outlaws: A semiotics of systemic interaction.* Bloomington, IN: Indiana University Press.

Kevelson, R. (1986). Law. In T. A. Sebeok (Ed.), *Encyclopedic dictionary of semiotics* (pp. 438–443) Berlin: Mouton de Gruyter.

Laczniak, G. R., & Caywood, C. L. (1987). The case for and against televised political advertising: Implications for research and public policy. *Journal of Public Policy and Marketing, 6,* 16–32.

Lieffers, J. (1986 Dec. 1). Negative advertising: Assessing the consequences and the Kasten-Garvey fray. *Milwaukee Magazine,* 12–14.

Lustig, T. (1986, March). Great Caesar's ghost. *Public Relations Journal,* 17–20.

Manasco v. Walley, 63 So.2d 91 (1953).

Matthews, L. (1984, Dec). President's message: Political advertising revisited. *American Association of Advertising Agencies Newsletter,* 3.

Meiklejohn, A. (1948). *Free speech and its relation to self-government.* New York: Harper.

Merritt, S. (1984). Negative political advertising: Some empirical findings. *Journal of Advertising, 13*(3), 27–38.

Metromedia v. City of San Diego, 453 U.S. 490 (1981).

Mick, D. G. (1986). Consumer Research and Semiotics: Exploring the Morphology of Signs, Symbols, and Significance. *Journal of Consumer Research, 13,* 196–213.

Miller v. California, 413 U.S. 15 (1973).

Mill, J. S. (1859). *On liberty.* London: Parker.

Mills v. Alabama, 384 U.S. 214 (1966).

Minneapolis Star & Tribune v. Minneapolis Commissioner of Revenue, 103 S.Ct. 1365 (1983).

Monitor Patriot Co. v. Roy, 401 U.S. 265 (1971).

Murphy, T. R., & Zeppos, E. N. (1987, July 22). Political consultants labor to present issues, not image. *Milwaukee Journal,* 13.

National Association of Broadcasters (1989). *Broadcast regulation '89—a mid-year report.* Washington, DC: National Association of Broadcasters.

Neel, R. F. (1985). Campaign hyperbole: The advisability of legislating false statements out of politics. *Journal of Law and Policy, 2,* 405–424.

New York Times v. Sullivan, 376 U.S. 254 (1964).

Nimmer, M. B. (1973). The meaning of symbolic speech under the first amendment. *UCLA Law Review, 21,* 29–62.

Nimmo, D. D., & Combs, J. E. (1983). *Mediated political realities.* New York: Longman.

Oreskes, M. (1988 Oct. 2). Talking heads: Weighing imagery in a campaign made for television. *New York Times,* Sec. 4, 1.

O'Toole, J. (1988, Nov. 28). Regulate political ads? They give us bad image. *Advertising Age,* p. 17.

Preston, I. L. (1975). *The great American blow-up: Puffery in advertising and selling.* Madison, WI: University of Wisconsin Press.

Preston, I. L., & Richards, J. I. (1986). Consumer miscomprehension as a challenge to FTC prosecutions of deceptive advertising. *John Marshall Law Review, 19,* 605–635.

Preston, I. L., & Richards, J. I. (1988). Consumer miscomprehension and deceptive advertising: A response to Professor Craswell. *Boston University Law Review, 68,* 431–438.

Reston, J. (1983, Nov. 20). The wrong stuff. *New York Times,* Sect. 4, p. 21, col. 2.

Richards, J. I. (1987). Clearing the air about cigarettes: Will advertisers' rights go up in smoke? *Pacific Law Journal, 19,* 1–70.

Richards, J. I. (1986). Obscenity and film: An empirical dilemma. *Loyola Entertainment Law Journal, 6,* 7–30.

Richards, J. I., & Zakia, R. D. (1981). Pictures: An advertiser's expressway through FTC regulation. *Georgia Law Review, 16,* 77–134.

Rosenstiel, T. B. (1988 Oct. 9). Campaigns leave no holds barred in negative ads. *Austin American-Statesman,* A4.

Rosenthal, A. (1988, Oct. 26). Dukakis at rally and in TV ads, presses theme that Bush is lying. *New York Times,* 10.

Rudisill v. Flynn, 619 F.2d 692 (1980).

Shaw, B., Hurd, S. N., & Bader, M. B. (1984). Corporate political speech and the first amendment. *Oklahoma City University Law Review, 9,* 271–291.

Shyles, L. (1986). The televised political spot advertisement: Its structure, content, and role in the political system. In L. L. Kaid, D. Nimmo, & K. R. Sanders (Eds.), *New perspectives on political advertising.* Carbondale, IL: Southern Illinois University Press.

Taylor, P. (1985, Nov. 28). Incumbents take negative view of election ads. *Milwaukee Journal,* 38.

Texas v. Johnson, 57 U.S.L.W. 4770 (U.S. Supreme Court, June 21, 1989).

Tolchin, M. (1984, Oct. 28). For some, low road is the only way to go. *New York Times,* sect. 4, p. 2, col. 3.

United States v. O'Brien, 391 U.S. 367 (1968).

United States Senate, S.137, 101st Congress, 1st Session (1989a).

United States Senate, S.340, 101st Congress, 1st Session (1989b).

United States Senate, S.999, 101st Congress, 1st Session (1989c).

Virginia Board of Pharmacy v. Virginia Citizens Consumer Council, 425 U.S. 748 (1976).

Walker v. City of Birmingham, 388 U.S. 307 (1967).

Will, G. F. (1988, Jan. 18). The other guy started it. *Advertising Age,* 66.

Will, G. F. (1986, Nov. 10). So much cash, so few ideas. *Newsweek,* 96.

Williamson, J. (1978). *Decoding advertisements: Ideology and meaning in advertising.* Southhampton, Great Britain: Camelot Press Ltd.

Winsbro, J. (1987). Misrepresentation in political advertising: The role of legal sanctions. *Emory Law Journal, 36,* 853–916.

Zakia, R. D. (1987). Alphapictorials. *Framework, 1,* 7–13.

Zauderer v. Office of Disciplinary Counsel, 471 U.S. 626 (1985).

Author Index

Subject Index